W9-AMX-859

FORMATIONS OF THE SECULAR

Cultural Memory
in
the
Present

Mieke Bal and Hent de Vries, Editors

FORMATIONS OF THE SECULAR

Christianity, Islam, Modernity

Talal Asad

STANFORD UNIVERSITY PRESS

STANFORD, CALIFORNIA 2003

BL
2747.8
.A75
2003

Stanford University Press
Stanford, California

© 2003 by the Board of Trustees of the
Leland Stanford Junior University.
All rights reserved.

Printed in the United States of America
on acid-free, archival-quality paper.

Library of Congress Cataloging-in-Publication Data

Asad, Talal.
    Formations of the secular : Christianity, Islam, modernity / Talal Asad.
        p.   cm. — (Cultural Memory in the Present)
    Includes bibliographical references and index.
    ISBN 0-8047-4767-9 (cloth : alk. paper) —
    ISBN 0-8047-4768-7 (pbk. : alk. paper)
        1. Secularism. 2. Islam and politics. 3. Christianity and politics.
    I. Title. II. Series.
    BL 2747.8 A75 2003
    291.1'7—DC21   2002011014

Original Printing 2003
Last figure below indicates year of this printing:
12   11   10   09   08   07   06   05   04   03

Typeset by Tim Roberts in 11/13.5 Garamond

EPISCOPAL DIVINITY SCHOOL LIBRARY
99 BRATTLE STREET
CAMBRIDGE, MA 02138

MAY 2 8 2003

Contents

Acknowledgments

Earlier versions of several of the chapters of this book have appeared before. Thus large parts of Chapter 4 were published in "What Do Human Rights *Do*?" *Theory and Event*, vol. 4, no. 4, December 2000 (Johns Hopkins University Press). Chapter 2 is a revised version of "Agency and Pain: An Exploration," published in *Culture and Religion*, vol. 1, no. 1, May 2000 (Curzon, UK). Chapter 3 is a revised and expanded version of "On Torture, or Cruel, Inhuman, and Degrading Treatment," first published in *Social Research*, vol. 63, no. 4, Winter 1996 (New School for Social Research). Chapter 5 first appeared under the title "Muslims and European Identity: Can Europe Represent Islam?" in *Cultural Encounters*, edited by E. Hallam and B. Street (Routledge, 2000). Chapter 6 first appeared in *Nation and Religion*, edited by P. Van der Veer and H. Lehmann (Princeton, 1999). The remaining portions of the book were not published previously, although Chapter 1 is based on the Rappaport Annual Distinguished Lecture in the Anthropology of Religion, delivered to the Religion Section of the American Anthropological Association in March 2000, and Chapter 7 on the ISIM Annual Lecture delivered in October 2000 to the International Institute for the Study of Islam in the Modern World in the University of Leiden.

Finally, I wish to express my gratitude to the many friends and colleagues who have read the book as a whole or in part: Hussein Agrama, Engin Akarli, Steven Caton, William Connolly, Veena Das, Charles Hirschkind, Baber Johansen, Webb Keane, Boris Nikolov, Saba Mahmood, John Milbank, David Scott, George Shulman, Hent de Vries, Jeremy Waldron, and Michael Warner. I have benefited much from exchanges with them, both written and oral. But I am also conscious of having failed to meet many of their criticisms, and to respond adequately to all their probing questions.

FORMATIONS OF THE SECULAR

Introduction: Thinking about Secularism

I

What is the connection between "the secular" as an epistemic category and "secularism" as a political doctrine? Can they be objects of anthropological inquiry? What might an anthropology of secularism look like? This book attempts, in a preliminary way, to address these questions.

The contemporary salience of religious movements around the globe, and the torrent of commentary on them by scholars and journalists, have made it plain that religion is by no means disappearing in the modern world. The "resurgence of religion" has been welcomed by many as a means of supplying what they see as a needed moral dimension to secular politics and environmental concerns. It has been regarded by others with alarm as a symptom of growing irrationality and intolerance in everyday life. The question of secularism has emerged as an object of academic argument and of practical dispute. If anything is agreed upon, it is that a straightforward narrative of progress from the religious to the secular is no longer acceptable. But does it follow that secularism is not universally valid?

Secularism as political doctrine arose in modern Euro-America. It is easy to think of it simply as requiring the separation of religious from secular institutions in government, but that is not all it is. Abstractly stated, examples of this separation can be found in medieval Christendom and in the Islamic empires—and no doubt elsewhere too. What is distinctive about "secularism" is that it presupposes new concepts of "religion," "ethics," and "politics," and new imperatives associated with them. Many people have sensed this novelty and reacted to it in a variety of ways. Thus the opponents of secularism in the Middle East and elsewhere have rejected it as specific to the West, while its advocates have insisted that its particular origin does not detract from its contemporary global relevance. The eminent philosopher Charles Taylor is among those who insist that although secularism emerged in response to the political problems of Western Christian society in early modernity—beginning with its devastating wars of religion—it is applicable to non-Christian societies everywhere that have become modern. This elegant and attractive argument by a highly influential social philosopher demands the attention of everyone interested in this queston.[1]

Taylor takes it for granted that the emergence of secularism is closely connected to the rise of the modern nation-state, and he identifies two ways in which secularism has legitimized it. First, there was the attempt to find the lowest common denominator among the doctrines of conflicting religious sects, and second, the attempt to define a political ethic independent of religious convictions altogether. It is this latter model that is applicable throughout the world today, but only after we have adapted to it the Rawlsian idea of an *overlapping consensus*, which proceeds on the assumption that there can be no universally agreed basis, whether secular or religious, for the political principles accepted in a modern, heterogeneous society. Taylor agrees with Rawls that the political ethic will be embedded in some understanding or other of the good, but argues against Rawls that background understandings and foreground political principles need not be tightly bound together as the latter maintains. This model of secularism is not only intellectually appealing, it is also, Taylor believes, one that the modern democratic state cannot do without.

Taylor likes Benedict Anderson's thought that a modern nation is an "imagined community" because it enables him to emphasize two features of the modern imaginary that belongs to a democratic state. These are: first, the horizontal, direct-access character of modern society; and second, its grounding in secular, homogeneous time. Direct access is reflected in several developments: the rise of the public sphere (the equal right of all to participate in nationwide discussions), the extension of the market princi-

1. Charles Taylor, "Modes of Secularism," in Rajeev Bhargava, ed., *Secularism and Its Critics*, Delhi: Oxford University Press, 1998.

ple (all contracts are between legal equals), and the emergence of citizenship (based on the principle of individualism). Apart from the idea of a direct-access society, homogeneous time is a prerequisite for imagining the totality of individual lives that comprise a (national) community in which there are no privileged persons or events, and therefore no mediations. This makes the sources of political legitimacy in a modern direct-access, temporally homogeneous state radically different from the sources in a traditional temporally and politically mediated one. "Traditional despotisms could ask of people only that they remain passive and obey the laws," he writes. "A democracy, ancient or modern, has to ask more. It requires that its members be motivated to make the necessary contributions: of treasure (in taxes), sometimes blood (in war), and always some degree of participation in the process of governance. A free society has to substitute for despotic enforcement a certain degree of self-enforcement. Where this fails, the system is in danger."[2]

Is this account persuasive? Some doubts arise at this point. Surely, the payment of taxes and induction into the army depend not on self-enforcement but on enforcement by the state? "Some degree" of participation in governance (by which Taylor means taking part in elections once every four or five years) explicitly refers to a statistical measure of the entire population and not to a measure of how strong individual motivation is. It depends, therefore, on the political skill with which large numbers are managed—including the organization and financing of electoral campaigns—rather than on the ethics of individual self-discipline. The distinctive feature of modern liberal governance, I would submit, is *neither* compulsion (force) *nor* negotiation (consent) *but* the statecraft that uses "self-discipline" and "participation," "law" and "economy" as elements of political strategy. In spite of the reference to "democracy, ancient or modern," which suggests a comparability of political predicaments, the problems and resources of modern society are utterly different from those of a Greek polis. Indeed Taylor's statement about participation is not, so one could argue, the way most individuals in modern state-administered populations justify governance. It is the way ideological spokespersons theorize "political legitimacy." If the system is in danger it is not because of an absence of self-enforcement by citizens. Most politicians are aware that "the system is in danger" when the general population ceases to enjoy any sense of prosperity, when the regime is felt to be thoroughly unre-

2. Ibid., p. 43.

sponsive to the governed, and when the state security apparatuses are grossly inefficient. Policing techniques and an economy that avoids disappointing too many in the general population too seriously are more important than self-discipline as an autonomous factor.

In today's liberal democracies a strong case can be made for the thesis that there is less and less of a direct link between the electorate and its parliamentary representatives—that the latter are less and less representative of the socio-economic interests, identities, and aspirations of a culturally differentiated and economically polarized electorate. And the absence of a direct reflection of the citizen in his political representation is not compensated for through the various extra-parliamentary institutions connected to governance. On the contrary. The influence of *pressure groups* on government decisions is more often than not far greater than is warranted by the proportion of the electorate whose interests they directly promote (for example, the Farmers Union in Britain; AIPAC and the oil lobby in the United States). *Opinion polls*, continuously monitoring the fragile collective views of citizens, keep the government informed about public sentiment between elections, and enable it to anticipate or influence opinion independently of the electoral mandate. Finally, *the mass media*, increasingly owned by conglomerates and often cooperating with the state, mediate the political reactions of the public and its sense of guarantee and threat. Thus in crucial ways this is not at all a direct-access society.[3] There is no space in which all citizens can negotiate freely and equally with one another. The existence of negotiation in public life is confined to such elites as party bosses, bureaucratic administrators, parliamentary legislators, and business leaders. The ordinary citizen does not participate in the process of formulating policy options as these elites do—his or her participation in periodic elections does not even guarantee that the policies voted for will be adhered to.

The modern nation as an imagined community is always mediated through constructed images. When Taylor says that a modern democracy must acquire a healthy dose of nationalist sentiment[4] he refers to the national media—including national education—that is charged with culti-

3. See the interesting article by Bernard Manin, "The Metamorphoses of Representative Government," *Economy and Society*, vol. 23, no. 2, May 1994.

4. "In other words, the modern democratic state needs a healthy degree of what used to be called patriotism, a strong sense of identification with the polity, and a willingness to give of oneself for its sake" (Taylor, p. 44).

vating it. For the media are not simply the means through which individuals simultaneously imagine their national community; they *mediate* that imagination, construct the sensibilities that underpin it.[5] When Taylor says that the modern state has to make citizenship the primary principle of identity, he refers to the way it must transcend the different identities built on class, gender, and religion, replacing conflicting perspectives by unifying experience. In an important sense, this transcendent mediation *is* secularism. Secularism is not simply an intellectual answer to a question about enduring social peace and toleration. It is an enactment by which a *political medium* (representation of citizenship) redefines and transcends particular and differentiating practices of the self that are articulated through class, gender, and religion. In contrast, the process of mediation enacted in "premodern" societies includes ways in which the state mediates local identities without aiming at transcendence.

So much for questions of space in modern secular society—the alleged absence of hierarchy and supposed dependence on horizontal solidarity. What about time? Here, too, the reality is more complex than Taylor's model suggests. The homogeneous time of state bureaucracies and market dealings is of course central to the calculations of modern political economy. It allows speed and direction to be plotted with precision. But there are other temporalities—immediate and mediated, reversible and nonreversible—by which individuals in a heterogeneous society live and by which therefore their political responses are shaped.

In short, the assumption that liberal democracy ushers in a direct-access society seems to me questionable. The forms of mediation characteristic of modern society certainly differ from medieval Christian—and Islamic—ones, but this is not a simple matter of the absence of "religion" in the public life of the modern nation-state. For even in modern secular countries the place of religion varies. Thus although in France both the highly centralized state and its citizens are secular, in Britain the state is linked to the Established Church and its inhabitants are largely nonreligious, and in America the population is largely religious but the federal state is secular. "Religion" has always been publicly present in both Britain and America. Consequently, although the secularism of these three countries have much in common, the mediating character of the modern imag-

5. See Hent de Vries, "In Media Res: Global Religion, Public Spheres, and the Task of Contemporary Comparative Religious Studies," in *Religion and Media*, ed. H. de Vries and S. Weber, Stanford, CA: Stanford University Press, 2001.

inary in each of them differs significantly. The notion of toleration between religiously defined groups is differently inflected in each. There is a different sense of participation in the nation and access to the state among religious minorities in the three countries.

So what does the idea of *an overlapping consensus* do for the doctrine of secularism? In a religiously diverse society, Taylor claims, it allows people to have different (even mutually exclusive) reasons for subscribing to the independent, *secular* ethic. For example, the right to life may be justified by secular or religious beliefs—and the latter may come in several varieties that belong to different traditions. This means that political disagreements will be continuous, incapable of being authoritatively resolved, and that temporary resolutions will have to depend on negotiated compromise. But given that there will be quarrels about what is to count as *core political principles* and as *background justifications*, how will they be resolved? Taylor answers: by persuasion and negotiation. There is certainly a generous impulse behind this answer, but the nation-state is not a generous agent and its law does not deal in persuasion. Consider what happens when the parties to a dispute are unwilling to compromise on what for them is a matter of principle (a principle that articulates action and being, not a principle that is justifiable by statements of belief). If citizens are not reasoned around in a matter deemed nationally important by the government and the majority that supports it, the threat of legal action (and the violence this implies) may be used. In that situation negotiation simply amounts to the exchange of unequal concessions in situations where the weaker party has no choice.[6] What happens, the citizen asks, to the principles of equality and liberty in the modern secular imaginary when they are subjected to the necessities of the law? It emerges then that although she can choose her happiness, she may not identify her harms.

Or to put it another way: When the state attempts to forcibly establish and defend "core political principles," when its courts impose a *particular* distinction between "core principles" and "background justifications" (for the law always *works through* violence), this may add to cumulative disaffection. Can secularism then guarantee the peace it allegedly ensured in

6. Intimidation can take many forms, of course. As Lord Cromer, consul-general and agent of the British government and informal ruler of Egypt at the end of the nineteenth century, put it, "advice could always take the substance, if not the form, of a command" (cited in Afaf Lutfi al-Sayyid, *Egypt and Cromer*, London: John Murray, 1968, p. 66).

Euro-America's early history—by shifting the violence of religious wars into the violence of national and colonial wars? The difficulty with secularism as a doctrine of war and peace in the world is not that it is European (and therefore alien to the non-West) but that it is closely connected with the rise of a system of capitalist nation-states—mutually suspicious and grossly unequal in power and prosperity, each possessing a collective personality that is differently mediated and therefore differently guaranteed and threatened.

Thus a number of historians have noted the tendency of spokespersons of the American nation, a tendency that has dramatically resurfaced since the September 11 tragedy, to define it as "good" in opposition to its "evil" enemies at home and abroad. "It is an outlook rooted in two distinctive American traditions," says Eric Foner, a historian at Columbia University. "The country's religious roots and its continuing high level of religious faith make Americans more likely to see enemies not just as opponents but as evil. Linked to that is the belief that America is the world's last best hope of liberty, so that those who oppose America become the enemies of freedom."[7] Included in this pattern, these historians tell us, is the tendency to denounce public dissent as treason and to subject various immigrant groups to legalized suppression. The historians have traced this recurring pattern of American nationalism (where internal difference, especially when it is identified as "foreign," becomes the focus of intolerance) from the end of the eighteenth century—that is, from the foundation of the republic—to the present. Is it to be understood in relation to its religious origins? But in the twentieth century the political rhetoric and repressive measures have been directed at real and imagined secular opponents. Regardless of the religious roots and the contemporary religiosity that historians invoke in explanation of this pattern, America has—as Taylor rightly observes—a model secular constitution. My point is that whatever the cause of the repeated explosions of intolerance in American history—however understandable they may be—they are entirely compatible (indeed intertwined) with secularism in a highly modern society. Thus it seems to me there has been scarcely any sustained public *debate* on the significance of the September 11 tragedy for a superpower-dominated world. On the whole the media have confined themselves to two kinds of question: on the one hand the requirements of national security and the danger

7. Robert F. Worth, "A Nation Defines Itself by Its Evil Enemies: Truth, Right and the American Way," in the *New York Times*, February 24, 2002.

to civil liberties of the "war on terror," and, on the other, the responsibility of Islam as a religion and Arabs as a people for acts of terror. (A number of thoughtful articles on the September tragedy have been published, but they do not appear to have affected the dominant intellectual discourse.) This absence of public debate in a liberal democratic society must be explained in terms of the mediating representations that define its national personality and identify the discourses that seem to threaten it.

Another instructive example is India, a country that has a secular constitution and an outstanding record as a functioning liberal democracy—perhaps the most impressive in the Third World. And yet in India "communal riots" (that is, between Hindus and various minorities—Muslim, Christian, and "Untouchable") have occurred frequently ever since independence in 1947. As Partha Chatterjee and others have pointed out, the publicly recognizable personality of the nation is strongly mediated by representations of a reconstituted high-caste Hinduism, and those who do not fit into that personality are inevitably defined as religious minorities. This has often placed the "religious minorities" in a defensive position.[8] A secular state does not guarantee toleration; it puts into play different structures of ambition and fear. The law never seeks to eliminate violence since its object is always to *regulate* violence.

II

If secularism as a doctrine requires the distinction between private reason and public principle, it also demands the placing of the "religious" in the former by "the secular." Private *reason* is not the same as private *space*; it is the entitlement to difference, the immunity from the force of public reason. So theoretical and practical problems remain that call for each of these categories to be defined. What makes a discourse and an action "religious" or "secular"?

A book entitled *The Bible Designed to Be Read as Literature*, published in England before the Second World War,[9] has a format that does away with the traditional double columns and numbered verses, and through

8. See, in this connection, Partha Chatterjee, "History and the Nationalization of Hinduism," *Social Research*, vol. 59, no. 1, 1992.

9. *The Bible Designed to Be Read as Literature*, ed. and arranged by E. S. Bates, London: William Heineman, undated.

modern page layout and typography aims to produce the effect of a continuous narrative with occasional breaks for lines of poetry. As the Introduction explains: "although a great part of the Bible is poetry, the poetry is printed as prose. The prose, on the other hand, instead of being printed continuously, is broken up into short 'verses,' and arbitrarily divided into 'chapters.' The Bible contains almost all the traditional types of literature; lyric poetry, dramatic and elegiac poetry, history, tales, philosophic treatises, collections of proverbs, letters, as well as types of writing peculiar to itself, what are called the Prophetic Books. Yet all these are presented in print as if, in the original, they had the same literary form" (page vii). The changes in layout certainly facilitate a reading of the Bible as "literature." But as the passage quoted implicitly acknowledges, "literature" has an ambiguous sense—at once "art," "texts dealing with a particular subject," and simply "printed matter."

If the Bible is read as art (whether as poetry or myth or philosophy) this is because a complicated historical development of disciplines and sensibilities has made it possible to do so. Hence the protest the Introduction makes to the effect that a concern for literary reading is no derogation of its sacred status ("And indeed, to make a rigid division between the sacred and the secular is surely to impoverish both") is itself a secular expression of the text's malleability. An atheist will not read it in the way a Christian would. Is this text essentially "religious" because it deals with the supernatural in which the Christian believes—either a text divinely revealed or a true record of divine inspiration? Or is it really "literature" because it can be read by the atheist as a human work of art? Or is the text neither in itself, but simply a reading that is either religious or literary—or possibly, as for the modern Christian, both together? For over the last two or three centuries it has become possible to bring a newly emerging concept of *literature* to the aid of religious sensibilities. However, until someone decides this question authoritatively, there can be no authorized allocation of what belongs to private reason and what to "a political ethic independent of religious belief" (a public ethic that is said to be subscribed to for diverse private reasons—that thus become little more than *rationalizations*).

Let me pursue this point briefly with reference to what is described in our media, and by many of our public intellectuals, as "the Islamic roots of violence"—especially since September 2001. Religion has long been seen as a source of violence,[10] and (for ideological reasons) Islam has been represented in the modern West as peculiarly so (undisciplined, arbitrary, singularly oppressive). Experts on "Islam," "the modern world," and "political philosophy" have lectured the Muslim world yet again on its failure to embrace secularism and enter modernity and on its inability to break off from its violent roots. Now some reflection would show that violence does not *need* to be justified by the Qur'an—or any other scripture for that matter. When General Ali Haidar of Syria, under the orders of his secular president Hafez al-Assad, massacred 30,000 to 40,000 civilians in the rebellious town of Hama in 1982 he did not invoke the Qur'an—nor did the secularist Saddam Hussein when he gassed thousands of Kurds and butchered the Shi'a population in Southern Iraq. Ariel Sharon in his indiscriminate killing and terrorizing of Palestinian civilians did not—so far as is publicly known—invoke passages of the Torah, such as Joshua's destruction of every living thing in Jericho.[11] Nor has any government (and rebel group), whether Western or non-Western, *needed* to justify its use of indiscriminate cruelty against civilians by appealing to the authority of sacred scripture. They might in some cases do so because that seems to them just—or else expedient. But that's very different from saying that they are *constrained* to do so. One need only remind oneself of the banal fact that innumerable pious Muslims, Jews, and Christians read their scriptures without being seized by the need to kill non-believers. My point here is simply to emphasize that the way people engage with such complex and multifaceted texts, translating their sense and relevance, is a complicated business involving disciplines and traditions of reading, personal habit, and temperament, as well as the perceived demands of particular social situations.

The present discourse about the roots of "Islamic terrorism" in Islamic texts trails two intriguing assumptions: (a) that the Qur'anic text will

10. "In the case of the Bible the tradition handed down from the Middle Ages has been to regard it as a collection of texts, any of which could be detached from its surroundings and used, regardless of the circumstances in which it was written or by whom it was spoken, as divine authority for conduct; often (as we know) with devastating consequences. Texts have been set up as idols, as cruel as ever were worshiped by savage idolaters" (ibid., p. viii).

11. The Torah is, of course, replete with God's injunctions to his chosen people to destroy the original inhabitants of the Promised Land. But it would be incredibly naive to suggest that religious Jews who read such passages are thereby incited to violence.

force Muslims to be guided by it; and (b) that Christians and Jews are free to interpret the Bible as they please. For no good reason, these assumptions take up contradictory positions between text and reader: On the one hand, the religious *text* is held to be determinate, fixed in its sense, and having the power to bring about particular beliefs (that in turn give rise to particular behavior) among those exposed to it—rendering readers passive. On the other hand, the religious *reader* is taken to be actively engaged in constructing the meaning of texts in accordance with changing social circumstances—so the texts are passive. These contradictory assumptions about agency help to account for the positions taken up by orientalists and others in arguments about religion and politics in Islam. A magical quality is attributed to Islamic religious texts, for they are said to be both essentially univocal (their meaning *cannot* be subject to dispute, just as "fundamentalists" insist) and infectious (except in relation to the orientalist, who is, fortunately for him, immune to their dangerous power). In fact in Islam as in Christianity there is a complicated history of shifting interpretations, and the distinction is recognized between the divine text and human approaches to it.

Those who think that the *motive* for violent action lies in "religious ideology" claim that any concern for the consequent suffering requires that we support the censorship of religious discourse—or at least the prevention of religious discourse from entering the domain where public policy is formulated. But it is not always clear whether it is pain and suffering as such that the secularist cares about or the pain and suffering that can be attributed to religious violence because that is pain the modern imaginary conceives of as gratuitous. Nor is it always clear how a "religious motive" is to be unequivocally identified in modern society. Is motivated behavior that accounts for itself by religious discourse ipso facto religious or only when it does so *sincerely*? But insincerity may itself be a construction of religious language. Is it assumed that there is always an *unconscious* motive to a religious act, a motive that is therefore secular, as Freud and others have done? But that begs the question of how to distinguish between the religious and the secular. In short, to identify a (religious) motive for violence one must have a theory of motives that deals with concepts of character and dispositions, inwardness and visibility, the thought and the unthought.[12] In modern, secular society this also means *authoritative* theories and practices—as

12. Two excellent conceptual investigations appeared in 1958: G. E. M. Anscombe, *Intention*, Oxford: Blackwell; and R. S. Peters, *The Concept of Motivation*,

in law courts, or in the hegemonic discourse of the national media, or in parliamentary forums where the intentions of foreign friends and enemies are assessed and policies formulated.

It would be easy to point to innumerable "secular" agents who have perpetrated acts of great cruelty. But such attempts at defending "religion" are less interesting than asking what it is we do when we assign responsibility for "violence and cruelty" to specific agents. One answer might be to point out that when the CIA together with the Pakistani Secret Service encouraged, armed, and trained religious warriors to fight against the Soviets in Afghanistan, when the Saudi government facilitated the travel of volunteer fighters from Arabia to that country, we had an action with several part-agents, networks of actors in an evolving plot. There was no single or consistent motive for that complex action not only because there were several part-agents but also because of the diverse desires, sensibilities, and self-images involved. But beyond this recognition of agentive complexity we can press the question further: When do we look for a clear motive? When we identify an unusual outcome that seems to us to call for justification or exoneration—and therefore for moral or legal *responsibility*. As I said above, there are theories as to how this attribution should be done (the law being paradigmatic here), and it is important to understand them and the circumstances in which they are applied in the modern world. In brief, although "religious" intentions are variously distinguished from "secular" ones in different traditions, the identification of *intentions* as such is especially important in what scholars call modernity for allocating moral and legal accountability.

III

Many critics have now taken the position that "modernity" (in which secularism is centrally located) is not a verifiable object.[13] They argue that contemporary societies are heterogeneous and overlapping, that they contain disparate, even discordant, circumstances, origins, valences, and so

London: Routledge & Kegan Paul. Herbert Morris, *On Guilt and Innocence* (published by University of California Press in 1976), looks at the question of motivation from an explicitly juridical perspective.

13. For example, Bernard Yack's *The Fetishism of Modernities: Epochal Self-Consciousness in Contemporary Social and Political Thought*, Notre Dame, IN: University of Notre Dame Press, 1997.

forth. My response is that in a sense these critics are right (although the heuristic value of looking for necessary connections should not be forgotten) but that what we have here is not a simple cognitive error. Assumptions about the integrated character of "modernity" are themselves part of practical and political reality. They direct the way in which people committed to it act in critical situations. These people *aim* at "modernity," and expect others (especially in the "non-West") to do so too. This fact doesn't disappear when we simply point out that "the West" isn't an integrated totality, that many people in the West contest secularism or interpret it in different ways, that the modern epoch in the West has witnessed many arguments and several irreconcilable aspirations. On the contrary, those who assume modernity *as a project* know that already. (An aspect of modern colonialism is this: although the West contains many faces at home it presents a single face abroad.[14]) The important question, therefore, is not to determine why the idea of "modernity" (or "the West") is a misdescription, but why it has become hegemonic *as a political goal*, what practical consequences follow from that hegemony, and what social conditions maintain it.

It is right to say that "modernity" is neither a totally coherent object nor a clearly bounded one, and that many of its elements originate in relations with the histories of peoples outside Europe. Modernity is a *project*— or rather, a series of interlinked projects—that certain people in power seek to achieve. The project aims at institutionalizing a number of (sometimes conflicting, often evolving) principles: constitutionalism, moral autonomy, democracy, human rights, civil equality, industry, consumerism, freedom of the market—and secularism. It employs proliferating technologies (of production, warfare, travel, entertainment, medicine) that generate new experiences of space and time, of cruelty and health, of consumption and knowledge. The notion that these experiences constitute "disenchantment"—implying a direct access to reality, a stripping away of myth, magic, and the sacred—is a salient feature of the modern epoch. It is, arguably, a product of nineteenth-century romanticism, partly linked to

14. "Simultaneously, and despite the parochialism of the governments at home," wrote Count Carlo Sforza, "a sort of international solidarity was slowly evolving in the colonies. . . . Out of interest if not out of good will, an embryonic European understanding had at last been found in Africa. We could hate one another in Europe, but we felt that, between two neighbouring colonies, the interest in common was as great as between two white men meeting in the desert" (*Europe and Europeans*, 1936).

the growing habit of reading imaginative literature[15]—being enclosed within and by it—so that images of a "pre-modern" past acquire in retrospect a quality of enchantment.

Modern projects do not hang together as an integrated totality, but they account for distinctive sensibilities, aesthetics, moralities. It is not always clear what critics mean when they claim that there is no such thing as "the West" because its modern culture has diverse genealogies taking it outside Europe. If Europe has a geographical "outside" doesn't that itself presuppose the idea of a space—at once coherent and subvertible—for locating the West? In my view that is not the best way of approaching the question. Modernity is not primarily a matter of cognizing the real but of living-in-the-world. Since this is true of every epoch, what is distinctive about modernity *as a historical epoch* includes modernity as a political-economic project. What interests me particularly is the attempt to construct categories of the secular and the religious in terms of which modern living is required to take place, and nonmodern peoples are invited to assess their adequacy. For representations of "the secular" and "the religious" in modern and modernizing states mediate people's identities, help shape their sensibilities, and guarantee their experiences.

But what evidence is there that there is such a thing as "a modern project"? In a review article on the new edition of *The Communist Manifesto*, the political scientist Stephen Holmes recently claimed that "the end of Communism has meant the collapse of the last world power officially founded on the Hegelian belief in capital-H History, loudly echoed by the *Manifesto*. The end of the Cold War means that, today, no single struggle spans the globe."[16] Yet this attribution of a universal historical teleology solely to a defeated Communism is less than convincing. Leaving aside neo-Hegelian apologists for the New World Order such as Francis Fukuyama, Holmes's disregard of U.S. attempts to promote a single social model over the globe is puzzling. Especially over the past fifteen years, the

15. Benedict Anderson's discussion of "print-capitalism" focuses on the significance of newspaper reading for imagining the nation as a community (1983), but he does not consider the simultaneous growth of serialized novels published in periodicals and the enormous expansion in the market for imaginative "literature"—both prose and poetry—that mediated people's understanding of "real" and "imagined." See Per Gedin, *Literature in the Marketplace*, London: Faber and Faber, 1982 (Swedish original 1975).

16. S. Holmes, "The End of Idiocy on a Planetary Scale," *London Review of Books*, vol. 20, no. 21, October 29, 1998, p. 13.

analyses and prescriptions by international agencies dominated by the United States (OECD, IMF, the World Bank) have been remarkably similar regardless of the country being considered. "Seldom," observes Serge Halimi, "has the development of the whole of humanity been conceived in terms so closely identical and so largely inspired by the American model." As Halimi notes, that model is not confined to matters of free trade and private enterprise but includes moral and political dimensions—prominent among them being the doctrine of secularism.[17] If this project has not been entirely successful on a global scale—if its result is more often further instability than homogeneity—it is certainly not because those in a position to make far-reaching decisions about the affairs of the world reject the doctrine of a singular destiny—a transcendent truth?—for all countries. (That the opponents of this project are themselves often driven by totalizing ideologies and intolerant attitudes is undoubtedly true. However, it is as well to stress—in the aftermath of the September 11 tragedy—that my point here is not to "blame America" and "justify its enemies," but to indicate that as the world's only superpower, the protection of its interests and commitment to "freedom" require America to intervene globally and to help reform local conditions according to what appear to be universal values. The reformed local conditions include new styles of consumption and expression. Whether these are best described as "freely chosen" or "imposed" is another question.)

We should look, therefore, at *the politics* of national progress—including the politics of secularism—that flow from the multifaceted concept of modernity exemplified by "the West" (and especially by America as its leader and most advanced exemplar). But should we not also inquire about the politics of the contrary view? What politics are promoted by the notion that the world is *not* divided into modern and nonmodern, into West and non-West? What practical options are opened up or closed by the notion that the world has *no* significant binary features, that it is, on the contrary, divided into overlapping, fragmented cultures, hybrid selves, continuously dissolving and emerging social states? As part of such an understanding I believe we must try to unpack the various assumptions on which secularism—a modern doctrine of the world in the world—is based. For it is precisely the process by which these conceptual binaries are established or subverted that tells us how people live the secular—how

17. See S. Halimi, "Liberal Dogma Shipwrecked," *Le Monde diplomatique*, Supplement to *The Guardian Weekly*, October 1998.

they vindicate the essential freedom and responsibility of the sovereign self in opposition to the constraints of that self by religious discourses.

IV

It is a major premise of this study that "the secular" is conceptually prior to the political doctrine of "secularism," that over time a variety of concepts, practices, and sensibilities have come together to form "the secular." In the chapters that follow I therefore begin with a partial genealogy of that concept, an effort aimed at questioning its self-evident character while asserting at the same time that it nevertheless marks something real. My resort to genealogy obviously derives from ways it has been deployed by Foucault and Nietzsche, although it does not claim to follow them religiously. Genealogy is not intended here as a substitute for social history ("real history," as many would put it) but as a way of working back from our present to the contingencies that have come together to give us our certainties.

But precisely for this reason, because the secular is so much part of our modern life, it is not easy to grasp it directly. I think it is best pursued through its shadows, as it were. That is why in the first chapter I pay special attention to the notion of myth (central to the modern idea of "enchantment") in some of its historical guises—and then, in Chapters 2 and 3, I discuss agency, pain, and cruelty in relation to embodiment. From these explorations of the secular, I move to aspects of secularism—to conceptions of the human that underlie subjective rights (Chapter 4), the notion of "religious minorities" in Europe (Chapter 5), and the question of whether nationalism is essentially secular or religious (Chapter 6). In the final chapter I deal at some length with some transformations in religious authority, law, and ethics in colonial Egypt that illuminate aspects of secularization not usually attended to.

Finally: Can anthropology as such contribute anything to the clarification of questions about secularism? Most anthropologists are taught that their discipline is essentially defined by a research technique (participant observation) carried out in a circumscribed field, and that as such it deals with particularity—with what Clifford Geertz, following the philosopher Gilbert Ryle, called "thick description." And isn't secularism a universal concept, applicable throughout the modern world—capable at once of explaining and moderating the volatility of cultural multiplicities?

In my view anthropology is more than a method, and it should not be equated—as it has popularly become—with the direction given to inquiry by the pseudoscientific notion of "fieldwork." Mary Douglas once proposed that although conventional accounts of the rise of modern anthropology locate it in the shift from armchair theorizing to intensive fieldwork (with invocations of Boas, Rivers, and Malinowski), the real story was very different. The account of modern anthropology that she favors begins with Marcel Mauss, pioneer of the systematic inquiry into cultural concepts ("Foreword" to Marcel Mauss, *The Gift*, London: Routledge, 1990, p. x). Douglas herself has been a distinguished contributor to this tradition of anthropology. But conceptual analysis as such is as old as philosophy. What is distinctive about modern anthropology is the comparison of embedded concepts (representations) between societies differently located in time or space. The important thing in this comparative analysis is not their origin (Western or non-Western), but the forms of life that articulate them, the powers they release or disable. Secularism—like religion—is such a concept.

An anthropology of secularism should thus start with a curiosity about the doctrine and practice of secularism regardless of where they have originated, and it would ask: How do attitudes to the human body (to pain, physical damage, decay, and death, to physical integrity, bodily growth, and sexual enjoyment) differ in various forms of life? What structures of the senses—hearing, seeing, touching—do these attitudes depend on? In what ways does the law define and regulate practices and doctrines on the grounds that they are "truly human"? What discursive spaces does this work of definition and regulation open up for grammars of "the secular" and "the religious"? How do all these sensibilities, attitudes, assumptions, and behaviors come together to support or undermine the doctrine of secularism?

Trying to formulate such questions in detail is a more important task for anthropology than hasty pronouncements about the virtues or vices of secularism.

SECULAR

1

What Might an Anthropology of Secularism Look Like?

Sociologists, political theorists, and historians have written copiously on secularism. It is part of a vigorous public debate in many parts of the world—especially in the Middle East. Is "secularism" a colonial imposition, an entire worldview that gives precedence to the material over the spiritual, a modern culture of alienation and unrestrained pleasure? Or is it necessary to universal humanism, a rational principle that calls for the suppression—or at any rate, the restraint—of religious passion so that a dangerous source of intolerance and delusion can be controlled, and political unity, peace, and progress secured?[1] The question of how secularism as a political doctrine is related to the secular as an ontology and an epistemology is evidently at stake here.

In contrast to the salience of such debates, anthropologists have paid scarcely any attention to the idea of the secular, although the study of religion has been a central concern of the discipline since the nineteenth century. A collection of university and college syllabi on the anthropology of religion prepared recently for the Anthropological Association of America,[2]

1. These two points of view are represented in a recent debate on this subject between Abdel-Wahab al-Messiri and Aziz al-Azmeh, published as *Al-'almāniyya taht al-mijhar*, Damascus: Dar al-Fikr al-Mu'asir, 2000. I take up the theme of secularism and law in Egypt under British rule in Chapter 7.

2. Andrew Buckser, comp., *Course Syllabi in the Anthropology of Religion*, Anthropology of Religion Section, American Anthropological Association, December 1998.

shows a heavy reliance on such themes as myth, magic, witchcraft, the use of hallucinogens, ritual as psychotherapy, possession, and taboo. Together, these familiar themes suggest that "religion," whose object is the sacred, stands in the domain of the nonrational. The secular, where modern politics and science are sited, makes no appearance in the collection. Nor is it treated in any of the well-known introductory texts.[3] And yet it is common knowledge that religion and the secular are closely linked, both in our thought and in the way they have emerged historically. Any discipline that seeks to understand "religion" must also try to understand its other. Anthropology in particular—the discipline that has sought to understand the strangeness of the non-European world—also needs to grasp more fully what is implied in its being at once modern and secular.

A number of anthropologists have begun to address secularism with the intention of demystifying contemporary political institutions. Where previous theorists saw worldly reason linked to tolerance, these unmaskers find myth and violence. Thus Michael Taussig complains that the Weberian notion of the rational-legal state's monopoly of violence fails to address "the intrinsically mysterious, mystifying, convoluting, plain scary, mythical, and arcane cultural properties and power of violence to the point where violence is very much an end in itself—a sign, as Benjamin put it, of the existence of the gods." In Taussig's opinion the "institutional interpenetration of reason by violence not only diminishes the claims of reason, casting it into ideology, mask, and effect of power, but [it is] also . . . *precisely the coming together of reason-and-violence in the State that creates, in a secular and modern world, the bigness of the big S*—not merely its apparent unity and the fictions of will and mind thus inspired, but the auratic and quasi-sacred quality of that very inspiration . . . that now stands as ground to our being as citizens of the world."[4] Once its rational-legal mask is re-

3. Take, for example, Brian Morris's *Anthropological Studies of Religion*, Cambridge: Cambridge University Press, 1987, and Roy Rappaport's *Ritual and Religion in the Making of Humanity*, Cambridge: Cambridge University Press, 1999, neither of which makes any mention of "secular," "secularism," or "secularization," but both, of course, have extensive references to the concept of "the sacred." Benson Saler's survey entitled *Conceptualizing Religion*, Leiden: E. J. Brill, 1993, refers only—and symptomatically—to "secular humanism as a religion," that is, to the secular that is also religious. Recent anthropological interest in secularism is partly reflected in a number of brief statements on the subject in a special section of *Social Anthropology*, vol. 9, no. 3, 2001.

4. M. Taussig, *The Nervous System*, New York: Routledge, 1992, p. 116, italics in original.

moved, so it is suggested, the modern state will reveal itself to be far from secular. For such critics the essential point at issue is whether our belief in the secular character of the state—or society—is justified or not. The category of the secular itself remains unexamined.

Anthropologists who identify the sacred character of the modern state often resort to a rationalist notion of myth to sharpen their attack. They take myth to be "sacred discourse," and agree with nineteenth-century anthropologists who theorized myths as expressions of beliefs about the supernatural world, about sacred times, beings, and places, beliefs that were therefore opposed to reason. In general the word "myth" has been used as a synonym for the irrational or the nonrational, for attachment to tradition in a modern world, for political fantasy and dangerous ideology. Myth in this way of thinking stands in contrast to the secular, even for those who invoke it positively.

I will refer often to myth in what follows, but I am not interested in theorizing about it. There are several books available that do that.[5] What I want to do here is to trace practical consequences of its uses in the eighteenth, nineteenth, and twentieth centuries in order to investigate some of the ways the secular was constituted. For the word "myth" that moderns have inherited from antiquity feeds into a number of familiar oppositions—*belief* and *knowledge, reason* and *imagination, history* and *fiction, symbol* and *allegory, natural* and *supernatural, sacred* and *profane*—binaries that pervade modern secular discourse, especially in its polemical mode. As I am concerned with the shifting web of concepts making up the secular, I discuss several of these binaries.

The terms "secularism" and "secularist" were introduced into English by freethinkers in the middle of the nineteenth century in order to avoid the charge of their being "atheists" and "infidels," terms that carried suggestions of immorality in a still largely Christian society.[6] These epithets

5. For example: Ivan Strenski, *Four Theories of Myth in Twentieth-Century History: Cassirer, Eliade, Levi-Strauss and Malinowski,* Iowa City: University of Iowa Press, 1987; Robert Segal, *Theorizing About Myth,* Amherst: University of Massachusetts Press, 1999; and Bruce Lincoln, *Theorizing Myth,* Chicago: University of Chicago Press, 2000.

6. The word "secularism" was coined by George Jacob Holyoake in 1851. "Secularism was intended to differentiate Holyoake's anti-theistic position from Bradlaugh's atheistic pronouncements, and, although Bradlaugh, Charles Watts, G. W. Foote, and other atheists were identified with the secular movement, Holyoake always endeavoured to make it possible that the social, political, and

mattered not because the freethinkers were concerned about their personal safety, but because they sought to direct an emerging mass politics of social reform in a rapidly industrializing society.[7] Long-standing habits of indifference, disbelief, or hostility among individuals toward Christian rituals and authorities were now becoming entangled with projects of total social reconstruction by means of legislation. A critical rearticulation was being negotiated between state law and personal morality.[8] This shift presupposed the new idea of society as a total population of individuals enjoying not only subjective rights and immunities, and endowed with moral agency, but also possessing the capacity to elect their political representatives—a shift that occurred all at once in Revolutionary France (excluding women and domestics), and gradually in nineteenth-century England. The extension of universal suffrage was in turn linked—as Foucault has pointed out—to new methods of government based on new styles of classification and calculation, and new forms of subjecthood. These principles of government are secular in the sense that they deal solely with a worldly disposition, an arrangement that is quite different from the medieval conception of a social body of Christian souls each of whom is endowed with equal dignity—members at once of the City of God and of divinely created human society. The discursive move in the nineteenth century from thinking of a fixed "human nature" to regarding humans in terms of a constituted "normality" facilitated the secular idea of moral progress defined and directed by autonomous human agency. In short, secularism as a political and governmental doctrine that has its origin in nineteenth-century liberal society seems easier to grasp than the secular. And yet the two are interdependent.

What follows is not a social history of secularization, nor even a his-

---

ethical aims of secularism should not necessitate subscription to atheistic belief, in the hope that liberal-minded theists might, without prejudice to their theism, join in promoting these ends—an attitude to which he persisted in clinging, despite the small success which it achieved." Eric S. Waterhouse, "Secularism," *Encyclopedia of Religion and Ethics*, vol. 11, ed. James Hastings, p. 348.

7. Owen Chadwick, *The Secularization of the European Mind in the 19th Century*, Cambridge: Cambridge University Press, 1975.

8. That moment was a critical part of a much longer history. See the account of the gradual withdrawal of legal jurisdiction over what comes retrospectively to be seen as the domain of private ethics from the Middle Ages through the nineteenth century in James Fitzjames Stephen's *A History of the Criminal Law of England*, London: MacMillan, 1883, vol. 2, chapter 25, "Offences Against Religion."

tory of it as an idea. It is an exploration of epistemological assumptions of the secular that might help us be a little clearer about what is involved in the anthropology of secularism. The secular, I argue, is neither continuous with the religious that supposedly preceded it (that is, it is not the latest phase of a sacred origin) nor a simple break from it (that is, it is not the opposite, an essence that excludes the sacred). I take the secular to be a concept that brings together certain behaviors, knowledges, and sensibilities in modern life. To appreciate this it is not enough to show that what appears to be necessary is really contingent—that in certain respects "the secular" obviously overlaps with "the religious." It is a matter of showing how contingencies relate to changes in the grammar of concepts—that is, how the changes in concepts articulate changes in practices.[9] My purpose in this initial chapter, therefore, is not to provide the outline of a historical narrative but to conduct a series of inquiries into aspects of what we have come to call the secular. So although I follow some connections at the expense of others, this should not be taken to imply that I think there was a single line of filiation in the formation of "the secular." In my view the secular is neither singular in origin nor stable in its historical identity, although it works through a series of particular oppositions.

I draw my material almost entirely from West European history because that history has had profound consequences for the ways that the doctrine of secularism has been conceived and implemented in the rest of the modernizing world. I try to understand the secular, the way it has been constituted, made real, connected to, and detached from particular historical conditions.

The analyses that I offer here are intended as a counter to the triumphalist history of the secular. I take the view, as others have done, that the "religious" and the "secular" are not essentially fixed categories. However, I do not claim that if one stripped appearances one would see that some apparently secular institutions were *really* religious. I assume, on the contrary, that there is nothing *essentially* religious, nor any universal essence that defines "sacred language" or "sacred experience." But I also assume that there were breaks between Christian and secular life in which words and practices were rearranged, and new discursive grammars replaced previous ones. I suggest that the fuller implications of those shifts need to be

9. The notion of grammar here is of course derived from Wittgenstein's idea of grammatical investigation. This notion pervades all his later writing. But see especially *Philosophical Investigations*, section 90.

explored. So I take up fragments of the history of a discourse that is often asserted to be an essential part of "religion"—or at any rate, to have a close affinity with it—to show how the sacred and the secular depend on each other. I dwell briefly on how religious myth contributed to the formation of modern historical knowledge and modern poetic sensibility (touching on the way they have been adopted by some contemporary Arab poets), but I argue that this did not make history or poetry essentially "religious."

That, too, is the case with recent statements by liberal thinkers for whom liberalism is a kind of redemptive myth. I point to the violence intrinsic to it but caution that liberalism's secular myth should not be confused with the redemptive myth of Christianity, despite a resemblance between them. Needless to say, my purpose is neither to criticize nor to endorse that myth. And more generally, I am not concerned to attack liberalism whether as a political system or as an ethical doctrine. Here, as in the other cases I deal with, I simply want to get away from the idea that the secular is a mask for religion, that secular political practices often simulate religious ones. I therefore end with a brief outline of two conceptions of "the secular" that I see as available to anthropology today, and I do this through a discussion of texts by Paul de Man and Walter Benjamin, respectively.

A reading of origins: myth, truth, and power

West European languages acquire the word "myth" from the Greek, and stories about Greek gods were paradigmatic objects of critical reflection when mythology became a discipline in early modernity. So a brief early history of the word and concept is in order.

In his book *Theorizing Myth*, Bruce Lincoln opens with a fascinating early history of the Greek terms *mythos* and *logos*. Thus we are told that Hesiod's *Works and Days* associates the speech of *mythos* with truth (*alethea*) and the speech of *logos* with lies and dissimulation. *Mythos* is powerful speech, the speech of heroes accustomed to prevail. In Homer, Lincoln points out, *logos* refers to speech that is usually designed to placate someone and aimed at dissuading warriors from combat.

In the context of political assemblies *mythoi* are of two kinds— "straight" and "crooked." *Mythoi* function in the context of law much as *lo-*

goi do in the context of war. *Muthos* in Homer, "is a speech-act indicating authority, performed at length, usually in public, with a full attention to every detail."[10] It never means a symbolic story that has to be deciphered— or for that matter, a false one. In the Odyssey, Odysseus praises poetry— asserting that it is truthful, that it affects the emotions of its audience, that it is able to reconcile differences—and he concludes his poetic narration by declaring that he has "recounted a *mythos*."[11]

At first, poets tended to authorize their speech by calling it *mythos*— an inspiration from the gods (what moderns call, in a new accent, the *supernatural world*); later, the Sophists taught that all speech originated with humans (who lived in *this world*). "Whereas the Christian world-view increasingly separates God from this world," writes Jan Bremmer, "the gods of the Greeks were not transcendent but directly involved in natural and social processes. . . . It is for such connections as between the human and divine spheres that a recent study has called the Greek world-view 'interconnected' against our own 'separative' cosmology."[12] But there is more at stake here than the immanence or transcendence of divinity in relation to the natural world. The idea of "nature" is itself internally transformed.[13] For the representation of the Christian God as being sited quite apart in "the supernatural" world signals the construction of a secular space that begins to emerge in early modernity. Such a space permits "nature" to be reconceived as manipulatable material, determinate, homogeneous, and subject to mechanical laws. Anything beyond that space is therefore "supernatural"—a place that, for many, was a fanciful extension of the real

10. Richard Martin, *The Language of Heroes*, Ithaca, NY: Cornell University Press, 1989, p. 12, cited in Bruce Lincoln, *Theorizing Myth*, Chicago: University of Chicago Press, 2000.

11. Marcel Detienne notes that Herodotus calls his stories *logoi*, or *hiroi*, and never *mythoi*. "The famous 'sacred discourses' which our usage interprets as 'myths' all the more easily since these traditions are often connected with ritual gestures and actions—these are never called *mythoi*." Marcel Detienne, "Rethinking Mythology" in *Between Belief and Transgression*, ed. M. Izard and P. Smith, Chicago: University of Chicago Press, 1982, p. 49.

12. Jan Bremmer, *Greek Religion* (published for the Classical Association, Oxford University Press, 1994), p. 5.

13. For an early account of such transformations see the study by R. G. Collingwood, *The Idea of Nature*, Oxford: Clarendon, 1945, in which Greek cosmology is contrasted with later views of nature.

world, peopled by irrational events and imagined beings.[14] This transformation had a significant effect on the meaning of "myth."

The *mythoi* of poets, so the Sophists said, are not only emotionally affecting, they are also lies in so far as they speak of the gods—although even as lies they may have a morally improving effect on an audience. This line is taken up and given a new twist by Plato who argued that philosophers and not poets were primarily responsible for moral improvement. In the course of his attack against poetry, Plato changed the sense of myth: it now comes to signify a socially useful lie.[15]

Enlightenment founders of mythology, such as Fontenelle, took this view of the beliefs of antiquity about its gods. Like many other cultivated men of his time, he regarded the study of myth as an occasion for reflecting on human error. "Although we are incomparably more enlightened than those whose crude minds invented Fables in good faith," he wrote, "we easily reacquire the same turn of mind that made those Fables so attractive to them. They devoured them because they believed in them, and we devour them with just as much pleasure yet without believing in them. There is no better proof that the imagination and reason have little commerce with each other, and that things with which reason has first become disillusioned lose none of their attractiveness to the imagination."[16] Fontenelle was a great naturalizer of "supernatural" events in the period when "nature" emerges as a distinctive domain of experience and study.[17]

But in the Enlightenment epoch as a whole myths were never only objects of "belief" and of "rational investigation." As elements of high culture in early modern Europe they were integral to its characteristic sensibility: a cultivated capacity for delicate feeling—especially for sympathy—and an ability to be moved by the pathetic in art and literature. Poems,

14. Amos Funkenstein's *Theology and the Scientific Imagination: From the Middle Ages to the Seventeenth Century*, Princeton: Princeton University Press, 1986, traces the new scientific worldview, with its ideals of the univocation of signs and the homogeneity of nature, as well as of mathematization and mechanization, that emerged in the seventeenth century. Funkenstein shows—especially in Chapter 2, entitled "God's Omnipresence, God's Body, and Four Ideals of Science"—how this required of theology a new ontology and epistemology of the deity.

15. Lincoln, p. 42.

16. Cited in Jean Starobinski, *Blessings in Disguise; or, The Morality of Evil*, Cambridge, MA: Harvard University Press, p. 186.

17. Fontenelle's debunking *Histoire des oracles* (1686) was rapidly published in English as *The History of Oracles, and the Cheats of Pagan Priests*, London, 1688.

paintings, the theater, public monuments, and private decoration in the homes of the rich depicted or alluded to the qualities and quests of Greek gods, goddesses, monsters, and heroes. Knowledge of such stories and figures was a necessary part of an upper-class education. Myths allowed writers and artists to represent contemporary events and feelings in what we moderns call a fictional mode. The distanced idealization of profane love, the exaggerated praise for the sovereign, were equally facilitated by a fabulous style. And this in turn facilitated a form of satire that aimed to unmask or literalize. Ecclesiastical authority could thus be attacked in an indirect fashion, without immediately risking the charge of blasphemy. In general, the literary assault on mythic figures and events demonstrated a preference for a sensible life of happiness as opposed to the heroic ideal that was coming to be regarded as less and less reasonable in a bourgeois society. But, as Jean Starobinski reminds us, myth was more than a decorative language or a satirical one for taking a distance from the heroic as a social ideal. In the great tragedies and operas of the seventeenth and eighteenth centuries, myths provided the material through which the psychology of human passions could be explored.[18]

So the question of whether people did or did not *believe* in these ancient narratives—whether (as Fontenelle suggested) by appealing to the imagination untruths were made attractive—does not quite engage with the terrain that mythic discourse inhabited in this culture. Myth was not merely a (mis)representation of the *real*. It was material for shaping the possibilities and limits of action. And in general it appears to have done this by feeding the desire to display the actual—a desire that became increasingly difficult to satisfy as the experiential opportunities of modernity multiplied.

Some modern commentators have observed that statements such as Fontenelle's signaled a mutation of the older opposition between sacred and profane into a new opposition between imagination and reason, principles that inaugurate the secular Enlightenment.[19] This change, they suggest, should be seen as the replacement of a religious hegemony by a secular one. But I think what we have here is something more complicated.

The first point to note is that in the newer binary Reason is endowed with the major work of defining, assessing, and regulating the human imagination to which "myth" was attributed. Marcel Detienne puts it this

18. Starobinski, p. 182.
19. Among them, Starobinski.

way: "exclusionary procedures multiply in the discourse of the science of myths, borne on a vocabulary of scandal that indicts all figures of otherness. Mythology is on the side of the primitive, the inferior races, the peoples of nature, the language of origins, childhood, savagery, madness—always the *other*, as the excluded figure."[20] But the *sacred* had not been endowed with such a function in the past, and there was as yet no unitary domain in social life and thought that the concept of "the sacred" organized. Instead there were disparate places, objects, and times, each with its qualities, and each requiring conduct and words appropriate to it. This point requires elaboration, so I will now discuss the sacred/profane binary before returning to the theme of myth.

A digression on the "sacred" and the "profane"

In the Latin of the Roman Republic, the word *sacer* referred to anything that was owned by a deity, having been "taken out of the region of the *profanum* by the action of the State, and passed on into that of the *sacrum*."[21] However, even then there was an intriguing exception: the term *homo sacer* was used for someone who, as the result of a curse (*sacer esto*), became an outlaw liable to be killed by anyone with impunity. Thus while the sacredness of property dedicated to a god made it inviolable, the sacredness of *homo sacer* made him eminently subject to violence. This contradictory usage has been explained by classicists (with the acknowledged help of anthropologist colleagues) in terms of "taboo," a supposedly primitive notion that confounds ideas of the sacred with those of the unclean, ideas that "spiritual" religion was later to distinguish and use more logically.[22] The conception that "taboo" is the primordial origin of "the sacred"

20. Detienne, pp. 46–47, italics in original.
21. W. W. Fowler, "The Original Meaning of the Word *Sacer*," in *Roman Essays and Interpretations*, Oxford: Clarendon Press, 1920, p. 15.
22. "If this is the right meaning of the word *sacer* in *sacer esto*, we may, I think, trace it back to the older stage in which it meant simply 'taboo' without reference to a deity; and we have seen that it seems to be so used in one or two of the ancient laws" (Fowler, p. 21). But the evolutionary explanation offered here is at once dubious and unnecessary. Giorgio Agamben has more interestingly argued that the "sacred man," object of the curse *sacer esto*, must be understood in relation to the logic of sovereignty, which he regards as the absolute power over life and death in *Homo Sacer: Sovereign Power and Bare Life*, Stanford, CA: Stanford University Press, 1998.

has a long history in anthropology, from which it was borrowed not only by classics to understand antique religion but also by Christian theology to reconstruct a "true" one. The anthropological part of that history is critically examined in a study by Franz Steiner in which he shows that the notion "taboo" is built on very shaky ethnographic and linguistic foundations.[23]

According to the *Oxford English Dictionary*, "sacred" in early modern English usage generally referred to individual things, persons, and occasions that were set apart and entitled to veneration. Yet if we consider the examples given in the dictionary—the poetic line "That sacred Fruit, sacred to abstinence," the inscription "sacred to the memory of Samuel Butler," the address-form "your sacred majesty," the phrase "a sacred concert"—it is virtually impossible to identify the setting apart or the venerating as being the same act in all cases. The subject to whom such things, occasions, or persons are said to be sacred does not stand in the same relation to them. It was late nineteenth-century anthropological and theological thought that rendered a variety of overlapping social usages rooted in changing and heterogeneous forms of life into a single immutable essence, and claimed it to be the object of a universal human experience called "religious."[24] The supposedly universal opposition between

23. In fact Steiner claimed that the problem of taboo was a Victorian invention, occasioned by ideological and social developments in Victorian society itself. See Franz Steiner, *Taboo*, London: Cohen & West, 1956.

24. The classic statement is Durkheim's. "All known religious beliefs, whether simple or complex, present one common characteristic," writes Durkheim. "They presuppose a classification of all things, real and ideal, of which men think, into two classes or opposed groups, generally designated by two distinct terms which are translated well enough by the words *profane* and *sacred* (*profane, sacré*). The division of the world into two domains, the one containing all that is sacred, the other all that is profane, is the distinctive trait of religious thought; the beliefs, myths, dogmas and legends are either representations or systems of representations which express the nature of sacred things, the virtues and powers that are attributed to them, or their relations with each other and with profane things. But by sacred things one must not understand simply those personal beings which are called gods or spirits; a rock, a tree, a spring, a pebble, a piece of wood, a house, in a word, anything can be sacred. A rite can have this character; in fact, the rite does not exist which does not have it to a certain degree. There are words, expressions and formulae which can be pronounced only by the mouths of consecrated persons; there are gestures and movements which everybody cannot perform" (*Elementary Forms of the Religious Life*, 1915, p. 37). Critics have objected that Durkheim was wrong to claim that

"sacred" and "profane" finds no place in premodern writing. In medieval theology, the overriding antinomy was between "the divine" and "the satanic" (both of them transcendent powers) or "the spiritual" and "the temporal" (both of them worldly institutions), not between a supernatural sacred and a natural profane.

In France, for example, the word *sacré* was not part of the language of ordinary Christian life in the Middle Ages and in early modern times.[25] It had learned uses, by which reference could be made to particular things (vessels), institutions (the College of Cardinals), and persons (the body of the king), but no unique *experience* was presupposed in relation to the objects to which it referred, and they were not set apart in a uniform way. The word and the concept that mattered to popular religion during this entire period—that is, to practices and sensibilities—was *sainteté*, a beneficent quality of certain persons and their relics, closely connected to the common people and their ordinary world. The word *sacré* becomes salient at the time of the Revolution and acquires intimidating resonances of secular power. Thus the Preamble to the *Déclaration des Droits de l'homme* (1789) speaks of "droits naturels, inaliénables et sacrés." The right to property is qualified *sacré* in article 17. "L'amour sacré de la patrie" is a common nineteenth-century expression.[26] Clearly the individual experience denoted by these usages, and the behavior expected of the citizen claiming to have it, were quite different from anything signified by the term "sacred" during the Middle Ages. It was now part of the discourse integral to functions and aspirations of the modern, secular state, in which the sacralization of individual citizen and collective people expresses a form of naturalized power.[27]

François Isambert has described in detail how the Durkheimian

---

profane and sacred are mutually exclusive domains because profane things can become sacred and vice versa. (See William Paden, "Before 'The Secular' Became Theological: Rereading The Durkheimian Legacy," *Method and Theory in the Study of Religion*, vol. 3, no. 1, 1991, who defends Durkheim against this charge.) More recently, critics have protested that in ordinary life sacred and profane are typically "scrambled together." But even such critics accept the universality of the sacred, which they represent as a special kind of power. What they object to is the idea of its rigid separation from "the materiality of everyday life" (see Colleen McDannell, *Material Christianity*, New Haven, CT: Yale University Press, 1995, chapter 1).

25. See Michel Despland, "The Sacred: The French Evidence," *Method and Theory in the Study of Religion*, vol. 3, no. 1, 1991, p. 43.

26. Ibid.

27. See the excellent history of universal suffrage in France: Pierre Rosanvallon, *Le sacre du citoyen*, Paris: Gallimard, 1992.

school, drawing upon Robertson Smith's notion of "taboo" as the typical form of primitive religion, arrived at the scholarly concept of "the sacred" as a universal essence.[28] The sacred came to refer to everything of social interest—collective states, traditions, sentiments—that society elaborates as representations, and was even said to be the evolutionary source of cognitive categories.[29] The sacred, constituted first by anthropologists and then taken over by theologians, became a universal quality hidden in things and an objective limit to mundane action. The sacred was at once a transcendent force that imposed itself on the subject and a space that must never, under threat of dire consequence, be violated—that is, profaned. In brief, "the sacred" came to be constituted as a mysterious, mythic thing,[30] the focus of moral and administrative disciplines.

It was in the context of an emerging discipline of comparative religion that anthropology developed a transcendent notion of the sacred. An interesting version of this is to be found in the work of R. R. Marett,[31] who proposed that ritual should be regarded as having the function of regulating emotions, especially in critical situations of life, an idea that enabled him to offer a well-known anthropological definition of the sacraments: "For anthropological purposes," he wrote, "let us define a sacrament as any rite of which the specific object is to consecrate or make sacred. More explicitly, this means any rite which by way of sanction or positive blessing invests a natural function with a supernatural authority of its own."[32]

This notion of the sacrament as an institution designed to invest life-cycle crises ("mating," "dying," and so forth) with "supernatural authority,"

28. F. Isambert, *Le sens du sacré*, Paris: Les Éditions de Minuit, 1982.

29. But this original inclusiveness, Isambert points out, was precisely what made it useless for identifying the particularity of religion: "On voit ainsi que cette expression du domaine sacré était bien faite pour fonder l'idée d'une évolution des divers secteurs de la pensée à partir de la religion. Mais, pour la même, la notion devenait impropre à la détermination de la spécificité du domaine religieux" (op. cit., p. 221).

30. "C'est ainsi que le sacré en arrive à être constitué en objet mythique" (op. cit., p. 256).

31. Marett is famous for the claim that "savage religion is something not so much thought out as danced out." R. R. Marett, *The Threshold of Religion*, 2nd ed., Oxford: Clarendon Press, 1914, p. xxxi. He was also the authority for Fowler's venture into evolutionary anthropology (see above, p. 30, n. 22).

32. R. R. Marett, *Sacraments of Simple Folk*, Oxford: Clarendon Press, 1933, p. 4.

of its being essentially a "religious psychotherapy" as Marett also puts it, is presented as having general comparative application. But it stands in marked contrast, for example, to the medieval Christian concept of the sacrament. Thus the twelfth-century theologian Hugh of St. Victor, responding to the question "What is a sacrament?" first considers the conventional definition: "A sacrament is a sign of a sacred thing," but then goes on to point out that it will not do, because various statues and pictures as well as the words of Scripture are all, in their different ways, signs of sacred things without being sacraments. So he proposes a more adequate definition: "A sacrament is a corporeal or material element [sounds, gestures, vestments, instruments] set before the senses without, representing by similitude and signifying by institution and containing by sanctification some invisible and spiritual grace." For example, the water of baptism represents the washing of sins from the soul by analogy with the washing of impurities from the body, signifies it for the believer because of Christ's inaugurating practice, and conveys—by virtue of the words and actions of the officiating priest who performs the baptism—spiritual grace. The three functions are not self-evident but must be identified and expounded by those in authority. (Medieval Christians learnt the meanings of elaborate allegories used in the mass through authorized commentaries.) Thus according to Hugh, a sacrament—from the moment of its authoritative foundation—was a complex network of signifiers and signifieds that acts, like an icon, commemoratively. The icon is both itself and a sign of what is already present in the minds of properly disciplined participants; it points backward to their memory and forward to their expectation as Christians.[33] It does not make sense to say, with reference to the account Hugh gives, that in the sacraments "natural" functions are endowed with "supernatural" authority (that is, a transcendent endowment), still less that the sacraments are a psychotherapy for helping humans through their life-crises (a useful myth). Hugh insists that there are conditions in which the sacraments are not recognized for what they are: "This is why the eyes of infidels who see only visible things despise venerating the sacraments of salvation, because beholding in this only what is contemptible without invisible species they do not recognize the invisible virtue within and the fruit of obedience."[34] The authority of the sacraments is itself an engagement of the Christian subject

33. I discuss Hugh of St. Victor's account of the sacraments in some detail in *Genealogies of Religion*, Baltimore: Johns Hopkins University Press, pp. 153–58.

34. Hugh of St. Victor, *On the Sacraments of the Christian Faith*, ed. R. J. Defarrari, Cambridge, Mass.: Harvard University Press, 1951, p. 156.

with what his eyes see as an embodiment of divine grace.[35] Grace is conceived of as a particular state of unawareness within a relationship, not as a divine payment for ritual assiduity.

What facilitated the essentialization of "the sacred" as an external, transcendent power? My tentative answer is that new theorizations of the sacred were connected with European encounters with the non-European world, in the enlightened space and time that witnessed the construction of "religion" and "nature" as universal categories. From early modern Europe—through what is retrospectively called the secular Enlightenment and into the long nineteenth century, within Christian Europe and in its overseas possessions—the things, words, and practices distinguished or set apart by "Nature Folk" were constituted by Europeans as "fetish" and "taboo."[36] What had been regarded in the sixteenth and seventeenth centuries in theological terms as "idolatry" and "devil-worship"[37] (devotion to false gods) became the secular concept of "superstition" (a meaningless survival)[38] in the framework of eighteenth- and nineteenth-century evolutionary thought. But they remained objects and relations falsely given truth status, wrongly endowed with virtuous power. They had to be constituted as categories of illusion and oppression before people could be liberated from them, as Freud knew when he used "fetish" and "taboo" to identify symptoms of primitive repressions in the psychopathology of modern individuals.

It may therefore be suggested that "profanation" is a kind of forcible emancipation from error and despotism. Reason requires that false things be either proscribed and eliminated, or transcribed and re-sited as objects to be seen, heard, and touched by the properly educated senses. By successfully unmasking pretended power (profaning it) universal reason dis-

35. According to John Milbank, a profound shift occurred in the later Middle Ages in the way the "sacrament" was understood, making it the external dress of spiritual power, a semantic shift that had far-reaching consequences for modern religiosity (personal communication). See also Michel de Certeau, *The Mystic Fable*, Chicago: University of Chicago Press, 1992, especially chapter 3.

36. William Pietz, "The problem of the fetish, I," *Res*, no. 9, 1985; Steiner, op. cit.

37. Margaret T. Hodgen, *Early Anthropology in the Sixteenth and Seventeenth Centuries*, Philadelphia: Pennsylvania University Press, 1964.

38. See Nicole Belmont, "Superstition and Popular Religion in Western Societies," in *Between Belief and Transgression*, ed. M. Izard and P. Smith, Chicago: Chicago University Press, 1982.

plays its own status as legitimate power. By empowering new things, this status is further confirmed. So the "sacred right to property" was made universal after church estates and common lands were freed. And the "sanctity of conscience" was constituted a universal principle in opposition to ecclesiastical authority and the rules casuistry authorized. At the very moment of becoming secular, these claims were transcendentalized, and they set in motion legal and moral disciplines to protect themselves (with violence where necessary) as universal.[39] Although profanation appears to shift the gaze from the transcendental to the mundane, what it does is re-arrange barriers between the illusory and the actual.

Developing a Durkheimian insight, Richard Comstock has suggested that "the sacred, as a kind of behaving, is not merely a number of immediate appearances, but a set of rules—prescriptions, proscriptions, interdictions—that determine the shape of the behavior and whether it is to count as an instance of the category in question."[40] This is helpful, but I think one also needs to attend to the tripartite fact that (1) all rule-governed behavior carries social sanctions, but that (2) the severity of the social sanctions varies according to the danger that the infringement of the rule constitutes for a particular ordering of society, and that (3) such assessments of danger do not remain historically unchanged. Attention to this fact should shift our preoccupation with definitions of "the sacred" as an object of experience to the wider question of how a heterogeneous landscape of power (moral, political, economic) is constituted, what disciplines (individual and collective) are necessary to it. This does not mean that "the sacred" must be regarded as a mask of power, but that we should look to what makes certain practices conceptually possible, desired, mandatory—including the everyday practices by which the subject's experience is disciplined.[41] Such

39. Thus Durkheim on secular morality: "Ainsi le domaine de la morale est comme entouré d'une barrière mystérieuse qui en tient à l'écart les profanateurs, tout comme le domaine religieux est sustrait aux atteintes du profane. C'est un domaine *sacré*." Cited in Isambert, p. 234.

40. "A Behavioral Approach to the Sacred: Category Formation in Religious Studies," *The Journal of the American Academy of Religion*, vol. XLIX, no. 4, 1981, p. 632.

41. It is of some interest that attempts to introduce a unified concept of "the sacred" into non-European languages have met with revealing problems of translation. Thus although the Arabic word *qadāsa* is usually glossed as "sacredness" in English, it remains the case that it will not do in all the contexts where the English term is now used. Translation of "the sacred" calls for a variety of words (*muhar-*

an approach, I submit, would give us a better understanding of how the sacred (and therefore the profane) can become the object not only of religious thought but of secular practice too.

Myth and the Scriptures

I referred above to some functions of myth as secular discourse in Enlightenment art and manners. The part played by myth as sacred discourse in religion and poetry during the nineteenth and twentieth centuries is more complicated. Inevitably, in what follows I must select and simplify.

It has been remarked that the German Higher Criticism liberated the Bible from "the letter of divine inspiration" and allowed it to emerge as "a system of human significances."[42] We should note, however, that that liberation signals a far-reaching change in the sense of "inspiration"—from an authorized reorientation of life toward a telos, into a psychology of artistry whose *source* is obscure—and therefore becomes the object of speculation (belief / knowledge).[43] It was a remarkable transformation. For in the former, the divine word, both spoken and written, was necessarily also material. As such, the inspired words were the object of a particular person's reverence, the means of his or her practical devotions at particular times and places. The body, taught over time to listen, to recite, to move, to be still, to be silent, engaged with the acoustics of words, with their sound, feel,

---

ram, mutahhar, mukhtass 'bi-l-'ibāda, and so on), each of which connects with different kinds of behavior. (See below, my discussion of the self-conscious resort to myth in modern Arabic poetry.)

42. E. S. Shaffer, *"Kubla Khan" and* The Fall of Jerusalem: *The Mythological School in Biblical Criticism and Secular Literature, 1770–1880*, Cambridge: Cambridge University Press, 1975, p. 10.

43. In the middle of the twentieth century, T. S. Eliot attempted a formulation that embraced both religious and secular senses of the notion: "if the word 'inspiration' is to have any meaning, it must mean just this, that the speaker or writer is uttering something which he does not wholly understand—or which he may even misinterpret when the inspiration has departed from him. This is certainly true of poetic inspiration. . . . [The poet] need not know what his poetry will come to mean to others, and a prophet need not understand the meaning of his prophetic utterance." "Virgil and the Christian World" [1951], in *On Poetry and Poets*, New York: Farrar, Straus and Cudahy, 1957, p. 137.

and look. Practice at devotions deepened the inscription of sound, look, and feel in his sensorium. When the devotee heard God speak, there was a sensuous connection between inside and outside, a fusion between signifier and signified. The proper reading of the scriptures that enabled her to *hear* divinity speak depended on disciplining the senses (especially hearing, speech, and sight).

In contrast, the mythic method used by the Higher Biblical Criticism rendered the materiality of scriptural sounds and marks into a *spiritual* poem whose effect was generated inside the subject as believer independent of the senses. An earlier change had assisted this shift. As John Montag has argued, the notion of "revelation" signifying a statement that issues from a supernatural being and that requires mental assent on the part of the believer dates only from the early modern period. For medieval theologians, he writes, "revelation has to do primarily with one's perspective on things in light of one's final end. It is not a supplementary packet of information about 'facts' which are round the bend, as it were, from rational comprehension or physical observation."[44] According to Thomas Aquinas, the prophetic gift of revelation is a passion to be undergone, not a faculty to be used, and among the words he uses to refer to it is *inspiratio*.[45] A neo-Platonic hierarchy of mediations linked divinity to all creatures, allowing the medium of language to facilitate the union of the divine with the human.

With the Reformation (and the Counter-Reformation) an unmediated divinity became scripturally disclosable, and his revelations pointed at once to his presence and his intentions. Thus language acquired the status of being extra-real, capable of "representing" and "reflecting"—and therefore also of "masking" the real. "The *experiment*, in the modern sense of the word," notes Michel de Certeau, "was born with the deontologizing of language, to which the birth of a linguistics also corresponds. In Bacon and many others, the experiment stood opposite language as that which guaranteed and verified the latter. This split between a deictic language (it shows and/or organizes) and a referential experimentation (it escapes and/or guarantees) structures modern science, including 'mystical science.'"[46] Where *faith* had once been a virtue, it now acquired an epistemological sense. Faith became a way of knowing supernatural objects, parallel

44. John Montag, "Revelation: The False Legacy of Suárez," in *Radical Orthodoxy*, ed. J. Milbank, C. Pickstock, and G. Ward, New York: Routledge, 1999, p. 43.

45. Montag, p. 46.

46. Michel de Certeau, *The Mystic Fable; Volume One: The Sixteenth and Seventeenth Centuries*, Chicago: Chicago University Press, 1992, p. 123.

to the knowledge of nature (the *real* world) that reason and observation provided. This difference in the economy of "inspiration" needs to be investigated further, but it may be suggested that the modern poetic conception of "inspiration" is a subjectivized accommodation to the transformations here referred to.

Of course, I do not intend a simple historical generalization. For on the one hand the idea of an inner dialogue with God has deep roots in the Christian mystical tradition (as it has in non-Christian traditions), and on the other, a fusion between physical and significant sound has been a part of modern evangelical experience since at least the eighteenth century.[47] But my interest is in genealogy. I do not claim that Protestant culture was uniquely interested in inner spiritual states—as though medieval Christian life, with its rich tradition of mystical experience, had had no interest in them. My concern is primarily with a conceptual question: What were the epistemological implications of the different ways that varieties of Christians and freethinkers engaged with the Scriptures through their senses? (Discounting, suppressing, marginalizing one or more of the senses are also, of course, ways of engaging with its materiality.) How did Scrip-

47. But for opponents of the evangelical movement (whether Christian, deist, or atheist) the need to identify deceptive sensory effects was pressing. "To liberal-minded opponents like Chauncy, the vocal immediacy of evangelical piety was not in harmony with the Puritan fathers and genuine reformed devotion; it smacked of the Quakers and the French Prophets. 'The *Spirituality* of Christians does not lie in *secret Whispers*, or *audible Voices*,' Chauncy pronounced confidently. If stalwart evangelicals lacked such blanket clarity, they had similar misgivings. Ever wary of the dangers of enthusiasm and the claims of immediate revelation, many evangelical ministers would have been ready to concur with the Anglican rector Benjamin Bayly, who in 1708, maddened by inspired sectaries, dismissed 'this way of Revelation, *by Calls and Voices*,' as 'the lowest and most dubious of all.' 'It becomes Men of Learning and Piety, methinks, . . . not to ground their Belief upon so idle a thing as a *hollow Voice*, or *little Noise*, coming from behind a Wall, or no Body can tell whence.' Even as Bayly wanted to protect the unique persuasiveness of the divine voice that spoke to the biblical prophets, he did all he could to delegitimate these slippery, disembodied soundings among his contemporaries" (Leigh Eric Schmidt, *Hearing Things: Religion, Illusion, and the American Enlightenment*, Cambridge, Mass.: Harvard University Press, 2000, p. 71). Schmidt describes how the pursuit of practical knowledge about sound and hearing in the Enlightenment was linked to the unmasking of religious imposture, and how it included the construction of ingenious auditory devices by which (so the secular critics claimed) priests in antiquity had produced "supernatural" effects.

ture as the medium in which divinity could be experienced come to be viewed as information about or from the supernatural? Alternatively: In what ways did the newly sharpened opposition between the merely "material"sign and the truly "spiritual" meaning become pivotal for the reconfiguration of "inspiration"?

Robertson Smith, theologian, anthropologist, and devotee of the Higher Criticism, provides an example of the shifting direction and character of inspiration in his essay on the Old Testament as poetry, where he distinguishes poetry as force from poetry as art. This enables him to speak of all *genuine* poetry, whether secular or religious, as "spiritual." For when poetry moves "from heart to heart"[48] it becomes the manifestation of a

48. Contrasting Robert Lowth, who was among the first to approach the Old Testament as poetry, with Johann Gottfried Herder, Robertson Smith writes: "While Lowth busies himself with the *art* of Hebrew poetry, the theologian of Weimar expressly treats of its *spirit*. If the former professed only to commend a choice poetry to students of polite letters . . . , the latter seeks to introduce his readers, through the aesthetic form, into the inmost spirit of the Old Testament. . . . Lowth proposed to survey the streams of sacred poetry, without ascending to the mysterious source. Herder's great strength lies in his demonstration of the way in which the noble poetry of Israel gushes forth with natural unconstrained force from the depths of a spirit touched with divinely inspired emotion. Lowth finds in the Bible a certain mass of poetical material, and says: 'I desire to estimate the sublimity and other virtues of this literature—*i.e. its power to affect men's minds*, a power that will be proportional to its conformity to the true rules of poetic art.' Nay, says Herder, the true power of poetry is that it speaks from the heart to the heart. True criticism is not the classification of poetic effects according to the principles of rhetoric, but the unfolding of the living forces which moved the poet's soul. To enjoy a poem is to share the emotion that inspired its author" (William Robertson Smith, "Poetry of the Old Testament" in *Lectures and Essays*, London: Adam and Charles Black, 1912, p. 405, italics in original). All early poets, says Robertson Smith, united inner feeling with outer nature, and among the ancient Greeks and heathen Semites this union is differently reflected in each religion. In the latter "Always we find a religion of passionate emotion, not a worship of the outer powers and phenomena of nature in their sensuous beauty, but of those inner powers, awful because unseen, of which outer things are only the symbol" (ibid., p. 425). The evolutionary thought here is that the Semitic worship of inner (spiritual) powers as opposed to outer (material) forms enabled them to become the recipients of divine revelation (a communication *from* the deity), although the advance of the Hebrews from formal to spiritual religion was continually retarded by lapses into idolatry.

transcendent force that secular literary critics now refer to by the theological term "epiphany."

But as skepticism about *the source* of inspiration thought of as communication led to a questioning of the idea that the scriptures were divinely given, a concern with their historical authenticity—with true origins—became increasingly urgent. If God did not directly inspire the Gospels, then Christian *belief* demanded that at least the accounts of Jesus they contained should be "reliable," because only then would they guarantee the life and death of Christ in this world, and thus bear witness to the truth of the Incarnation.[49]

Much has been written on the way Protestant historians helped to form the notion of history as a collective, singular subject. "If the new view of History and the historian secularized revealed religion," observes John Stroup, "it also tended to sacralize profane events and the universal historian. . . . By the end of the Enlightenment sacred and profane history were so intertwined that it was hard to disentangle them."[50] In the same vein, Starobinski writes of the mythicization of modern history as progress: "It is not enough to note, as many have done, the existence of a 'secularizing' process in enlightenment philosophy, a process in which man claims for reason prerogatives that had belonged to the divine *logos*. An opposite tendency also existed: myth, at first excluded and declared to be absurd, was now endowed with full and profound meaning and prized as revealed truth."[51]

But I turn from the old themes of historical teleology and of the sacralization of history to focus on the project of historical authenticity. In that connection one should note that it was not an already constituted dis-

49. "If the question is whether the Christian religion is divinely inspired," noted the eighteenth-century theologian Johann David Michaelis, "authenticity, or lack of authenticity, of Scripture turns out to be more important than one might assume at first glance. . . . Assuming that God did not inspire any of the books of the New Testament but simply left Matthew, Mark, Luke, John and Paul the freedom to write what they knew, provided only that their writings are old, authentic and reliable, the Christian religion would still be the true one" (cited in Peter Bietenholz, *Historia and Fabula: Myths and Legends in Historical Thought from Antiquity to the Modern Age*, Leiden: Brill, 1994, p. 315–16).

50. J. Stroup, "Protestant Church Historians in the German Enlightenment," in H. E. Bödeker et al., eds., *Aufklärung und Geschichte*, Göttingen: Vandenhoeck & Ruprecht, 1986, p. 172.

51. Starobinski, p. 192.

cipline of secular history that was endowed with sacredness. On the contrary, it was Christian doubt and anxiety[52]—the discontinuities of Christian life—that drove biblical scholars to develop textual techniques that have since become part of the foundation of modern, secular historiography.[53] Herbert Butterfield, in his history of modern historiography, puts it this way: "the truth of religion was so momentous an issue, and the controversies about it so intense, that the critical methods were developing in ecclesiastical research before anybody thought of transposing them into the field of modern history."[54] But this move should not, strictly speaking, be thought of as a transposition. A secular critique developed, accidentally as it were, out of a concern with the apparent unviability of Christian traditional practice and *that in itself* helped to constitute the field of written secular history. The result was a clearer split between "scientific" history

52. There were other conditions as well. "The rise of the central state implied the emergence of a literate group whose horizons were not determined by the ideas of particularistic society," writes Stroup. "In accord with this emergence was the origin of the Pietist and Enlightenment Christianity placing great emphasis on public toleration and private religiosity: the institutional church and its dogma were to be of secondary importance. What mattered was arriving at a Christianity that transcended existing factions: one immune from the machinations of the clerical estate. The related attack on the divine legitimation, apostolic foundation, and juridical privilege of the existing institutional church and its dogma and clergy, utilized an appeal to history. The effort was made to reshape Christianity so as to remove any rough edges disturbing to the central state and its social allies" (op. cit., p. 170). However, it is not so much the alleged motives of theologians that interest me as the techniques they devised—such as "source criticism"—that helped to produce the field of modern secular history.

53. There were, of course, earlier moments in the construction of modern history that can be identified retrospectively. Thus, significant steps were taken in that direction during the Counter-Reformation by the Dominican theologian Melchior Cano when he sought to defend the traditional authorities under assault (see Julian Franklin, *Jean Bodin and the Sixteenth-Century Revolution in the Methodology of Law and History*, New York: Columbia, 1963, "Chapter VII. Melchior Cano: The Foundations of Historical Belief"). But my concern here is with eighteenth- and nineteenth-century developments when the idea of "secular" history separated itself definitively from "religious."

54. Herbert Butterfield, *Man on His Past: The Study of the History of Historical Scholarship*, Cambridge: Cambridge University Press, 1955, pp. 15–16. Butterfield is summarizing Lord Acton.

(including ecclesiastical history)[55] that depended on an attitude of skeptical inquiry in pursuit of authenticity, and "imaginative" literature (or religion and the arts generally) that depended on setting aside the question of propositional validity. This growing split was what consolidated "secular history"—history as the record of "what really happened" in this world—and in the same moment, it shaped the modern understanding of "myth," "sacred discourse," and "symbolism." As textualized memory, secular history has of course became integral to modern life in the nation-state. But although it is subject, like all remembered time, to continuous re-formation, reinvestment, and reinvocation, secular history's linear temporality has become the privileged measure of all time. The rereading of the scriptures through the grid of myth has not only separated the sacred from the secular, it has helped to constitute the secular as *the* epistemological domain in which history exists as history—and as anthropology.

In the mythic rereading of the scriptures, Christ's suffering, death, and resurrection could still be represented as foundational. But in the course of this reconstruction, Christian faith sought a reconsideration of the question of inspiration. God might not have literally dictated to the Old Testament prophets and to the apostles of the New, but the faithful Christian sought some sense in which they could still be said to be "inspired"—that is, literally breathed into by the Holy Spirit. Herder had initiated an answer by attributing to the Old Testament prophets a gift for giving expression to the power of the spirit, but it was his follower Eichhorn who applied this thought systematically. It was Eichhorn, too, who provided a new solution to the irreconcilable claims of skeptics and believers—the claim, on the one hand, that the prophets were charlatans, and on the other, that they were spokesmen for the divinity. Prophets, Eichhorn proposed disarmingly, were inspired artists. But what appears to have gone largely unnoticed was that while prophets were *called*, artists were not. Artists might commune with God's creation—but they could not hear his voice. Not, at any rate, in their capacity as poets.

Given that inspiration was no longer to be thought of as direct divine communication, romantic poets identified it in a way that could be accepted by skeptics and believers alike. Elaine Shaffer observes that Coleridge used sleep, waking dream, and opium (which he took for the relief

55. The collapse of ecclesiastical history into the general history of mankind was a crucial step in the constitution of comparative religion (see Stroup, p. 191).

of pain) to suspend normal perception and to attain to a state that could be described as an illuminated trance.[56] In this, as in other cases, there was more than a simple attempt to reassure skeptical opinion: a new twist was given to problematize further the notion of a unitary, self-conscious subject by attributing to fragmented states access to radically different kinds of experience.[57]

According to Coleridge's theory of imagination, poetic vision presupposed the alteration of ordinary perception, regardless of how it might be attained.[58] No longer opposed to reason, as in the secular Enlightenment, "imagination" now acquired some of reason's functions, and stood in contrast to "fancy."[59] For Coleridge, himself deeply read in German Biblical Criticism, prophets were not men who sought to predict the future but creative poets who expressed a vision of their community's past—the past both as a renewal of the present and as a promise for the future. And a "re-

56. There is an interesting discussion of "anaesthetic revelation" in William James's *The Varieties of Religious Experience*, Fontana Books, 1960 [1902], Lectures XVI and XVII. James is agnostic about the source of the mystical experiences reported by many subjects who had undergone total anesthesia for a surgical operation. But commenting on the ecstasies of Saint Teresa, he writes: "To the medical mind these ecstasies signify nothing but suggested and imitated hypnoid states, on an intellectual basis of degeneration and hysteria. Undoubtedly these pathological conditions have existed in many and possibly in all cases, but that fact tells us nothing about the value for knowledge of the consciousness which they induce. To pass a spiritual judgment upon these states, we must not content ourselves with superficial medical talk, but inquire into their fruits for life" (p. 398). James's religious philosophy requires that the idea of a governing consciousness be retained so that actions attributed to a unitary subject can be assessed overall on a pragmatic basis. In his assumption of a unitary subject James is closer to Freud—with his concept of a consciousness that misreads the language of its suppressed unconscious, an unconscious that needs to be unmasked through the practice of analysis—than either is to the notion of a decentered self whose successive experiences can never be recovered. True, Freud greatly complicated his earlier picture of id and ego as occupying respectively the domain of the unconscious and of consciousness, so that ego eventually came to be seen as itself partly unconscious. But it remains the case that the therapeutic work of analysis cannot take place if the self is taken to be horizontally decentered.

57. Eighteenth-century sensationalist psychology of Condillac and Hartley had begun, in its own way, to do this.

58. E. S. Shaffer, p. 90.

59. Samuel Taylor Coleridge, *Biographia Literaria* [1817].

newal," as the Durkheimian Henri Hubert was to point out much later, is a repetition, a participation in mythic time.[60]

Not only was it conceded that prophets and apostles were not super-human, they were even credited with an awareness of their personal inadequacy as channels of revelation. In the romantic conception of the poet, the tension between authentic inspiration and human weakness allowed for moments of subjective illusion—and thus accounted for evidence of exaggeration and insufficiency. In this regard the prophets and apostles were no different. What mattered was not the authenticity of facts about the past but the power of the spiritual idea they sought to convey as gifted humans.[61]

I now move from the history of Christian theology briefly to the history of ethnography, where we find changing concepts of inspiration entangled with an emerging experimental physiology and concepts of artistic genius.

Shamanism: inspiration and sensibility

An accumulating ethnography of shamans in the eighteenth century contributed to the recrafting of the idea of "inspiration" in secular terms.

60. See François Isambert, "At the Frontier of Folklore and Sociology: Hubert, Hertz and Czarnowski, Founders of a Sociology of Religion," in *The Sociological Domain: The Durkheimians and the Founding of French Sociology*, ed. P. Besnard, Cambridge: Cambridge University Press, 1983.

61. As the Hegelian David Strauss wrote in the preface to his epochal *Life of Jesus* (1835): "Orthodox and rationalists alike proceed from the false assumption that we have always in the gospels testimony, sometimes even that of eye-witnesses, to fact. They are, therefore, reduced to asking themselves what can have been the real and natural fact which is here witnessed to in such extraordinary ways. We have to realize that the narrators testify sometimes, not to outward facts, but to ideas, often most practical and beautiful ideas, constructions which even eye-witnesses had unconsciously put upon facts, imagination concerning them, reflections upon them, reflections such as were natural to the time and the author's level of culture. What we have here is not falsehood, but misrepresentation of the truth. It is a plastic, naive, and, at the same time, often most profound apprehension of the truth, within the area of religious feeling and poetic insight. It results in narrative, legendary, mythical in nature, illustrative often of spiritual truth in a manner more perfect than any hard, prosaic statement could achieve" (cited in W. Neil, "The Criticism and Theological Use of the Bible, 1700–1950," in *The Cambridge History of the Bible*, vol. 3, Cambridge: Cambridge University Press, p. 276).

This involved not only the shifting of all causation from outside the world of material bodies entirely into that world, but also an "inside" that had to be progressively redefined. That shift also served to separate healthy from unhealthy states of mind and behavior, and led—in the thought of Enlightenment rationalism—to the doctrine that morality be based on medical science rather than the other way around, as the older Christian view had it.

From the very beginnings of the encounter between Europeans and aboriginal peoples, Christian doctrine and rationalist skepticism tended to describe shamans[62] as demon worshipers, magicians, charlatans, or quacks, and the shamanic séance, with its drumming, its contorted gestures and strange cries, as merely grotesque attempts at deception. The shaman's claims to be able to divine and prognosticate were invariably dismissed and classed with the priests and soothsayers of antiquity who had pretended to commune with gods and spirits. But Enlightenment demystification did not preclude a curiosity, in some reports at least, about shamanic healing abilities. Greater attention was therefore given to the theatricality of séances, which were sometimes acknowledged to be remarkable performances in which music and rhythm helped to enrapture an audience and soothe the sufferer. There was some interest, too, in the natural substances used by shamans to cure or alleviate pain or illness.[63] However, such interest came from a culture in which pain was increasingly regarded as having an origin entirely internal to a mechanistic world and therefore susceptible only to the action of elements in that world. The shaman was a striking example of occult powers that appeared to elude the world of nature. As inhabitants of the supernatural they had to be explained—or explained away.

In eighteenth-century Europe the understanding of pain was undergoing momentous changes that have been retrospectively labeled "secularization."[64] Roselyne Rey, in her medical history of pain, describes a signif-

62. Michael Taussig has written an interesting study, partly historical and partly ethnographic, on the subject in *Shamanism, Colonialism and the Wild Man*, Chicago: Chicago University Press, 1987. Taussig's book is one of the sources of inspiration for Caroline Humphrey's *Shamans and Elders: Experience, Knowledge, and Power Among the Daur Mongols*, Oxford: Clarendon Press, 1996.

63. Gloria Flaherty, *Shamanism and the Eighteenth Century*, Princeton: Princeton University Press, 1992.

64. A triumphalist history of the secularization of pain describes the process as a move from the premodern resignation to suffering and cruelty justified or condoned by religious beliefs, to the accumulation of scientific knowledge and the

icant transformation in the deliberations of physicians belonging to the vitalist school. The myth of punishment for original sin was translated by the latter into the myth of punishment for transgressions against the laws of nature (for example, following a wrong diet or failing to exercise.)[65] This was a simple metaphorical translation, by which Nature was personified and endowed with an agency originally possessed by God.[66] But there was another and more interesting shift that Rey also identifies, one that was not merely a matter of metaphorical substitution but of a change in the grammar of the concept.

Citing attacks by the philosophes on the Christian justification of pain (a celebration of pain that begins with the myth of Christ's suffering) she notes that the discourse of sin and punishment was being set aside in favor of another.[67] In this newer discourse pain began to be objectified, set in the framework of a mechanistic philosophy, and sited within an accumulating knowledge of the living body acquired through the discipline of vivisection: "even a religious or indeed devout figure such as Haller," writes Rey of one of the great early experimenters, "could approach the question of pain without introducing religious obsessions; it is true that this was easier for someone whose work involved experimenting on animals, rather

---

growth of humanitarian attitudes that lead to the discovery and use of anesthesia in the nineteenth century. See Donald Caton, M.D., "The Secularization of Pain," *Anesthesiology*, vol. 62, no. 4, 1985.

65. "Their pain became totally secular since pain as well as illness were seen as nature's punishment for omissions in one's regimen, while mental illness was perceived as a sign of conflict between the demands of each individual character and the constraints of the social order; this interpretation called for a fundamental social reorganization when its standards (chastity in particular) went against nature. This explains why, as a leitmotiv, the physician of the Enlightenment maintained that in order to be a good moralist, one must first be a good physician, thus reversing the traditional relationship between medicine and morality" (Roselyne Rey, *The History of Pain*, Cambridge, Mass.: Harvard University Press, 1993, p. 107).

66. See Basil Willey's *The 18th Century Background: Studies on the Idea of Nature in the Thought of the Period*, London: Chatto & Windus, 1940.

67. Rey claims that "essentially, the main change occurred elsewhere. . . . This change lay precisely in the fact that for the physician or the physiologist, the problematical question of pain could be placed outside the problem of sin, evil and punishment" (Rey, p. 90). Strictly speaking the question of pain now becomes a "human evil"—a secular concept that lacks a supporting theology.

than being a physician [that is, being someone who cultivated in himself the arts of healing and comforting]. With Haller and the beginning of the experimental method, the definition of sensibility and the respective functions of the nerves and the muscles found themselves based on more scientific foundations."[68] That is to say, *activity* and *passivity* are distinguished in empiricist terms, by which *feeling* is attributed to the former and denied to the latter.

In this example the secularization of pain signals not merely the abandonment of a transcendental language ("religious obsessions") but the shift to a new preoccupation—from the personal attempt at consoling and curing (that is, inhabiting a social relationship) to a distanced attempt at investigating the functions and sensations of the living body. Pain is inflicted in systematic fashion on animals in order to understand its physiological basis.[69] So on the one hand we have pain inhabiting a discourse between patient and physician; on the other, pain is the reading made through experimental observation in a context where—as de Certeau noted—language has become de-ontologized. It is this latter model that informs Enlightenment skepticism toward the shaman's curative claims (mixed up as they are with ecstatic displays and "inspiration" by *invisible* spirits) and helps to constitute the secular domain of physiological knowledge through written reports of experimental results.[70] The contrast is not properly described in terms of "disenchantment" when what is at stake are different patterns of sensibility about pain, and different ways of objectifying it. Thus a question that preoccupied Haller in his animal experiments was whether pain was the product of the stimulus or of the body part to which it was applied: "It was in order to resolve this problem that, in his experiments, Haller multiplied and diversified the types of reagent and means used to stimulate a given part, using a process of elimination: thus he successively applied thermal stimulants, mechanical stimulants (tearing,

68. Ibid., p. 91.

69. "In Haller's work," Rey observes, "the animal's pain became an instrument of physiological investigation which allowed him to establish that only the nerves and the innervated parts are sensitive, whilst only muscle fibres are irritable" (ibid., p. 110).

70. Ibid., p. 109. In a review article on Roy Porter's history of medicine, Thomas Laqueur notes ruefully the counterpoint of violence, the pain inflicted experimentally on animals and on humans, that has accompanied the triumphant story of modern medicine (T. Laqueur, "Even Immortality," *London Review of Books*, July 29, 1999).

cuts, etc.) and chemical stimulants (oil of vitriol, spirit of nitrate) to each part. Electricity, and particularly galvanism when it was discovered, also provided a means of measuring the irritability of the parts and their residual vitality after death. The entire body was thoroughly investigated from head to toe: membranes, cellular tissue, tendons and aponeuroses, bones and cartilages, muscles, glands, nerves, etc." The concept of "experience" that had from early on had the sense of putting something to the test was now being used to identify an internal state through an external manipulation ("experiment").[71]

However, the claims of quacks (to whom shamans were often likened) were not always dismissed. Jerome Gaub, member of the Royal Society and professor of medicine, regarded their rhetoric and the credulity it addressed as valuable for healing: "It is this faith that physicians greatly wish for, since if they know how to procure it for themselves from the ill, they render them more obedient and are able to breathe new life into them with words alone, moreover they find the power of their remedies to be increased and the results made more certain." The extravagant performances of mountebanks who promised cures aroused wonder, and wonder led to hope. "The arousal of the bodily organs is sometimes such that the vital principles cast off their torpidity, the tone of the nervous system is restored, the movements of the humors are accelerated, and nature then attacks and overcomes with her own powers a disease that prolonged treatment has opposed in vain. Let those fortunate enough to have more rapidly recovered by means of these empty arts than by means of approved systems of healing congratulate themselves, I say, on having regained their health, regardless of the reason!"[72] For Gaub healing was a social process in which the inspiration of the healer was validated not by its occult *source* but by its salutary *effect.*

Interest in the mind-altering substances used by shamans was to develop much later.[73] But in the eighteenth century another aspect of the

71. For an account of the new grammar of "experience" in seventeenth-century natural science, see Peter Dear, *Discipline and Experience: The Mathematical Way in the Scientific Revolution,* Chicago: University of Chicago Press, 1995.

72. Cited in Flaherty, p. 99.

73. In her study of shamanism and poetic inspiration, Nora Chadwick refers to a nineteenth-century ethnographer of Siberian life: "According to Niemojowski children consecrated for the office of shaman are taught by old men, doubtless shamans themselves, not only the outward form and ceremonies, but the medical

shaman figure was being taken much more seriously: the shaman as poet, myth-recounter, and performing artist. Gloria Flaherty summarizes the reports of Johann Georgi, who described Central Asian shamanism and connected it to the origin of the verbal arts. "Like the oracles of antiquity, he wrote, contemporary shamans and shamankas [women shamans] spoke in an extraordinarily flowery and unclear language so that what they said could be applicable in all cases, whatever the outcome. Actually, he added, it was necessary that they did so because their believers, who had only hieroglyphs, no alphabet, themselves only knew how to communicate by sharing images and sensations. The litany was one favored form because its rhythms and tones affected the body directly, without appeal to the higher faculty of reason. . . . Georgi cited their particular kind of nervous system as the cause: 'People of such makeup and such irritability must be rich in dreams, apparitions, superstitions, and fairy tales. And they are, too.'"[74] Shamans, far from being mere charlatans were, as Herder more famously declared, oral poets, sacred musicians and healing performers who—for all the tricks they might use—enabled their audiences to sense in their own souls a force greater than themselves.[75]

If shamanic rhetoric and behavior were to be viewed as art, some artists could be viewed as shamans. If ecstasy had been a sign of mantic inspiration, it was becoming an indication of artistic genius. Flaherty writes of the evolving theory of genius in eighteenth-century Europe that drew on the classical myths of Orpheus as well as the ethnographic descriptions of shamans, a theory that eventually focused on the extraordinary international phenomenon of Mozart.[76] That he was often likened to Orpheus by his audiences was, says Flaherty, part of the mythologization of the great artist, of his healing and "civilizing" powers acquired through inspiration. Thus she cites, among other contemporaries, the physician Simon Tissot, who described "the stamp of genius" that Mozart's music making displayed: "He was sometimes involuntarily driven to his harpsichord, as by a sudden force," Tissot wrote, "and he drew from it sounds that were the living expression of the idea that had just seized him. One might say that at

properties of plants and herbs, with the different ways of forecasting the weather by the behaviour and migration of animals" (*Poetry and Prophecy*, Cambridge: Cambridge University Press, 1952, p. 53).

74. Flaherty, pp. 74–75.
75. Ibid., chapter 6.
76. Ibid., p. 150.

such moments he is an instrument at the command of music, imagining him like a set of strings, harmoniously arranged with such art that a single one cannot be touched without all others being set in motion; he plays all the images, as a Poet versifies and a Painter colours them."[77] This idea of inspiration was thus deduced from the artist's extraordinary *performance*, best described as a consequence of his being seized by an external force.

Johann Sulzer, a theorist of the fine arts, wrote in more general terms: "All artists of any genius claim that from time to time they experience a state of extraordinary psychic intensity which makes work unusually easy, images arising without great effort and the best ideas flowing in such profusion as if they were the gift of some higher power. This is without doubt what is called inspiration. If an artist experiences this condition, his object appears to him in an unusual light; his genius, as if guided by a divine power, invents without effort, shaping his invention in the most suitable form without strain; the finest ideas and images occur unbidden in floods to the inspired poet; the orator judges with the greatest acumen, feels with the greatest intensity, and the strongest and most vividly expressive words rise to his tongue."[78] Such statements, Flaherty argues, are strongly reminiscent of accounts of shamanism—in this case of a shaman described not skeptically but in wonderment. They employ the idea of inspiration metaphorically—as control of an "instrument" from outside the person, or as a "gift" from a "higher power." But these remain metaphors, covering an inability to explain a this-worldly phenomenon in natural terms.

But when the physician Melchior Weickard locates his explanation entirely in terms of human physiology, a genuine change in the language has taken place: "A Genius, a human being with exalted imaginative powers, must have more excitable brain fibers than other human beings," he speculates, "Those fibers must be set into motion quicker and more easily, so that lively and frequent images arise."[79]

Regardless of the adequacy of such explanations from the perspective of a later century, a secular discourse of inspiration now referred entirely to the abilities of "the natural body" and to their social demonstration. The genius, like the shaman, was at once object, performer, and reproducer of myth. For Immanuel Kant, a genius was simply someone who could naturally exercise his cognitive faculties wonderfully without having to be

77. Cited in ibid., p. 159.
78. Cited in ibid., pp. 151–52.
79. Cited in ibid., p. 153.

taught by anyone: "We say that he who possesses these powers to a supe-rior degree has a head; and he who has a small measure of these faculties is called a simpleton, because he always allows himself to be guided by other persons. But we call him a genius who makes use of originality and pro-duces out of himself what must ordinarily be learned under the guidance of others."[80] A genius was the product of nature, and what he produced was "natural," albeit singular. For this reason it could be appreciated by a cultivated audience exercising judgments of taste.

Myth, poetry, and secular sensibility

Poets from Blake and Coleridge on, "geniuses" in the romantic tradi-tion, experimented with the mythic method in their own religious poetry.[81] Myth was regarded in much early romantic thought as the original way of apprehending spiritual truth. If biblical prophets and apostles—as well as shamans in "the primitive world"—were now to be seen as performing, in mythic mode, a poetic function, then modern geniuses could reach into themselves and express spiritual truths by employing the same method. For this the virtue of faith was not necessary; all that was required was that one be sincere in one's intention, that one represent the deepest feelings truthfully in outer discourse. This may help to explain the prevalence among Victorian unbelievers of what Stefan Collini calls "a rhetoric of sin-cerity."[82] For not only was the idea of being true to oneself conceived of as a moral duty, it also presupposed the existence of a secular self whose sov-ereignty had to be demonstrated through acts of sincerity. The self's secu-larity consisted in the fact that it was the precondition of transcendent (po-etic or religious) experience and not its product.

Poets like Browning, who struggled to retain their religious convic-tions in an increasingly skeptical age, saw in mythic patterns a way to har-monize the findings of psychology and history—that's to say, to harmonize internal reality with external. Robert Langbaum observes that it was

80. I. Kant, *Anthropology from a Pragmatic Point of View*, Carbondale: Southern Illinois University Press, 1978, p. 22.

81. Coleridge's uncompleted epic *Kubla Khan* was a landmark—as Elaine Shaffer has so ably shown—in the development of modern religious poetry. But Blake (who was, incidentally, an inspiration for Coleridge) is also important here, although his work is not discussed by Shaffer.

82. *Public Moralists: Political Thought and Intellectual Life in Britain, 1850–1930*, Oxford: Clarendon, 1991, p. 276.

Browning who first outlined "what has come to be the dominant twenti-eth-century theory about poetry—that it makes its effect through the association in the reader's mind of disparate elements, and that this process of association leads to the recognition, in what has been presented successively, of static pattern. The recognition in the twentieth century is often called 'epiphany'"[83]—the sudden showing forth of the spiritual in the actual.

The mythic method continued to be important even among twentieth-century writers who disclaimed any religious faith, such as James Joyce. T. S. Eliot, in his laudatory review of *Ulysses*, writes that "In using the myth, in manipulating a continuous parallel between contemporaneity and antiquity, Mr. Joyce is pursuing a method which others must pursue after him. . . . [The mythic method] is simply a way of controlling, of ordering, of giving a shape and a significance to the immense panorama of futility and anarchy which is contemporary history. It is a method already adumbrated by Mr. Yeats. . . . Psychology . . . ethnology, and *The Golden Bough* have concurred to make possible what was impossible even a few years ago. Instead of narrative method, we may now use the mythical method. It is, I seriously believe, a step toward making the modern world possible for art, toward . . . order and form."[84]

T. S. Eliot famously used what he called the mythical method in his own poetry. However, this use of myth is not to be confused with Starobinski's reference to the mythicization of modern history that I cited earlier. There is no yearning for a lost plenitude in this literature. Here myth is invoked explicitly as a fictional grounding for secular values that are sensed to be ultimately without foundation.[85] It therefore marks a very different sensibility from the one to be found in the use of myth by Coleridge and other romantics. (Ironically, the fictional character of myth that led Enlightenment writers like Diderot to place "myth" together with "tradition" is precisely what leads early twentieth-century writers to link mythic fabrication to "modernity."[86])

83. Robert Langbaum, *The Modern Spirit: Essays on the Continuity of Nineteenth- and Twentieth-Century Literature*, Oxford: Oxford University Press, 1970, p. 87.

84. Cited in ibid., p. 82.

85. See also Joseph Frank, "Spatial Form in Modern Literature," in *The Idea of Spatial Form*, Brunswick, NJ: Rutgers University Press, 1991.

86. The *Encyclopaedie* entries begin with "Tradition" in the theological sense, proceed to "Tradition" in the religious sense (Christian and Jewish), on to

The importance of myth as a literary technique for imposing aesthetic unity on the disjointed and ephemeral character of individual experience the poet encounters in modern life has frequently been noted.[87] By a curious inversion, the "New" Arab poets, strongly influenced by modernist European poetry, have resorted to ancient Middle Eastern mythology in order to signify the authentically modern, indicating in this way their desire for escape from what they regard as the stifling traditions in the contemporary Islamic world. The most prominent among these poets is Adonis, the Phoenician pseudonym of the most eminent member of the *shi'r* group,[88] a self-declared atheist and modernist. Using devices familiar to Western symbolist and surrealist poetry, Adonis alludes to mythic figures in a self-conscious effort to disrupt Islamic aesthetic and moral sensibilities, to attack what is taken to be sacred tradition in favor of the new—that is, of the Western.[89] (These myths, incidentally, have had to be translated into Arabic from the writings of modern European scholars who transcribed and re-narrated them.) But in this respect Adonis's technique is figural rather than structural; it aims primarily to dislocate settled feelings, not to impose a sense of order and form where these are lacking. This use of myth in modern Arabic poetry is part of a response to the perceived failure of Muslim societies to secularize, and it is infused with a consciousness of "the West" as an object of emulation.

For Adonis, myth arises whenever human reason encounters perplexing questions about existence and attempts to answer them in what

"Tradition Mythologique," and end with "Tradition" in the jurisprudential sense (the action of transferring, giving up, a thing).

87. See Michael Bell and Peter Poellner, eds., *Myth and the Making of Modernity: The Problem of Grounding in Early Twentieth-Century Literature*, Amsterdam/Atlanta, GA: Rodopi, 1998.

88. So called after the periodical with that title, founded in 1956 in Beirut.

89. See the extended interview conducted by Saqr Abū Fakhr, "A Dialogue with Adūnīs: Childhood, Poetry, Exile," especially Part 9, in *al-Quds al-'Arabi* Daily, Friday, July 14, 2000, p. 13, which deals with enlightenment, secularism, religion, and tradition—and the role of myth (*astūra*) with respect to them. At one point, referring to a three-volume work on pre-Islamic myths edited by Adonis, the interlocutor asks him why myths and epics are absent in Islam. Adonis answers that Islam rejected prior texts as expressions of idolatry or superstition and magic, but it did, nevertheless, adopt many myths connected with Judaism—such as stories about the miraculous rod of Moses, the parting of the Red Sea, and so forth—which are themselves rewritings of earlier myths in the region.

can only be a non-rational way (*bi-tarīqa lā 'aqlāniyya*), thus producing a combination of poetry, history, and wonderment. The freedom to think in this way, to recognize publicly that myth is a necessary product of the secular mind, Adonis regards as integral to modernity. Hence in his poetry existential questions and historical ones are addressed in mythic terms. More specifically, his desire for salvation of the Arab people, held for a millennium in the grip of a "sacred language," is acted out through myths of alienation, of resurrection, and of redemption.[90] And yet in classical Islamic discourse the Arabic language of the Qur'an is never called "a sacred language" (*lugha muqaddisa*) as it is in modern secular discourse. For the latter idea presupposes an abstraction called "language" that it can then combine with a contingent quality called "sacredness."

Typically, Adonis uses the term myth both to celebrate human creativity (*ibdā'*) and to unmask the authority of divine texts. His concern is with Reason, and with restoring to humanity its essential sacredness (*qadāsa*). Echoing an earlier European (Feuerbachian) discourse, Adonis declares "Here the logic of atheism (*ilhād*) means the restoration of humanity to its true nature, to faith in it by virtue of its being human. . . . The sacred (*al-muqaddas*) for atheism is the human being himself, the human being of reason, and there is nothing greater than this human being. It replaces revelation by reason, and God by humanity."[91] But an atheism that deifies Man is, ironically, close to the doctrine of the incarnation. The idea that there is a single, clear "logic of atheism" is itself the product of a modern binary—belief or unbelief in a supernatural Being.

90. Myth (Greek and biblical) had also figured in the so-called romantic poets of the 1930s and 1940s, such as Abū Shādī, Nājī, Abū Shabaka, and others. Imitative of Western poetic styles, their self-absorption left them little scope for meditating on the problem of cultural salvation (see M. M. Badawi, "Convention and Revolt in Modern Arabic Poetry," in *Modern Arabic Literature and the West*, London: Ithaca Press, 1985). For the "New" poets it is precisely this latter preoccupation that gives their interest in myth its motive force. Thus in his famous 1992 "Declaration on Modernity," Adonis compares the Arab Self invidiously with the Western Other and finds everything of value in the latter. "It is not only modernity that is absent in Arab life," he concludes, "but poetry itself is similarly lacking" (cited in Muhammad Lutfi al-Yūsufi, "al-Qasīda al-mu'-āsira" in Fandi Salih, ed., *al-Mu'aththarāt al-ajnabiyya fī al-shi'r al-'arabi al-mu'āsir*, Beirut, 1995, p. 57).

91. Adonis (Ali Ahmad Sa'id), *al-Thābit wa-l-mutahawwal*, Beirut: Dar al-Awda, 4th ed., vol. I, 1983, p. 89.

Although the fundamentalist (*asūli*) form of Islamic thought that prevails today is itself mythic, he argues, it is a form of myth that has acquired for believers the character of law—of commandment—and so is not apparent to them as myth. For Adonis myth is plural, even anarchic, while the religious law is monotheistic and totalitarian. In marking the unconscious truth of contemporary religious discourse, myth clearly has a very different function from the one modernist European poets give it when they use it to ground secular experience.[92]

Democratic liberalism and myth

I began this chapter with the view of radical anthropologists who criticize the modern liberal state for pretending to be secular and rational when in fact it was heavily invested in myth and violence. I then proceeded to problematize the secular as a category by investigating its transformations. I now conclude with a contemporary liberal political theorist who argues that a secular, liberal state depends crucially for its public virtues (equality, tolerance, liberty) on political myth—that is, on origin narratives that provide a foundation for its political values and a coherent framework for its public and private morality. This brings us back to secularism as a political doctrine, and its connections with "the sacred" and "the profane."

Margaret Canovan maintains that if liberalism gives up its illusion of

92. In recent years Western scholars of Islam have produced some noteworthy analyses of myth in Islam. Thus Jaroslav Stetkevych claims that the Qur'an is a fragmentary presentation of an Arabian national myth that founds Muhammad's authority as an archetypal priest-king. I find his attempt at introducing Victorian assumptions about sacredness and nationalism into a very different cultural tradition ingenious but unconvincing (see J. Stetkevych, *Muhammad and the Golden Bough*, Bloomington: Indiana University Press, 1996). A very different approach to myth in the Qur'an has been tried—in my view more fruitfully—by Angelika Neuwirth. Unlike Stetkevych and Adonis, Neuwirth is not primarily concerned with mythic narratives but with the temporal structures of Qur'anic rhetoric. She describes in detail the way its style invokes as well as reenacts what she calls mythic time. In doing so she stresses the importance of the Qur'an as *recitation* and not merely as text—that is, as being not simply read for its informational content but read out and heard in a total engagement with the divine (see A. Neuwirth, "Qur'anic Literary Structure Revisited: *Surat al-Rahman* between Mythic Account and Decodation of Myth," in *Story-telling in the Framework of Non-fictional Arabic Literature*, ed. S. Leder, Wiesbaden: Harassowitz, 1998).

being the party of reason, it will be better placed to defend its political values against its conservative and radical critics.[93] The central principles of liberalism, she reminds us, rest on assumptions about the nature of mankind and the nature of society that are frequently questioned: "all men are created equal," "everyone possesses human rights," and so on. But no dispassionate observer of the human condition would find these descriptive propositions unproblematic, says Canovan. For men and women are not in fact equal, they do not all exercise human rights in the world as we know it.

Canovan points out that in the eighteenth century the ideas that eventually formed the core of liberal thinking were attached to a distinctive conception of nature as deep reality. In the succeeding century liberals invoked nature as a realm more real than the social world, an understanding that gave them grounds for optimism about political change. The terminology of natural rights referred not simply to what men (and later women too) *should* have, but to what they *do in fact* possess in the reality of human nature that lies beneath the distorted world as it now appears. However, for the conservative opponents of liberalism the inequalities and injustices in the world directly reflected the unregenerate nature of human beings.

Why did the ancestors of liberalism employ the terminology of nature in this way? Simply because in their thought the idea of "nature" served to explain and justify things. To insist that manifest social inequalities and constraints were "unnatural" was in effect to invoke an alternative world—a mythical world—that was "natural" because in it freedom and equality prevailed. But over time their assumptions about the nature of "man" exposed liberals to uncomfortable criticism. This weakness emerged most fully at the turn of the nineteenth century with the rise of sociological realism, and the simultaneous emergence of a new vision of nature as essentially violent and conflict ridden. What eventually resurrected the liberal idea of natural rights in the face of the vision of an essentially ruthless nature was not more effective theorization but Europe's experience of its own horrors in the shape of Nazism and Stalinism in the first half of the twentieth century. Thus the liberal myth has facilitated the entire project of human rights that is so much a part of our contemporary world, and that brings with it a moralism wrongly said to be uncongenial to secularism as a system of political governance.

93. Margaret Canovan, "On Being Economical with the Truth: Some Liberal Reflections," *Political Studies*, vol. 38, 1990, p. 9.

Canovan concedes that there are skeptical liberals who admit the fragility of liberal institutions and who stress the importance of secular citizenship and the need for conscious commitment to secular political arrangements in which religion is kept separate from the state. For them myth might seem less important. But there is no doubt—she insists—that in the beginnings of what we now recognize as liberalism, the myth of nature was inspirational, and that as such it enabled great transformations to be effected. Yet now liberal political discourse is again being exposed to attack. She thinks that liberal principles such as the universality of human rights are difficult to defend in the face of a sociologized nature. For when nature is interpreted positivistically in terms of statistical norms, then different norms of behavior and sentiment can claim to be equally natural. The result, we are informed, is a crippling relativism.

The defense of liberal principles in the modern world cannot, Canovan argues, be effectively carried out by making abstract arguments more rigorous, as Rawls has tried to do. This anticipates—albeit in another register—Stuart Hampshire's distrust of the use made of "reason" and "reasonable" in Rawls's exposition of political liberalism. "Why should an overlapping consensus among 'reasonable' persons about basic liberal values be either required or expected?" asks Hampshire. "The answer is to be found in the history of the myth of reason itself. Plato, discussing justice in *The Republic*, threw off the brilliant and entertaining idea that the soul is divided into three parts, just as the city-state is to be divided into three social classes, and in a just person's soul the upper part, reason, ensures harmony and stability, and in a just city the upper class, philosophers trained in mathematics, will impose order in a well-ordered society. . . . The corollary in ordinary and conventional speech has been that the desires and emotions of persons are supposed to issue from the quarrelsome and insubordinate underclass in the soul, and that they should be left in their proper place and kept away from the serious business of self-control."[94] The picture of human nature that has sustained liberalism from its inception, says Hampshire, is one in which passion and struggle, not reason and order, are central. Thus while Hampshire wants to do away with the myth of Reason in contemporary liberal theory, Canovan appeals to the reason of myth.

Canovan believes that liberalism can be defended only by recognizing and drawing openly on its great myth. "For liberalism never has been

94. S. Hampshire, "Liberalism: The New Twist," *The New York Review of Books*, vol. 40, August 12, 1993, pp. 45–46.

an account of the world," she writes, "but a project to be realized. The 'nature' of early liberalism, the 'humanity' of our own day, may be talked about as if they already exist but the point of talking about them is that they are still to be created. The essence of the myth of liberalism—its imaginary construction—is to assert human rights precisely because they are *not* built into the structure of the universe. The frightening truth concealed by the liberal myth is, therefore, that liberal principles go against the grain of human and social nature. Liberalism is not a matter of clearing away a few accidental obstacles and allowing humanity to unfold its natural essence. It is more like *making a garden in a jungle that is continually encroaching. . . .* But it is precisely the element of truth in the gloomy pictures of society and politics drawn by critics of liberalism that makes the project of realizing liberal principles all the more urgent. *The world is a dark place, which needs redemption by the light of a myth.*"[95] The liberal project of redemption in a world of injustice and suffering that Canovan urges us to recognize in mythic terms allows once again the sacred character of humanity to be affirmed, and the liberal project re-empowered. It permits the politics of certainty to be restored, and retrieves the language of prophecy for politics in place of moral relativism. Thus what has often been described as the political exclusion of women, the propertyless, colonial subjects, in liberalism's history can be re-described as the gradual extension of liberalism's incomplete project of universal emancipation.

The image Canovan employs to present and defend liberalism is striking: "making a garden in a jungle that is continually encroaching" and a "world [that] is a dark place, which needs redemption by the light of a myth." This image is not only an invitation to adopt a mythic approach; it is already part of the myth. It fixes on (explains and justifies) the violence lying at the heart of a political doctrine that has disavowed violence on principle. That is not to say, incidentally, that this violence is "intrinsically mysterious, mystifying, convoluting, plain scary, mythical" and "a sign of the existence of the gods," as Taussig has proposed. The liberal violence to which I refer (as opposed to the violence of illiberal regimes) is translucent. It is the violence of universalizing reason itself. For to make an enlightened space, the liberal must continually attack the darkness of the outside world that threatens to overwhelm that space.[96] Not only must that outside there-

95. Canovan, p. 16, italics added.
96. The gardening metaphor can also be found in nineteenth-century colonial discourse. Thus Lord Cromer, virtual British ruler of Egypt from 1883 to 1907,

fore be conquered, but in the garden itself there are always weeds to be destroyed and unruly branches to be cut off. Violence required by the cultivation of enlightenment is therefore distinguished from the violence of the dark jungle. The former is to be seen as an expression of law, the latter of transgression. Political and legal disciplines that forcefully protect sacred things (individual conscience, property, liberty, experience) against whatever violates them is thus underwritten by the myth. Liberalism is not merely the passion of civility, as Hampshire and others have asserted. It claims the right to exercise power, through the threat and the use of violence, when it redeems the world and punishes the recalcitrant. There is no fatality in all this—as Adorno and Horkheimer claimed—no necessary unfolding of an Enlightenment essence. It is just a way some liberals have argued and acted.

The liberal political scientist and Middle East specialist Leonard Binder reaches the same conclusion about the necessity of violence as Canovan but he does so through an explicit set of propositions about the possibilities and limits of *rational discourse*, apparently not through the invocation of myth: "1. Liberal government is the product of a continuous process of rational discourse. 2. Rational discourse is possible even among those who do not share the same culture nor the same consciousness. 3. Rational discourse can produce mutual understanding and cultural consensus, as well as agreement on particulars. 4. Consensus permits stable political arrangements, and is the rational basis of the choice of coherent political strategies. 5. Rational strategic choice is the basis of improving the

reviewing the reforms carried out under his authority, concludes, with imperial confidence: "Where once the seeds of true Western civilisation have taken root so deeply as is now the case in Egypt, no retrograde forces, however malignant they may be, will in the end be able to check germination and ultimate growth. The seeds which [Egyptian rulers prior to the British occupation] planted produced little but rank weeds. The seeds which have now been planted are those of true civilisation. They will assuredly bring forth fruit in due season. Interested antagonism, ignorance, religious prejudice, and all the forces which cluster round an archaic and corrupt social system, may do their worst. They will not succeed. We have dealt a blow to the forces of reaction in Egypt from which they can never recover, and from which, if England does her duty towards herself, towards the Egyptian people, and towards the civilised world, they will never have a chance of recovering" (*Modern Egypt*, vol. II, London: Macmillan, 1908, pp. 558–59). This trope of garden making in the heyday of imperialism clearly lacks the melancholy of Canovan's postimperial gardening myth.

human condition through collective action. 6. Political liberalism, in this sense, is indivisible. It will either prevail worldwide, or it will have to be defended by nondiscursive action."[97] But what Canovan calls the liberal myth is, I would suggest, part of the deep structure of Binder's abstract argument. Liberal politics is based on cultural consensus and aims at human progress. It is the product of rational discourse as well as its precondition. It must dominate the unredeemed world—if not by reason then, alas, by force—in order to survive.

In fact liberal democracy here expresses the two secular myths that are, notoriously, at odds with each other: the Enlightenment myth of politics as a discourse of public reason whose bond with *knowledge* enables the elite to direct the education of mankind, and the revolutionary myth of universal suffrage, a politics of large numbers in which the representation of "collective will" is sought by quantifying the *opinion* and *fantasy* of individual citizen-electors. The secular theory of state toleration is based on these contradictory foundations: on the one hand elite liberal clarity seeks to contain religious passion, on the other hand democratic numbers allow majorities to dominate minorities even if both are religiously formed.

The thought that the world needs to be redeemed is more than merely an idea. Since the eighteenth century it has animated a variety of intellectual and social projects within Christendom and beyond, in European global empires. In practice they have varied from country to country, unified only by the aspiration toward liberal modernity. But the similarity of these projects to the Christian idea of redemption should not, I submit, lead us to think of them as simple restatements of sacred myth, as projects that are only apparently secular but in reality religious. For although the New Testament myth may have assisted in the formation of these secular projects it does not follow that the latter are essentially Christian. They embrace a distinctive politics (democratic, anticlerical), they presuppose a different kind of morality (based on the sacredness of individual conscience and individual right), and they regard suffering as entirely subjective and accidental (as bodily damage to be medically treated, or as corrective punishment for crime, or simply as the unfinished business of universal empowerment).

In secular redemptive politics there is no place for the idea of a re-

97. Leonard Binder, *Islamic Liberalism*, Chicago: University of Chicago Press, 1988, p. 1.

deemer saving sinners through *his* submission to suffering. And there is no place for a theology of evil by which different kinds of suffering are identified. ("Evil" is simply the superlative form of what is bad and shocking.) Instead there is a readiness to cause pain to those who are to be saved by being humanized. It is not merely that the object of violence is different; it is that the secular myth uses the element of violence to connect an optimistic project of universal empowerment with a pessimistic account of human motivation in which inertia and incorrigibility figure prominently. If the world is a dark place that needs redemption, the human redeemer, as an inhabitant of *this world*, must first redeem himself. That the worldly project of redemption requires self-redemption means that the jungle is after all in the gardener's own soul. Thus the structure of this secular myth differs from the one articulating the story of redemption through Christ's sacrifice, a difference that the use of the term "sacred" for both of them may obscure. Each of the two structures that I touch on here articulates different kinds of subjectivity, mobilizes different kinds of social activity, and invokes different modalities of time.

And yet Christianity's missionary history managed to fuse the two—to fold the spiritual promise ("Christ died to save us all") into the political project ("the world must be changed for Christ")—making the modern concept of redemption possible.

A kind of ending: reading two modern texts on the secular

So how, finally, do we make anthropological sense of the secular? It is difficult to provide a short answer. Instead I conclude with two contrasting accounts that relate myth, symbol, and allegory to definitions of the secular: Paul de Man's essay "The Rhetoric of Temporality,"[98] and Walter Benjamin's book *The Origin of German Tragic Drama*.[99] Taken together, they indicate that even secular views of the secular aren't all the same.

De Man's famous essay is primarily concerned with the romantic movement and with the way it has been written about in modern histories. The romantic image, says de Man, has been understood as a relationship between self and nature (or subject and object), but this is mistaken. At

98. In P. de Man, *Blindness and Insight: Essays in the Rhetoric of Contemporary Criticism*, Minneapolis: University of Minnesota Press, 1983.

99. W. Benjamin, *The Origin of German Tragic Drama*, London: Verso, 1977.

first romantics rediscovered an older allegorical tradition from the Middle Ages, but that rediscovery occurred in a world where religious belief had begun to crumble faced with the discoveries of modern knowledge. It was—as Weber had said—increasingly a disenchanted world. In the medieval world allegory was simply one of a set of figures whose meanings were fixed by the Church's teachings for the purpose of biblical interpretation, and thus of exerting its authority. Because ecclesiastical disciplines were now no longer unchallenged, and belief in the sacred had begun to be undermined, de Man informs us that for the early romantics allegory was rediscovered in a different predicament. By virtue of the conventional succession of the signifier by the signified, allegory essentially played out an inescapable temporal destiny in which self and nonself could never coincide. *Early* romantic imagery therefore constituted the site of a reluctant coming to terms with the secular—a world in which there are no hidden depths, no natural continuities between the subject's emotions and the objects of these emotions, no fulfillment of time. It could be *seen* that the real was not sacred, not enchanted. And yet—so de Man puts it—this painful clarity about the *real* world that the early romantics at first had (in contrast to the mystified consciousness of religious believers) did not last. Very quickly a symbolic (or mythical) conception of language was established everywhere in nineteenth- and twentieth-century European literature and painting, allowing endlessly rich meanings to be recovered. Once again, de Man observes, symbolic imagination (or mythic interpretation) began to obscure the reality of this-world.

In his study of German baroque drama known as *Trauerspiel,* Walter Benjamin describes a different trajectory, one that directs the reader to a secular world that is not merely discovered (through clear-sighted knowledge of the real) but precariously assembled and lived in contradictory fashion. Although de Man also displays a sense of the precariousness of secular life in his writings, he retains a commitment to the secular as "the real" that Benjamin doesn't have.

Thus when Benjamin distinguishes between subject and object he begins not with the contrast between self and nature (as de Man does) but with the opposition between persons. It is the obscurity of intentions not of objects that generates suspicion, desire, and deceit in the exercise of power, and that makes a simple resort to sincerity impossible. Benjamin's baroque is a social world to which allegory and not symbol is central. The sixteenth- and seventeenth-century plays that Benjamin analyzes—primarily German but also English and Spanish—reflect a conception of history that is no longer integrated into the Christian myth of redemption. That is one aspect of their secularity. Another less obvious aspect is displayed in the emblematic character of Socrates' death. The legend of Socrates' judicially imposed suicide, Benjamin maintains, constitutes the secularization of classical tragedy, and hence of myth, because it substitutes a reasoned and exemplary death for the sacrificial death of a mythic hero. Although baroque drama does not quite represent the complete triumph of enlightened reason—thus Benjamin—it does signify the impossibility of classical tragedy and myth in the modern world. It aspires to *teach* the spectator. Its movement typically revolves around the person of the monarch, at once tyrant and martyr, a figure whose extravagant passions demonstrate the willfulness of sovereignty. Its theme is not tragic fate (from which nothing can be learned) but the mourning and sorrow that are invested in the dangerous exercise of social reason and social power.

Given the social instability and political violence of early modern times, there is a continuous tension in baroque drama between the ideal of restoration and the fear of catastrophe. The emphasis on *this-worldliness* is a consequence of that tension. Skeptical detachment from all contestable beliefs was conducive to self-preservation. In a striking sentence Benjamin observes that even "The religious man of the baroque era clings so tightly to the world because of the feeling that he is being driven along a cataract with it."[100] Thus Benjamin presents the emerging salience of the secular world in early modernity not by assuming the triumph of "common sense," or by invoking criteria acceptable to his secular readers for determining what is worthy of belief. He displays actualizing provincial rulers as they seek desperately to control an unruly world as allegorical performances.

Why is allegory the appropriate mode for apprehending this world? Because, says Benjamin, unlike romantic *symbol* (timeless, unified, and spiritualized) baroque *allegory* has a fluid temporality, it is always fragmented, and it is material. Allegory expresses well the uncontrollable, indeterminable, and yet *material* world of the baroque princely court with its intrigue, betrayal, and murder. In brief, this world is "secular" not because scientific knowledge has replaced religious belief (that is, because the "real" has at last become apparent) but because, on the contrary, it must be lived in uncertainly, without fixed moorings even for the believer, a world in

100. Ibid., p. 66.

which the real and the imaginary mirror each other. In this world the politics of certainty is clearly impossible.

That de Man attributes the secular attitude to the early romantics while Benjamin places it in the earlier, baroque period is really beside the point for my purposes. What is worth noting is that through his account of baroque allegory Benjamin provides a different understanding of "the secular" than the one de Man does in his discussion of romantic symbolism. For Benjamin takes allegory to be not merely a conventional relationship between an image and its meaning but a "form of expression." Citing Renaissance sources, Benjamin argues that emblems and hieroglyphs do not merely show something, they also instruct. (Language is not an abstraction that stands apart from "the real"; it embodies and mediates the life of people, gestures, and things in the world.) And what the emblems have to teach is more authoritative than purely personal preferences. The interweaving in such communication of what today many would separate as the sacred and the profane remains for Benjamin an essential feature of allegory.

This in at least two senses. To begin with, there is the *power* of a sign to signify: for in allegorical textuality, "all of the things that are used to signify derive, from the very fact of their pointing to something else, a power which makes them appear no longer commensurable with profane things, [a power] which raises them onto a higher plane, and which can, indeed, sanctify them." Actuality is never translucent even to the agent, says Benjamin. It must always be (provisionally) read. The representation (or signifier) and what it represents (signified) are interdependent. Each is incomplete, and both are equally real.

Second, the *interdependence* of religious and secular elements in allegorical writing implies a "conflict between theological and artistic intentions, a synthesis not so much in the sense of a peace as a *treuga dei* [Truce of God] between the conflicting opinions."[101] In other words, it is this conflict between the two poles that creates the space for allegory—so Benjamin maintains—and thus makes possible the particular form of sensibility called baroque.

In both de Man and Benjamin the secular is clearly opposed to the mythical. For de Man this means the exclusion of symbolism, for Benjamin the inclusion of allegory. The two approaches seem to me to have different implications for research as well as for politics. The one calls for

101. Ibid., op. cit., pp. 162–77.

unmasking a collective illusion, for seeing through an "enchanted world,"[102] the other for exploring the intricate play between representations and what they represent, between actions and the disciplines that aim to define and validate them, between language games and forms of life. Because Benjamin tries to maintain a continuous tension between moral judgment and open inquiry, between the reassurance of enlightenment and the uncertainties of desire, he helps one to address the ambiguous connections between the secular and modern politics.

102. I do not want to be taken as saying that de Man's views on unmasking are simple. Far from it. Thus in "Criticism and Crisis" he writes: "In the same manner that the poetic lyric originates in moments of tranquility, in the absence of actual emotions, and then proceeds to invent fictional emotions to create the illusion of recollection, the work of fiction invents fictional subjects to create the illusion of the reality of others. But the fiction is not myth, for it knows and names itself as fiction. It is not a demystification, it is demystified from the start. When modern critics think they are demystifying literature, they are in fact being demystified by it; but since this necessarily occurs in the form of a crisis, they are blind to what takes place within themselves" (de Man, p. 18). Literature, he maintains, is concerned with naming, but what it names is not an absence—as critics who seek to demonstrate its ideological function suppose—but "nothingness." However, it seems to me that there is, in de Man's statement, a wish to evoke an echo of the sacred within a "disenchanted" world.

2

Thinking about Agency and Pain

I suggested in the previous chapter that the secular is best approached indirectly. So I explored some ways in which the notion of myth was used through several centuries to shape knowledges, behaviors, and sensibilities we call secular. In this chapter I explore it through the concept of agency, especially agency connected to pain. Why agency? Because the secular depends on particular conceptions of *action* and *passion*. Why pain? For two reasons: First, because in the sense of passion, pain is associated with religious subjectivity and often regarded as inimical to reason; second, because in the sense of suffering it is thought of as a human condition that secular agency must eliminate universally.[1] In the latter part of this chapter I discuss some examples of agency from Christian, Muslim, and pre-Christian history in which pain is central. But I do so less for the sake of understanding the justifications some religious people give for the existence of

---

1. Lawrence Grossberg observes that "agency—the ability to make history as it were—is not intrinsic either to subjectivity or to subjects. It is not an ontological principle that distinguishes humans from other sorts of being. Agency is defined by the articulations of subject positions into specific places (sites of investment) and spaces (fields of activity) on socially constructed territorialities. Agency is the empowerment enabled at particular sites and along particular vectors" (Lawrence Grossberg, "Cultural Studies and/in New Worlds," *Critical Studies in Mass Communication*, vol. 10, 1993, p. 15). I agree with Grossberg that agency and subjectivity must be analytically separated, but I disagree that agency must be identified with "history-making" and "self-empowerment," as this chapter makes clear.

suffering than for investigating aspects of secularity. For if pain is the symptom of an afflicted body, it is first of all a limit to the body's ability to act effectively in the "real world." It is also the most immediate sign of this-world, of the senses through which its materiality, external and internal, is felt—and therefore it offers a kind of vindication of the secular. A crucial point about pain, however, is that it enables the secular idea that "history-making" and "self-empowerment" can progressively replace pain by pleasure—or at any rate, by the search for what pleases one.

The anthropological literature on the subject seems to me marked by a lack of adequate attention to the limits of the human body as a site of agency—and in particular by an inadequate sensitivity to the different ways that an agent engages with pain and suffering. When the word "body" is used, it is more often than not a synonym for the individual whose desire and ability to act are taken as unproblematic.[2] This is not so for those influenced by Freud, of course. In fact, although Freud's claim to have produced a comprehensive theory of the subject having universal applicability has been rightly contested by many, his concern with our incomplete knowledge of and mastery over our bodies-and-minds remains highly instructive. Thus, in her excellent study of early modern theories of the emotions, Susan James described the steps by which "desire" came to be thought of as the central force governing all actions. "As with most re-alignments of this sort, however, its achievements are bought at some cost," she observes. "On the one hand, an increasingly generic conception of desire paves the way for the modern orthodoxy that beliefs and desires are the antecedents of action. On the other hand, explanations of actions grounded on the view that the passions only move us to act in so far as they are kinds of desire, or are mixed with desire, are often comparatively blank. Taken generically, desires lack the inflections that would make them explanatory. Once we begin to expand them, we are drawn back into the intricate and sometimes baffling territory of the passions." This tension between "desire" as action and as passion, James suggests, has been uniquely addressed in our own time by Freud and his followers.[3] It should be added, however, that although Freudianism has an exceptionally sophisticated

2. A relevant collection that deserves wider critical attention is *Other Intentions: Cultural Contexts and the Attribution of Inner States*, ed. Lawrence Rosen, Santa Fe, NM: School of American Research, 1995.

3. *Passion and Action: The Emotions in Seventeenth-Century Philosophy*, Oxford: Clarendon Press, 1997, p. 292.

sense of the internal dynamics of the passions (mediators between mind and body), it holds out the problematic promise that the passions can ultimately be mastered by reason through systematic observation and interpretation, thereby giving rationality primacy in the constitution of the modern, secular subject.

In the last decade an increasing amount of research has been published on the centrality of emotion in cultural life, and this is certainly welcome for our understanding of agency. However, my interest in suffering as a passion is a little different from most of this literature. I ask first whether pain is not simply a *cause* of action, but can also itself be a *kind* of action.

There is no agreement among contemporary researchers on what emotions are.[4] Some insist that they are impulses occurring entirely in the part of the body called the brain, others that they are intersubjective, located in the social space individuals inhabit. Sometimes all emotion is equated with desire, at other times desire is regarded as one emotion among others. However, many theories apart from Freud's stress the unconscious character of emotions. And everyone, regardless of whether he or she has a theory of emotions or not, knows that some emotions ("passions") can and do disrupt or disguise intentions.[5] And yet conscious intention is assumed to be central to the concept of agency in most anthropological work.[6]

Even in the growing field of medical anthropology, where innovative work has given us a cultural understanding of health and disease, the standard meaning of agency is taken too much for granted. The sick body is of-

4. A useful discussion of various theories is contained in a recent book by the neuroscientist Joseph LeDoux, *The Emotional Brain*, New York: Simon & Schuster, 1996. I am grateful to William Connolly for directing me to it.

5. Collingwood argued that emotion is not essentially opposed to reason because all reasoning—and therefore reasoned action—is itself "charged" with emotion. See R. G. Collingwood, *The Principles of Art*, Oxford: Clarendon Press, 1938, especially the chapter on language that precedes Book III ("The Theory of Art").

6. Sherry Ortner complains of "the denial of the intentional subject, and of 'agency'" in contemporary social science writing (see S. Ortner, *Making Gender: The Politics and Erotics of Culture*, Boston: Beacon Press, 1996, p. 8). But I find agency talk very popular in anthropology and "the intentional subject" almost invariably part of it. The intimate anecdotal style of ethnographic writing now favored reflects a preoccupation with intentionality that isn't always carefully thought through.

ten represented no differently from the healthy body in that for both resistance to power is the form that agency typically takes.[7]

I find such views troubling because they attribute individual agency to the sick body by translating all its states and movements directly into "dissent." For when anthropologists talk of getting at the subject's experience of illness, they often refer not only to a patient's words but to his or her behavior as though it were a form of discourse. Rendering subjective reactions legible in this way seems to me unsatisfactory when we remain unclear as to how the behavioral "text" is to be decoded, when "dissent" or "resistance" is taken to be self-evident. Yet even in Freud "resistance" is a theoretically defined concept, one that has a particular place in the work of analysis. The sick body's suffering is not always to be read as resistance to the social power of others; it is sometimes the body's punishment of itself for desiring what it ought not to desire.

The anthropological use of the notion of "resistance" has rightly been criticized for underestimating the strength and diversity of power structures.[8] I am worried less by what has been called "the romance of resistance" than by the more inclusive category of "agency" presupposed by it. Of course in commonsense terms "resistance" occurs in everyday life, and it is often important to outcomes when it does so. My concern, however, is that our fascination with "resistance" itself comes from larger, support-

7. This can be illustrated by reference to a useful survey of recent work on the body by Margaret Lock who notes that "Bodily dissent has been interpreted until recently as marginal, pathological, or so much exotica, or else has been passed over, unnoticed and unrecorded. Historicized, grounded ethnography, stimulated by close attention paid for the first time to the everyday lives of women, children, and other 'peripheral' peoples has led to a reformulation of theory. The body, imbued with social meaning, is now historically situated, and becomes not only a signifier of belonging and order [as in the older anthropological work], but also an active forum for the expression of dissent and loss, *thus* ascribing it individual agency" (Margaret Lock, "Cultivating the Body: Anthropology and Epistemologies of Bodily Practice and Knowledge," *Annual Review of Anthropology*, 1993, vol. 22, p. 141. Italics supplied; the syntactic hiatus in the final clause is in the original). Like the oppressed working class, the sick body is seen as dissenting, and for that reason as an agent trying to assert its interests. A single psychological model of autonomy thus underlies both cases. The problem, however, is that to *read* the sick body's behavior as "expressions of dissent" we need different translation criteria from those we employ when we identify working-class dissent.

8. See, for example, the article by Lila Abu-Lughod, "The Romance of Resistance," *American Ethnologist*, vol. 17, no. 1, 1990.

ing ideas. The tendency to romanticize resistance comes from a metaphysical question to which this notion of "agency" is a response: Given the essential freedom, or the natural sovereignty, of the human subject, and given, too, its own desires and interests,[9] what should human beings do to realize their freedom, empower themselves, and choose pleasure? The assumption here is that power—and so too pain—is external to and repressive of the agent, that it "subjects" him or her, and that nevertheless the agent as "active subject" has both the desire to oppose power and the responsibility to become more powerful so that disempowerment—suffering—can be overcome.[10] I shall argue against this assumption. But to the extent that the task of confronting power is taken to be more than an individual one, it also defines a historical project whose aim is the increasing triumph of individual autonomy. The fact that "resistance" is a term used by theorists of culture for a number of disparate conditions (the unconscious behavior of patients, student protests in school, generalized movements for civil reform, the defensive strategies of labor unions, militants

9. The concept of "interest" (including "self-interest"), which agency theorists often invoke, is another psychological term that has a singular history and that presents itself to moderns as universal, natural, essential (see Albert Hirschman, *The Passions and the Interests: Political Arguments for Capitalism before Its Triumph*, Princeton: Princeton University Press, 1977). The complicated genealogies by which we have acquired our vocabularies for talking about agency and subjectivity, and the changing psychological theories they bring with them, should alert us to the dangers of applying them without careful thought and qualification to any or all social situations.

10. Although Foucault is often invoked by theorists of resistance, his use of that notion is quite distinctive. For example: "there is indeed always something in the social body, in classes, groups and individuals themselves which in some sense escapes relations of power, something which is by no means a docile or reactive primal matter, but rather a centrifugal movement, an inverse energy, a discharge. There is certainly no such thing as 'the' plebs; rather there is, as it were, a certain plebeian quality or aspect (*de la plèbe*). There is plebs in bodies, in souls, in individuals, in the proletariat, in the bourgeoisie, but everywhere in a diversity of forms and extensions, of energies and irreducibilities. This measure of plebs is not so much what stands outside relations of power as their limit, their underside, their counter-stroke, that which responds to every advance of power by a movement of disengagement" (*Power/Knowledge*, Brighton, UK: Harvester Press, 1980, p. 138). This notion of resistance as the "limit" of power has some resemblance to the Clausewitzian notion of "friction" (see Carl von Clausewitz, *On War* [1832], New York: Penguin Books, 1982, pp. 164–65).

struggling against an occupying power, and so on) points to one way in which a particular kind of deep motivation may become attributed to an essentialized subject-agent.

Theorists of culture sometimes find themselves at once asserting and denying the existence of such an essence. Thus the editors of a popular reader in contemporary social theory write in their Introduction: "From a theoretical point of view we need a subject who is at once culturally and historically constructed, yet from a political perspective, we would wish this subject to be capable of acting in some sense 'autonomously,' not simply in conformity to dominant cultural norms and rules, or within the patterns that power inscribes. But this autonomous actor may not be defined as acting from some hidden well of innate 'will' or consciousness that has somehow escaped cultural shaping and ordering. In fact, such an actor is not only possible but 'normal,' for the simple reason that neither 'culture' itself nor the regimes of power that are imbricated in cultural logics and experiences can ever be wholly consistent or totally determining."[11] Because they are progressive-minded (read: "constructivists"), these social theorists disapprove of any talk of "innateness." They also want to present struggle (resistance) and dissent (deviation) as normal to human behavior. But "normal" is a notoriously ambiguous notion, including both a descriptive statistical sense in which a *distribution* is normal and a prescriptive one in which being normal is being healthy, the opposite of pathological.[12] Sliding between these two senses, the editors can assert that there is nothing in the agent "that has somehow escaped cultural shaping and ordering," and yet insist that "culture" can never be "totally determining."

Of course anthropologists have written interestingly about the body, its emotions, and its engagement with the world through the senses. My concern is that because the human body has a changing life largely inaccessible to itself, because behavior depends on unconscious routine and habit, because emotions render the ownership of actions a matter of conflicting descriptions, because body and mind decay with age and chronic illness, we should not assume that every act is the act of a competent agent with a clear intention. Nor should we assume that a proper understanding of agency requires us to place it within the framework of a secular history

11. *Culture/Power/History*, ed. Nicholas B. Dirks, Geoff Eley, and Sherry B. Ortner, Princeton: Princeton University Press, p. 18.

12. See Ian Hacking, *The Taming of Chance*, Cambridge: Cambridge University Press, 1990, especially chapter 19.

of freedom from all coercive control, a history in which everything can be made, and pleasure always innocently enjoyed—a framework that allegedly enables us to see ordinary life as distorted or incomplete.

The paradox inadequately appreciated here is that the self to be liberated from external control must be subjected to the control of a liberating self already and always free, aware, and in control of its own desires. Susan Wolf identifies this metaphysical conundrum and the failure of recent philosophers to solve it. In place of the obsessive attempts to define the freedom of the subject as its ability to create its self, Wolf offers an alternative by drawing on the commonsense notion of being *sane*: "The desire to be sane," she writes, "is thus not a desire for another form of control; it is rather a desire that one's self be connected to the world in a certain way—we could even say it is a desire that one's self be *controlled by* the world in certain ways and not in others."[13] This notion of sanity presupposes knowing the world practically and being known practically by it, a world of accumulating probabilities rather than constant certainties. It allows us to think of moral agency in terms of people's habitual engagement with the world in which they live, so that one kind of moral insanity occurs precisely when the pain they know in this world is suddenly no longer an object of practical knowledge.

Thinking about agency

Assuming that agency need not be conceptualized in terms of individual self-empowerment and resistance, or of utopian history, how should it be understood? One might begin by looking at usages of the term (or what are taken to be its equivalents) in different historical contexts. This would indicate not merely that agency is not a natural category, but that the successive uses of this concept (their different grammars) have opened up or closed very different possibilities for acting and being. The secular, with its focus on empowerment and history-making, is merely one of those possibilities. I am unable to attempt a history of the concept of agency here, but I begin with some brief comments on contemporary usage.

Agency today serves primarily to define a completed personal action

13. Susan Wolf, "Sanity and the Metaphysics of Responsibility," in F. Schoeman, ed., *Responsibility, Character, and the Emotions*, Cambridge: Cambridge University Press, 1987, p. 55.

from within an indefinite network of causality by attributing to an actor responsibility *to* power. Paradigmatically, this means *forcing* a person to be accountable, to answer to a judge in a court of law why things were done or left undone. In that sense agency is built on the idea of blame and pain. A world of apparent accidents is rendered into a world of essences by attributing to a person moral/legal responsibility on whose basis guilt and innocence (and therefore punishment or exoneration) are determined. How did such a model of agency become paradigmatic? After all, human beings do, think, and feel all sorts of disparate things—what is it that brings all of them together? At least as far back as John Locke, "person" was theorized as a forensic term that called for the integration of a single subject with a continuous consciousness in a single body.[14] The development of property law in a nascent capitalism was important to this conception. But equally important was the way attributing an essence to him helped the human subject to become an object of social discipline.

Moderns tend to think of responsibility *for* something as being founded on a relation between an act and the law that defines the penalty attaching to its performance or nonperformance. Intention (in the sense of being a subjective cause) may have nothing to do with the matter, as when someone sustains an injury on another's property because of an accident. Agents need not necessarily coincide with individual biological bodies and the consciousness that is said to go with them. Corporations are both liable under the law and have the power to carry out particular tasks. But the projects of a corporation are distinguished from the intentions of the individuals who work for it and act in its name. Because "corporations never die,"[15] they can be described as agents but not as having subjectivity.

Agency also has the meaning of representation. In this sense the ac-

14. *Person*, writes Locke, "is a forensic term, appropriating actions and their merit, and so belongs only to intelligent agents, capable of a law, and happiness, and misery. This personality extends itself beyond present existence to what is past, only by consciousness, whereby it becomes concerned and accountable, owns and imputes to itself past actions, just upon the same ground and for the same reason as it does the present" (*An Essay Concerning Human Understanding*, Book Two, Essay XXVII, Section 26).

15. "Corporations never die," observed Henry Maine of their legal constitution. "The decease of individual members makes no difference to the collective existence of the aggregate body, and does not in any way affect its legal incidents, its faculties or liabilities" (*Ancient Law* [1861], Oxford [World Classics], 1931, p. 154).

tions of an agent are taken to be the actions of the principal whom the agent represents. The concept of representation, central to this meaning of agency, has been the subject of longstanding debate in Western political theory. Are elected representatives finally responsible to themselves (agents in their own right) or to their constituents (as their agents)? Whose wishes should they enact in the representative assembly? There does not seem to be a decisive answer. The idea of representation underlying agency is rooted in a paradox: that who or what is represented is both absent and present at the same time (re-presented).[16] Theatrical representation, where the actor's body makes present someone who is absent, exemplifies in a different way the same paradox.

Even when it refers to leaving undone what ought to have been done, the responsibility of individuals refers to an action in opposition to a passion. That is the reasoning behind the legal doctrine that "crimes of passion" are less culpable than calculated crimes since in them the agent's capacity for reason (and therefore, in the Kantian sense, for moral judgment) is diminished by the intrusion of an "external force." Like the act of an insane person, a crime of passion is not considered to be the consequence of an agent's *own* intention. Now that emotions are generally thought of as part of the internal economy of the self, the notion is reinforced that agency means the self-ownership of the individual to whom external power always signifies a potential threat.

Agency also has a theatrical context. Here the professional actor tries to set her self aside and inhabit the somatic world of her character—her gestures, passions, and desires. The actor's agency consists not in the actions of the role she performs but in her ability to *disempower* one self for the sake of another.[17] Her action is not solely her own. It is at the same

16. Hanna Pitkin, *The Concept of Representation*, Berkeley: University of California Press, 1967.

17. The actor Alla Nazimova puts this as follows: "The actor himself should be a creature of clay, putty, capable of being molded into another form, another shape. An actor must never see himself in [a] character. I study the woman. I look at her under a magnifying glass and say to myself: 'Is she right? Is she logical? Is she true to herself? Can *I* act that woman? Can I make *myself* over into *her*?' I am nothing. I am nobody. I have to reconstruct my whole self into this woman I am to portray—speak with her voice, laugh with her laughter—move with her motion. But if you can see the person as a living creature, quite removed from yourself, you can work objectively to adapt yourself to the part." ("The Actor as an Instrument," in Toby Cole and Helen K. Chinoy, eds., *Actors on Acting*, New York:

time that of the dramatist who has written the script and of the director who mediates between script and performance. It also belongs to the tradition of acting in which she has been schooled. In an important sense the actor is a part subject; her actions are not fully her own. That she is not the author of the story doesn't mean that she is therefore its passive object.

Writing about acting traditions, Edward Burns has made the interesting point that whereas the Elizabethan player sought to become an instrument of the text, to fuse himself directly with it by presenting a dramatic persona in an explicit, open-ended manner, the (modern) Stanislavskian actor by contrast constructs his own text—that of a being whose "character" he tries to represent through the script. Burns suggests that there is a tension between the actor's self and that of the substantive character he projects, a tension that creates the effect among the audience of realism ("human" subject positions available for imaginative occupation) as well as of profundity (hidden "human" meanings to be endlessly uncovered).[18] These are two very different ways in which actors' ability to disavow or *empty* themselves articulates their agency in relation to a particular acting tradition. Of these two traditions the second is not "truer" or "more developed" than the first; it is just that in a subjectivising literary culture people take to it more easily and regard it as "more natural."

A recent critic of modern styles of acting (identified as Strasbergian rather than Stanislavskian) makes the interesting claim that its strongly individualist bias leads to a devaluation of plot: "seeing a play as a collection of individualized character portraits," he maintains, "means that plot, themes, images, rhetorical figures, metrical forms, poetic motifs, and intellectual content of any kind become unimportant; they are . . . externals. As dozens of actors and directors have earnestly told me over the past three decades, 'You can't play an idea.' You can only play real, live, independent persons, so the theory goes, not literary constructs."[19] The assumption that

Crown, 1949, p. 512). What begins as the seemingly simple statement that the actor's role is to be *a mere instrument* quickly evolves into a claim that the actor must organize and stabilize for herself *a character* in relation to which her performance can be crafted.

18. Edward Burns, *Character: Acting and Being on the Pre-Modern Stage*, New York: St. Martin's Press, 1990.

19. Richard Hornby, *The End of Acting*, New York: Applause Books, 1992, pp. 6–7. The book is, among other things, an instructive account of the limits of conscious intention for effective acting.

real, live persons are independent of plots has interesting consequences. (I return to this point in the final section.)

It may be objected that professional actors disempower themselves voluntarily and temporarily, in the context of framed performances—that in "real life" we can and do represent ourselves. But one answer to this is that many, if not all, activities in social life are framed. The professional actor's concern to perfect a role on the stage is of a piece with the teaching and learning of rhetorical skills (speech, gesture, attitude, behavior)[20] by agents in other domains where their actions are not absolutely "their own." In modern, secular society these sites include law courts and political arenas, domains in which the self must be disavowed (whether sincerely or not) in the act of representing a client or "the law," a constituency or "an interest group"—domains in which state laws *disempower* as well as enable the active citizen. (Incidentally, critics drawing on psychoanalytic ideas have proposed that *acting* in modern society can offer relief to the painful effort of having to live up continuously to one's idealized self-image precisely by *disempowering* the self.[21]) In all such situations the partial owner-

20. Burns reminds us that in early modern Europe "Acting and rhetoric are never seen as distinct entities; the theory of acting is unnecessary, as are systematic manuals of its techniques, since the first is already present in the theory of rhetoric, and the second can be seen in one aspect as an aggregate of unclassifiable social and entertainment skills, and in another, in the special effects of master rhetoricians like Alleyn and Burbage, as a development from within a long-established rhetorical tradition. The dramatic traditions of the universities, the Inns of Court and the choir schools had long explored acting and rhetoric as, essentially, the same. We must not make the mistake of taking rhetoric in its modern colloquial sense as something strained, unreal, nearly ridiculous. To talk of acting in terms of rhetoric is to consider it as a branch of the study of human communication, of the development of the skills of 'moving', 'delighting', 'persuading' and 'teaching' other human subjects, as classical, mediaeval and renaissance culture conceived of it" (Burns, p. 10). Burns could have added that medieval and early modern rhetorical traditions had strong roots in Christian preaching and the performance of sacramental rites as well as passion plays.

21. "In a safe, socially approved situation (at a party, on a holiday, or in a play) you are allowed to drop, temporarily, the *pain* of living up to your idealized self-image. You can even be a despised figure—an idiot, a villain, a coward—and not only not be abused or ridiculed for it, but even receive laughter and applause. . . . The character weeps, but the actor feels ecstatic (from the Greek *ex histanai*, which means, literally, out of one's place) because he is liberated from his usual cabined, cribbed, confined everyday personality" (Hornby, pp. 17–18 [italics in original]).

ship of the agent's acts, and their continuously re-defined nature, become evident. As opposed to a dramatic plot, acts unfold and are subject to re-description in ways that are often unanticipated.

Ritual drama, such as the Passion of Christ or the Martyrdom of Hussain, has an added dimension. Participants here enact, identify with, undergo, the predetermined agony of figures in Christian and Islamic nar-ratives. In subjecting themselves to suffering (in some cases to self-inflicted wounds) they seek in part to extend themselves as subjects.[22]

Religious history is a discursive domain in which the notion of agency is richly played out. Thus in eighteenth-century England, a combi-nation of secular ideas about human perfectability with Christian ideas about Christ's suffering issued among evangelicals in a self that was at once active and passive. "The theology of the Atonement," writes Phyllis Mack, "taught women and men to be little children, passively resting in the arms (or wounds) of Christ, but the theology of universal perfectability pushed them toward a firmer sense of personal autonomy or self-mastery, which in turn made it more difficult to perceive themselves as dependent on God. The Methodists' attainment of self-control—the habits of diet, discipline, and reflection that helped them to manage suffering—thus had the poten-tial to threaten the very core of their faith and confidence: the power of the Atonement to wash away sin and conquer death. Agency both increased the desire for self-transcendence and made self-transcendence more diffi-cult to attain. For women as well as men, the problem was not in finding the authority to speak and act; it was in remembering that the authority didn't belong to them."[23] Because the tension was unstable, Mack believes that the unequivocal triumph of reformist activism over passivity—and therefore of a more secular, this-worldly outlook—was inevitable. But this causal drift did not render the possibility of "surrender to Christ" incon-ceivable, as the life of many Christians demonstrates.

Thus "agency" is a complex term whose senses emerge within se-mantic and institutional networks that define and make possible particular ways of relating to people, things, and oneself. Yet "intention," which is variously glossed as "plan," "awareness," "willfulness," "directedness," or

22. See the interesting article by David Pinault, "Shia Lamentation Rituals and Reinterpretations of the Doctrine of Intercession: Two Cases from Modern India," *History of Religions*, vol. 38, no. 3, 1999.

23. Phyllis Mack, "Religious Dissenters in Enlightenment England," *History Workshop Journal*, issue 49, 2000, pp. 16–17.

"desire" (terms whose linguistic opposites don't function grammatically in the same way: to be without desire is not to be without a plan nor to be in a state of unawareness) is often made to be central to the attribution of agency. "Empowerment," a legal term referring *both* to the act of giving power to someone *and* to someone's power to act, becomes a metaphysical quality defining secular human agency, its objective as well as precondition. Although the various usages of agency have very different implications that do not all hang together, cultural theory tends to reduce them to the metaphysical idea of a conscious agent-subject having both the capacity and the desire to move in a singular historical direction: that of increasing self-empowerment and decreasing pain.

Thinking about pain

There is a secular viewpoint held by many (including anthropologists) that would have one accept that in the final analysis there are only two mutually exclusive options available: either an agent (representing and asserting himself or herself) or a victim (the passive object of chance or cruelty).

When we say that someone is suffering, we commonly suppose that he or she is not an agent. To suffer (physical or mental pain, humiliation, deprivation) is, so we usually think, to be in a passive state—to be an object, not a subject. One readily allows that pain may be a cause for action (seeking to end the suffering, say), but one does not normally think of it as action itself. Pain is something that happens to the body or that afflicts the mind. Or so, at any rate, we tend to think. Yet one can think of pain not merely as a passive state (although it can be just that) but as itself agentive.

Physical pain is of course the object of passion—but also of action. In Paul Valéry's *Monsieur Teste* we have a remarkable account of the attempts by an ailing subject to control his bodily pain mentally. This includes the use of metaphors. The most pervasive of these is the dark image of pain as a hostile alien thing within the body. Jean Starobinski points to the fact that Valéry employs musical tropes, as when he writes that "Pain is due to the resistance of the consciousness to a local arrangement of the body.—A pain which we could consider clearly, and in some way circumscribe, would become sensation without suffering—and perhaps in this way we could succeed in knowing something directly about our deeper body—knowledge of the sort we find in music. Pain is a very musical thing, one can almost speak of it in terms of music. There are deep and high-pitched pains, andantes and furiosos, prolonged notes, fermatas and arpeggios, progressions—abrupt silences, etc. . . . " Starobinski observes that here the musical metaphor is closely connected to a plan for control because "every metaphorization implies an interpretation, and every interpretation involves a distance between an interpreting power and an object interpreted—even if that object is an event taking place in 'my body.' . . . For Valery, 'pain has no meaning,' hence its indefinitely interpretable nature."[24]

I offer, tentatively, a slightly different conclusion. Using musical metaphors (or indeed music itself) to fix the body's pain might be seen not exactly as giving meaning to brute experience but as a process of structuring that experience. I knew someone who found herself using numbers to anticipate and categorize her experience of pain. Although, unsurprisingly, severe pains were numbered higher, a less obvious structuration was also at work: only acute, irresolvable pains appeared as prime numbers. Furthermore, the numbering varied according to the social context she was in: prime numbers were more likely when she was alone. Such structuration doesn't necessarily make pain "meaningful"; it is simply a way of engaging with it. So the conclusion I offer contrasts with Elaine Scarry's position in her influential study *The Body in Pain*, according to which "the utter rigidity of pain itself" is universally reflected in the fact that "its resistance to language is not simply one of its incidental or accidental attributes but is essential to what it is."[25] For although musical or mathematical structuration (both of which have to be learned) may not constitute "language" in the ordinary sense, it problematizes the idea of pain-in-itself as necessarily a private, thought-destroying event.

Scarry asserts that pain is necessarily a private experience, and proposes that the experience of "one's own physical pain" is the very paradigm of certainty, and hearing about "another person's physical pain" the paradigm of doubt—because it can never be completely confirmed.[26] I suggest that this secular understanding of pain as inscrutable may arise in part

24. Jean Starobinski, "Monsieur Teste Confronting Pain," in M. Feher, ed., *Fragments for a History of the Human Body*, Part Two, New York: Zone, 1989, p. 386.

25. Elaine Scarry, *The Body in Pain: The Making and Unmaking of the World*, Oxford: Oxford University Press, 1985, p. 5.

26. Ibid., p. 4.

from the experience of animal experimentation of the kind I discussed in the previous chapter, in which observable reactions of the flesh that is subjected to experiment constitutes "pain." The question to consider here is whether this claim is true, and if it is, why it should apply solely to pain.[27]

Whether one can be certain of another's pain depends surely on who is expressing it to whom, how—verbally, for example, or through lamentation, or by facial signs, or by the way an agonized or impaired body is revealed—and for what purpose "certainty" is sought. One may suppress or cover up such signs (even unusual silence can be noted as significant, of course), but the point is that pain is not merely a private experience but a public relationship as Wittgenstein taught long ago.[28] Indeed, if doubt about another's pain were always irresolvable, as Scarry claims it is,[29] the repeated infliction of cruelty on victims of torture would be hard to understand—unless the *repeated* infliction of suffering is to be accounted for as an epistemological obsession. Scarry's statement that in the eyes of torturers "the objectified pain [of the victim] is denied as pain and read as power" strikes me as odd because the *denial* of a victim's pain implies a kind of certainty for the torturer, although Scarry's basic claim is that he must *always* be uncertain in the matter of another's pain. (Why is inflicted pain chosen as the medium for inscribing and reading power if its effect is essentially so doubtful?)

Of course error—and therefore doubt—may occur not only in the context of reports of pain but of reports of any feeling. (As Collingwood once put it, I can't be wrong if I *feel* something—although I might be wrong, or simply lying, in *saying* that I feel it.[30]) However, addressing an-

27. In their "Introduction" to Mary-Jo Delvecchio Good, Paul E. Brodwin, Byron J. Good, and A. Kleinman, eds., *Pain as Human Experience: An Anthropological Perspective* (Berkeley: University of California Press, 1992), the editors reveal an unresolved tension between two ideas. On the one hand, they regard pain as a prelinguistic experience that is to be represented (hence "pain resists symbolization"), and on the other, as an experience that is formulated in and through language *ab initio* (and is thus always "influenced by meanings, relationships, and institutions"). This paradox may be the result of assuming that there are two kinds of pain, psychological (mediated by the mind) and physical (objective, "raw") pain, when these may in fact be two aspects of the same event—subjective and objective.

28. Ludwig Wittgenstein, *Philosophical Investigations*, Oxford: Blackwell, 1953, especially p. 100.

29. Scarry, p. 28.

30. Collingwood maintained that feeling as opposed to thinking is a spontaneous state of passivity, to which the notion of failure doesn't apply because it isn't

other's pain is not merely a matter of judging referential statements. It is about how a particular kind of relationship can be inhabited and enacted.[31] An agent suffers because of the pain of someone she loves—a mother, say, confronted by her wounded child. That suffering is a condition of her relationship, something that includes her ability to respond sympathetically to the pain of the original sufferer. The person who suffers because of another's pain doesn't first assess the evidence presented to her and then decide on whether and how to react. She lives a relationship. The other's hurt—expressed in painful words, cries, gestures, unusual silences (in short, a recognizable rhetoric)—makes a difference to her in the sense of being the active reason for her own compassion and for her reaching out to the other's pain. It is a practical condition of who she and her suffering child are. (This applies equally, of course, to pleasures the two may share.) Only in law does the mother stand as an individual agent with responsibility toward the child regardless of her actual feelings.

It's not that one's own pain can never be convincingly conveyed to others, but that *when* one feels the urgent need to communicate one's pain, and the communication fails, *then* it may come to be thought of—with

---

intentional. Like suffering, one either feels or doesn't feel something. Furthermore, feelings are essentially private in a way that thought isn't. Although the act of thinking something may or may not be an entirely private act, depending on how one performs it, that which we think (a particular thought) is always in principle directly accessible by others, and therefore public (see R. G. Collingwood, *The Principles of Art*, Oxford: Oxford University Press, 1938, p. 158). According to Collingwood, as soon as any sensation is identified by the sufferer it becomes indissolubly linked to and stabilized by "thought"—and, of course, altered by it. One might extend him as saying that pain can be shared because thought doesn't simply *refer* to a feeling, it instigates, fashions, and perpetuates it within a social relationship.

31. Veena Das has made this point more elegantly in her article on women's suffering during the partition of India in 1947: "Following Wittgenstein, this manner of conceptualizing the puzzle of pain frees us from thinking that statements about pain are in the nature of questions about certainty or doubt over our own pain or that of others. Instead, we begin to think of pain as asking for acknowledgment and recognition; denial of the other's pain is not about the failings of the intellect but the failings of the spirit. In the register of the imaginary, the pain of the other not only asks for a home in language but also seeks a home in the body" ("Language and Body: Transactions in the Construction of Pain," in A. Kleinman, V. Das, and M. Lock, eds., *Social Suffering*, Berkeley: University of California Press, 1997, p. 88). See also her important essay "Witgenstein and Anthropology," *Annual Review of Anthropology*, vol. 27, 1998.

added anguish—as unshareable. "In order to construct self-narratives," notes Susan Brison discussing victims of rape and torture, "we need not only the words with which to tell our stories but also an audience able and willing to hear us and to understand our words as we intend them. This aspect of remaking a self in the aftermath of trauma highlights the dependency of the self on others and helps to explain why it is so difficult for survivors to recover when others are unwilling [or unable?] to listen to what they endured."[32] The ability to live sanely after a traumatic experience of pain is always dependent on the responses of others. Pain, one might venture, is neither a brute reality undermining thought nor an interpretation that is the occasion of ideological or scientific elaboration. It can be an active, practical relationship inhabiting time. But surely—so it may be objected—this applies only to "mental suffering" and not to bodily pain.

How clear is the distinction between physical pain and psychological (or social) suffering? All feelings of pain involve physical changes that are not only internal to the body (muscular, biochemical) but also externally visible (voice, demeanor, gait) and culturally readable. This fact alone complicates the too-neat distinction between physical pain and mental pain. Distressing emotions, too, are connected to chemical disturbances in the body. And chemical imbalances—whether associated with trauma or malignant cell growth—are as "physical" as torn ligaments. It may be that physical pain is typically located by the sufferer in particular parts of his or her body and that this is what distinguishes it from mental distress. But mental states—themselves closely connected to social circumstances—are central in the experience of physical pain.

It has long been known that tolerance to physical pain is culturally variable (I return to this in the next chapter). The latest research on the physiology of pain points to a more radical conclusion: physical injury to a specific part of the body is not necessary to activate the body's pain system. The notorious phenomenon of phantom-limb pain is not, it now seems, a curious anomaly. Pain is not merely experienced in the mind, researchers say, but generated by it.[33] The brain is the locus of complex in-

32. Susan Brison, "Outliving Oneself: Trauma, Memory, and Personal Identity", in D. Meyer, ed., *Feminists Rethink the Self*, Boulder, CO: Westview, 1997, pp. 21–22. (I am obliged to Susan James for this reference.)

33. Ronald Melzack, well known for his gate-theory of pain (Ronald Melzack and Patrick Wall, *The Challenge of Pain*, New York: Penguin, 1982), has now radically revised his view (see "Pain: Past, Present and Future," *Canadian Journal of Experimental Psychology*, vol. 47, no. 4, 1993). Because pain is generated

teractions—including interactions between distressing memories, perceptions, and emotions—whose result is the experience and behavior of pain. The familiar distinction between physical pain as something that is typically experienced in a particular part of the body, and mental suffering as a physically unlocatable experience, is not so clear-cut if we recall that in many cultures distressing emotions are experienced as being located in particular organs of the body (liver, belly, heart, and so forth).[34] Even in modern society people recognize that they can be "sick with anger" and "flushed with embarrassment," and that these unpleasant experiences are at once physically located and socially anchored.

If research now indicates that the brain is the source and not the terminus of pain sensations, the latter can be thought of as actions that are sited at once in cultural *and* neurophysiological contexts. In an important sense "cultural" and "physical" cease to be dichotomies, although for analytical purposes they can be distinguished. What a subject experiences as painful, and how, are not simply mediated culturally and physically, *they are themselves modes of living a relationship.* The ability to live such relationships over time transforms pain from a passive experience into an active one, and thus defines one of the ways of living sanely in the world. It does not follow, of course, that one cannot or should not seek to reform the social relations one inhabits, still less that pain is intrinsically "a valuable thing." My point is that one can live one's pain sanely or insanely, and (although ideas about insanity change) that the progressivist model of agency diverts attention away from our trying to understand how this is done in different traditions, because of the assumption that the agent always seeks to overcome pain conceived as object and as state of passivity. The secular emphasis on the integral human body as the locus of moral sovereignty makes it difficult to grasp the idea of pain as an imagined relationship in which such "internal" states as memory and hope mediate sociality.

I do not claim that the pain felt by a physically injured person can be

---

in the brain independently of damage to the body, says Melzack, it can be "felt" in locations of the body that do not exist. That explains the phenomena of phantom seeing and hearing. See R. Melzack, "Phantom Limbs," *Scientific American*, April 1992.

34. For cultures of antiquity, see R. B. Onians, *The Origins of European Thought About the Body, the Mind, the Soul, the World, Time, and Fate*, Cambridge: Cambridge University Press, 1951 (especially chapter 5).

experienced in the same way by an observer. There is always an irreproducible excess in pain. I argue that that is not all pain is. Sufferers are also social persons (animals) and their suffering is partly constituted by the way they inhabit, or are constrained to inhabit, their relationships with others. Pain is not always an insufferable agony or a chronic condition. There are varieties of incommensurable experiences we collect together under the label "pain" (or "suffering") as though it were, like agency, a single thing, an ultimate vindication of corporeal reality. But as a social relationship pain is more than an experience. It is part of what creates the conditions of action and experience, as I will now try to show in some examples of pain from religious history and ethnography.

Thinking about agentive pain in religious history and ethnography

Pain inflicted as punishment can be eagerly embraced by those on whom it is inflicted and transformed into something other than what was intended. Sadomasochism (which I discuss in the next chapter) is one example, although I shall argue that it should not be identified as merely a secular version of a phenomenon familiar to us from the domain of religion—and therefore as the pathology underlying particular religious practices. The presence of the word "pain" should not be taken as evidence that it refers to a single concept.

Historians of late antiquity have made us familiar with the fact that sovereignty in the early Roman empire was realized to a great degree through public demonstrations of the emperor's power and munificence. The theatrical torture of certain categories of criminal was part of this necessary display of power. Famously, among those so tortured were the early Christian martyrs. Judith Perkins in her book *The Suffering Self* states that early Christian martyrologies "refuse to read the martyrs' broken bodies as defeat, but reverse the reading, insisting on interpreting them as symbols of victory over society's power."[35] Far from shunning physical suffering, the martyrs actively sought to live it. Like Christ's passion on the cross, the martyrs' passivity was an act of triumph. *That* openness to pain was precisely part of the structure of their agency as Christians. This is what makes

35. Judith Perkins, *The Suffering Self: Pain and Narrative in the Early Christian Era*, New York: Routledge, 1995, p. 117.

its description as "a symbol of victory over society's power" (a secular motivation) inapposite. It was what it claimed to be: an empowerment through the endurance of what Christ was believed to have suffered on the cross.

However, it is not the symbolic significance of martyrdom that I want to focus on here but its effectiveness in creating new spaces for secular action. In Perkins's account, a search for the meanings of martyrdom leads to explanations in terms of false consciousness, and that is something I want to avoid.

In the world of late antiquity, the Christian community was positively oriented (as the ancient world had not been) to sickness and human suffering. Where sickness could not be healed, Christians insisted that pain could be understood as valuable. This was different from two traditions that were more or less contemporaneous with the early Christian persecutions related in the martyrologies: Stoic moral philosophy (with its emphasis on self-mastery, its denial of externals such as suffering), and Galenic medicine (that regarded pain as a bodily condition subject to appropriate technical intervention).

Perkins argues that Stoicism was a ruling ideology: "Epictitus' emphasis on the internal, on self-mastery, and self-formation, as well as his denial of the importance of externals [such as suffering], would have served to divert the attention of his students and others like them away from attending to social or material conditions. His teaching supported the status quo, and any affirmation of the status quo acts to affirm an elite's position. Stoic insistence that poverty and social position did not matter fitted into the elite agenda better than into an underprivileged one: as does the corresponding counsel that what did, in fact, matter was how well you did at being poor, imprisoned, or politically unpopular. This teaching, along with emphasis on control directed at the interior self, had significant relevance for the social body; it would work to restrain social as well as personal disturbances."[36] But this resort to the notion of false consciousness to explain political domination seems to me weak. In the first place Stoicism was an ethic intended for the elite rather than the masses. As such, it encouraged withdrawal from corrupt public life and inattention to social and material conditions. We may therefore question whether it was an ideology well suited to active involvement in imperial rule. Perkins overlooks the fact that although a pessimistic acceptance of suffering as an ineradicable part of life—and a recommendation to adjust to it rather than seeking to

36. Ibid., pp. 84–85.

change life—might well be mistaken, it is not in itself a denial that life is ultimately unjust. On the contrary, it is precisely because the world *is* viewed as unjust and filled with misfortune that Stoicism prescribes psychological remedies.

Perkins's discussion of ancient medicine is more interesting. Galen's understanding of the sick body, she tells us, was adapted by the early Christians in their distinctive treatment of pain. Thus by a paradoxical development, the Christian embrace of suffering led, she tells us, to a greater concern for—and therefore a new kind of secular activity directed at—the diseased, the poor, and the despised members of society. If Perkins is right, then we find here not merely another *meaning* of pain but also another *economy* of action. The self-subjection of these Christians to pain (at least as represented in the martyrologies on which Perkins draws) was itself a form of agency not because of their active intention (whatever that may have been), nor primarily because of the symbolic significance of suffering ("a text to be read"[37]). It was a form of agency because, as part of an emerging tradition, their public suffering made a difference not only to themselves (to their own potential actions) as members of a new faith but also to the world in which they lived: it required that one's own pain and the pain of others be engaged with differently.

The distinction between looking for the symbolic meaning of pain (as an ideology) and for its agentive function may be illustrated further by reference to an ethnography of pain in childbirth among North American religious women published by the anthropologist Pamela Klassen. Klassen tells us that many of the women she studied regarded giving birth without drugs to be an empowering act because—as one of them put it—"it's something that a man could never do." Klassen is aware that this claim to power might be criticized for presenting an essentialized category of woman because not all women give birth. She thinks nevertheless that it can help to subvert the gendered image of male strength and female weakness.

"Perhaps in late-twentieth-century America," Klassen writes, "where women are taught to be observers and critics of their own bodies from outside, the pain of childbirth puts women back *in* their bodies. In this specific context, the counter-cultural force of pain holds an empowering, and for some, salvific dimension. In accord with Carolyn Walker Bynum, I cautiously assert that 'our culture may finally need something of the medieval sense, reflected so clearly in the use of *birthing* and *nursing* as symbols for

37. Ibid., p. 152.

salvation, that generativity and suffering can be synonymous.' Many home-birthing women are working towards such a coupling."[38]

But I want to think of the pain of childbirth not as a meaningful experience, and not as an image subversive of male arrogance (on that score, alas, it has not been historically very effective). Pain may be thought of directly as a constitutive element of giving birth. My point is not that birthing should be accepted as a moral basis of the female claim to empowerment. Still less that her ability to face pain courageously is a virtue. It is that particular women in particular places and particular times actually give birth in pain—and this creates a new situation for the mother herself and for others. For those who can exercise it, the power to bring another life and therefore other relations into the world in pain is no less agentive for being particularized as well as unwilled (I refer, of course, not to the decision to have a child but to the process of conception, pregnancy, and birth).

Of course mothering is possible when physical pain is prevented or alleviated by analgesics. I do not wish to be taken as saying that painful birth is intrinsically valuable (even though the religious women studied by Klassen preferred giving birth at home among family members and without the presence of professional doctors). My point is only that when pain is a constitutive part of birthing it is not simply the negative *experience* of a patient, as biomedicine tends to regard it, but an aspect of a distinctive social act in which others assist. What I want to emphasize is that in the cases Klassen describes, pain is not the isolable condition of an individual body to be finally eliminated by chemical or surgical intervention. It is integral to an activity that reproduces and sustains human relationships. For how pain is felt is in some measure dependent on how it is expressed, and how it is expressed is dependent on social relationships.

It is not the *symbolic meaning* attributed to motherhood (or to pain) that concerns me here, any more than the self-interpretation of individuals as mothers. What I think matters is the becoming and being "a mother" by means of the practical methods employed in various traditions. For the act of birthing doesn't merely produce another living body, it also creates a vital relationship that is imbued with sensitivity to pain, the relationship that binds mother and child actively together. The mother is an agent as a consequence of what she has done in a particular social situation—after the

38. Pamela Klassen, "'Sliding Around between Pain and Pleasure': Home Birth and Visionary Pain," *Scottish Journal of Religious Studies*, vol. 19, no. 1, 1998, p. 66.

event, as it were—and not because of her conscious intention. (The desire that she have a child is not the mother's alone; other relatives are also involved.)

Our tendency to think of childbirth as passive because unwilled and uncontrolled is deep-rooted. Even Simone de Beauvoir, observes Susan Brison, "views childbirth and nursing as completely passive—and thus dehumanizing—processes, which keep women mired in immanence."[39] Such a view, in its highly transcendental and intentionalist perspective, rejects that birthing has anything to do with agency, with doing. References to pain in birthing tend to underscore its passivity.

I discuss a final example of the role of pain in the economy of action—this time from the Islamic tradition, aspects of which have been described in relation to movements of piety in contemporary Cairo in two ethnographic studies by Saba Mahmood and Charles Hirschkind.[40] Both studies are concerned with a tradition that is based on the idea of the soul that is at least as old as Aristotle and that has been absorbed into Judaism and Christianity as well as Islam. This tradition requires us to attend not merely to the idea of embodiment (that human action and experience are sited in a material body) but also to the idea of ensoulment—the idea that the living human body is an integrated totality having developable capacities for activity and experience unique to it, the capacities for sensing, imagining, and doing that are culturally mediated.

Although the living body is the object of sensations (and in that sense passive), its ability to suffer, to respond perceptually and emotionally to external and internal causes, to use its own pain in unique ways in particular social relationships, makes it active. Many traditions therefore attribute to the living human body the potential to be shaped (the power to shape itself) for good or ill.

Whether passive or active, the living body's materiality is regarded as an essential means for cultivating what such traditions define as virtuous conduct and for discouraging what they consider as vice. The role of fear and hope, of felicity and pain, is central to such practices. According to this view of the living body, the more one exercises a virtue the easier it be-

39. Susan J. Brison. Brison herself takes a view opposed to de Beauvoir's.

40. Charles Hirschkind, "Technologies of Islamic Piety: Cassette-Sermons and the Ethics of Listening" (Ph.D. diss., Johns Hopkins University, 1999); Saba Mahmood, "Women's Piety and Embodied Discipline: The Islamic Resurgence in Contemporary Egypt" (Ph.D. diss., Stanford University, 1998).

comes. On the other hand, the more one gives in to vice, the harder it is to act virtuously. This is precisely how many Muslims interpret the repeated Qur'anic declaration to the effect that God seals the hearts of stubborn sinners. The punishment for repeated wickedness is to become the sort of person one is: unable to distinguish true speech from false, and divine speech from human speech—a person who cannot live the virtuous life that God requires of her or him. Time is not reversible.

Conscious intentionality typically is here seen as important where inexperience or vice prevails, for it is in those conditions that the inertial resistance of the body, as well as its fragility, need to be addressed deliberately by responsible practice. Note that I speak here of the formation of virtues (*fadā'il*) and sensibilities (*hisās*). Rites of worship (*'ibādāt*)—whose regular practice is in fact necessary to the cultivation of the virtues and sensibilities required of a Muslim—always require the silent enunciation of one's intention (*niyya*) to perform the prayer (*salāt*), and so forth, at the commencement of the rite. The *niyya* is therefore an integral part of the rite, a form of conscious commitment initiating acts of worship that must itself be cultivated as an aspect of one's continuous faith. *Imān*—usually translated into English as "faith"—is not a singular epistemological means that guarantees God's existence for the believer. It is better translated as the virtue of faithfulness toward God, an unquestioning habit of obedience that God requires of those faithful to him (*mu'minīn*), a disposition that has to be cultivated like any other, and that links one to others who are faithful, through mutual trust and responsibility.

Both Mahmood and Hirschkind provide detailed descriptions of practices directed at the cultivation of Islamic conduct in which painful emotions—fear and remorse, for example—are seen as central to the practice of moral discrimination. In different ways, their accounts reveal that "virtuous fear" (*taqwa*) is regarded not simply as a spur to action but as integral to action itself. Apart from being necessary to the development of moral discrimination, the endurance of pain is considered to be a necessary means of cultivating the virtue of *sabr* (endurance, perseverance, self-control) that is itself basic to all processes of virtue-acquisition.

Physical pain and damage to the body are not celebrated in the central Sunni tradition of Islam, as they are for example among the early Christian martyrs—nor does pain have the same role in its religious discipline. But forms of suffering are nonetheless intrinsic to the kind of agent a devout Muslim aspires to be. The most important of these is the universal experience of dying and death. When "the time comes" the devout Muslim is required *to let go*. The suffering among survivors generated by the loss of those they love is shared through prescribed practices of burial and bereavement (although the entire structure of burial practices makes it more difficult for mourning women to achieve closure than for men). The devout Muslim seeks to cultivate virtue and repudiate vice by a constant awareness of his or her own earthly finitude, trying to achieve the state of equilibrium that the Qur'an calls *an-nafs al-mutma'inna*, "the self at peace."

Penalties, whether emerging as incapacity from within the living body's functions, or imposed as punishment on the body externally, are regarded as a necessary part of learning how to act appropriately. This formative process is set within the Islamic tradition of mutual discipline: *al-amr bil-ma'rūf wan-nahy 'an al-munkar* (literally, "the requiring of what is good and the rejection of what is reprehensible").[41] The individual's acquisition of appropriate agency and its exercise are articulated by responsibility, a responsibility not merely of the agent but of the entire community of Muslims severally and collectively. If religious behavior is to be defined in terms of responsibility, then we have here a case of behavior that acquires its sense not from a historical teleology but from a biographical one in which the individual seeks to acquire the capacities and sensibilities internal to a religious tradition (*al-sunna al-dīniyya*) that is oriented by an eschatology according to which he or she stands alone on the Day of Judgment to account for his or her life. In this tradition, the body-and-its-capacities is not owned solely by the individual but is subject to a variety of obligations held by others as fellow Muslims. There is therefore a continuous, unresolved tension between responsibility as individual and metaphysical on the one hand, and as collective and quotidian on the other—that is, between eschatology and sociology.

In referring sketchily to aspects of Islamic corporal discipline I do not wish to repeat the old secularist prejudice that religion is essentially about fear of punishment. My concern is to point to the way in which certain traditions use pain to create a space for moral action that articulates this-world-in-the-next. Thus pain is used and justified by modern state law (including the law of war) to uphold order and attain security. Muslim and

41. The thirteenth-century theologian Ibn Taymiyya's *Amr bi al-ma'rūf wa al-nahy 'an al-munkar* has been reprinted in Cairo several times since 1979, together with a long explanatory introduction by the modern Egyptian editor Muhammad Jamil Ghazi.

Christian princes have also used pain for this purpose. But in addition, Christian and Islamic traditions have, in their different ways, regarded suffering as the working through of worldly evil. For the suffering subject, not *all* pain is to be avoided; *some* pain must be actively endured if evil is to be transcended. According to Christian and Islamic traditions "evil" is an intrinsic part of the way this world is constituted. As long as the world lasts, evil can never be permanently eliminated, only temporarily overcome.[42]

Thus pain does not simply constitute irrefutable evidence of the corporeal ground of experience, it is also a way of constituting the epistemological status of "the body." As well as its moral potentialities.

Moral agency, responsibility, and punishment

In conclusion I want to speculate on whether intention, responsibility, and punishment are together necessary to the notion of agency with which we have become familiar in secular ethics. I do this by discussing briefly the example of Oedipus for whom pain was intermingled with *moral* action—an action that, arguably, is not to be described in terms of "responsibility."

The tragedy of *Oedipus* depicts a story of suffering and disempowerment that is neither voluntary nor involuntary. For Oedipus is an agent who, not knowing what he has done, makes a deep difference in the world. On gradually learning the secret of his past acts he inflicts terrible wounds on the body that performed them, on the self that can neither be recognized nor repudiated. Oedipus' final acts consist of his public renunciation of kingly power as both expression and consequence of pain. They embody and extend his passion—his agony—not of his conscious intention. Oedipus' agency is constituted by the conflicting definitions of his predicament that is the outcome of his insistence on uncovering the truth of his origin. The act of disempowering himself is performed because, as the slayer of his father and the husband of his mother (a double transgression, both unknowingly committed), he is the cause of his subjects' unique suffering, which will cease when he exiles himself from Thebes—that is, when he disempowers himself.

42. I am grateful to John Milbank for helping me get a clearer understanding of the early church fathers' views on suffering. See especially "The Force of Identity" and "Can Morality Be Christian," in his *The Word Made Strange*, Oxford: Blackwell, 1997.

Michael Dillon,[43] whose impressive analysis of disempowerment has led me to write this section, observes that by finally "taking responsibility" for himself, Oedipus becomes an agent in his own right. His is a suggestive interpretation, but I am not persuaded that the notion of "responsibility" is appropriate here. If we take that notion as containing the elements of imputability and liability to punishment it seems to me that Oedipus is not responsible *to* any authority. He does not have to answer to any court (human or divine) for his actions—not even to what Christian casuistry would later call "the internal court of conscience," a concept quite foreign to the Greeks.[44]

In *Colonus* Oedipus explicitly denies that his transgressions were his own acts, and interrupts the Chorus, who refers to what he has done, by insisting that it was "No doing of mine." What he denies is not that he caused the death of a man at the crossroads (*that* he had always known) but that he murdered his father, which is a different act, and one which he had tried specifically to avoid. In what sense was he responsible for *this* act? By disowning the terrible thing done (parricide) he isn't saying that he didn't intend to kill. In that sense he recognizes himself as the owner of a responsible act (as an agent). But he also claims that the act turned out to be not his own, that he was an unwitting instrument (agent) of the gods, and that as such his own intention was irrelevant. Yet when he discovers what has been done, he knows he must act—not because he admits or claims "responsibility," but because he cannot live in the knowledge of who he is and what, being who he is, he has done to his father and his mother. That knowledge demands some resolution. Although Oedipus did not know "the moral meaning" of his transgressive act at the time it was performed he nonetheless suffers for it. His subjects aren't immune from suffering either even though *they* have done nothing "to deserve it."

(Is Oedipus the same man at the end of the drama as he was at the beginning? By the end he has undergone horrendous experiences—the mental trauma of self-discovery and the bodily trauma of self-blinding. The self that now becomes visible is also the self that deliberately destroys

43. Michael Dillon, "Otherwise than Self-Determination: The Mortal Freedom of *Oedipus Asphaleos*," in Hent de Vries and Samuel Weber, eds., *Violence, Identity, and Self-Determination*, Stanford, CA: Stanford University Press, 1997.

44. I stress that my purpose is *not* to argue that the Greeks had no concept of responsibility. I have not the scholarly competence to make or defend such a thesis. My skeptical questions relate only to the case of Oedipus as presented by Dillon—and (see below) by Bernard Williams.

its own capacity for sight. From a powerful, admired, and protective king to a homeless, blinded, despised exile. Does this rupture allow a continuous personal identity for Oedipus, a Lockean self-identifying consciousness? And without that continuity, can we really say that at last Oedipus takes up responsibility for what he has done—or has responsibility ascribed to him?[45])

I am not implying that what Oedipus does is best explained by relating it to magic as opposed to moral agency—that since he believed he had unwittingly released a dangerous pollution by killing his father he then sought to stop it by punishing and exiling himself. (This is what Freud saw in the Oedipus story—transgressions against magically conditioned prohibitions that *therefore* have nothing to do with morality.)[46] I am urging that acts *can* have an ethical significance without necessarily having to be interpreted in terms of "answerability."

Victorian anthropologists held the view that "magic," being essentially the deployment of mistaken understandings of natural causality, was a kind of pseudoscience—and therefore not to be confused with morality. "Religion," on the other hand, when purified of its "magical" elements, was held to be the original site of morality, because religious morality had to do with the responsibility of agents *for* their actions and *to* their God. Secular morality could simply replace God by the individual conscience of men and women. Hence the "primitive" belief that a human death automatically triggers a polluting substance contact with which causes harm to liv-

45. See Susan James, "Feminism and Philosophy of Mind: The Question of Personal Identity," in M. Fricker and J. Hornsby, eds., *The Cambridge Companion to Feminist Philosophy*, Cambridge: Cambridge University Press, 2000, for an insightful review of debates about psychological continuity, personal identity, and the body.

46. "Taboo restrictions are distinct from religious or moral prohibitions. They are not based upon any divine ordinance, but may be said to impose themselves on their own account. They differ from moral prohibitions in that they fall into no system that declares quite generally that certain abstinences must be observed and gives reasons for that necessity. Taboo prohibitions have no grounds and are of unknown origin. Though they are unintelligible to *us*, to those who are dominated by them they are taken as a matter of course" (*Totem and Taboo*, London: Routledge & Kegan Paul, 1960, p. 18). (The explicit references to Oedipus are at pp. 68 and 80.) According to Freud, not only are no reasons given for taboos, there is also no point in giving reasons for breaking them. This irrationality is what puts taboo prescriptions outside the domain of moral agency.

ing humans is at once an erroneous understanding of natural causality and an idea incompatible with "responsible" action. Because moral action, for Victorian theorists as well as their present-day heirs, is the action par excellence of a "free agent" who is answerable to God, or society, or conscience (the three being identical according to Durkheim). The opposition of magic/science to religion/morality appears plausible even now to many. But anthropologists in the twentieth century have problematized the concept of "magic," and, more recently, of "religion." There are also good reasons to be skeptical of the sharp opposition between the realm of nature and that of society. Historians, sociologists, and philosophers have now given us a deeper understanding of the ways in which the realm of nature is dependent on and even replicates human activity.[47] In short: if our understanding of "moral action" is formed in contrast to certain ideas of "magic" and "religion," can it remain unaffected when the latter are shown to be outmoded?

The nature of Oedipus' moral action may thus not depend on a sequence of natural causality to which "responsibility" can be attached. One might say that Oedipus' actions on discovering what he has done (beginning with "self-punishment") arise from virtues that depend on what Marcel Mauss called *habitus*—an embodied capacity that is more than physical ability in that it also includes cultivated sensibilities and passions, an orchestration of the senses. Thus Oedipus' self-inflicted pain should not, I think, be regarded as the outcome of a judgment about his responsibility. It is perhaps best not thought of as "punishment" (a notion that has pretensions to being a reasoned and reasonable action), but as itself the passionate performance of an embodied ethical sensibility. Oedipus suffers not because he is guilty but because he is virtuous.

In the modern sense to be responsible is to be accountable to an authority, to be prepared to give justifications and excuses for one's actions, to know that one deserves punishment for the failure to do one's duty—a duty that one could and should have done, and therefore another's right that that duty be performed. Richard McKeon notes that the first use of the word "responsibility" in English and French was in 1787, in the context of the American and French revolutions, and that since then its primary use has remained political.[48] Thus the notion of "responsible govern-

47. See, for example, Ilya Prigogine, *The End of Certainty: Time, Chaos, and the New Laws of Nature*, New York: The Free Press, 1997.

48. Richard McKeon, "The Development and the Significance of the Concept of Responsibility," in *Freedom and History, and Other Essays*, Chicago: University of Chicago Press, 1990.

ment"—meaning constitutionalism, the rule of law, and self-determination—has come to be the model not only for political behavior that is imbued with a certain moral quality, but for morality itself.

Habitus, in contrast to this political model of ethics, is not something one accepts or rejects, it is part of what one essentially is and must do. (The ethics of passionate necessity encompasses tragedy.) Oedipus puts out his own eyes not because his conscience or his god considers that he deserves to be punished for failing to be responsible—or because *he* thinks he does—but because (as he says) he cannot bear the thought of having to look his father and his mother in the eyes when he joins them beyond the grave, or to see his children, "begotten as they were begotten." He acts as he does necessarily, out of the passion that is his *habitus*. I am therefore puzzled by Dillon's representation of Oedipus as a paradigm of moral "responsibility."

Bernard Williams too maintains that the story of Oedipus illustrates the concept of moral responsibility.[49] Williams regards the idea of responsibility to be essential to the concept of agency, thereby virtually equating morality with criminal law. His account is not always as clear as it might be. Thus at page 55 he identifies "cause, intention, state, and response" as the "basic elements of *any* conception of responsibility," but at page 57 he concedes that modern law holds people responsible "in some cases, for outcomes they did not even cause." So here cause is a basic element by virtue of its absence. This attribution of responsibility without causality rests, he thinks, on a distinction that is "analogous" to the one found in the ritual of "the scapegoat," in being "a substitute for someone who is responsible."

Typically, this mode of explanation by analogy presents "the secular" (the law) as a desacralized version of "the religious" (the ritual). Yet the internal structure of the two cases is not the same. Modern law defines the liability of legal persons such as landlords prior to any tort, whereas scapegoats are constituted in relation to specific transgressions. The landlord's liability for damage to others that occurs on his property is quite different from the scapegoat's role in carrying people's sins away into the desert. To begin with, the concept of "negligence," which made a property owner legally liable, is entirely a modern one—and therefore the concept of

49. Bernard Williams, *Shame and Necessity*, Berkeley: University of California Press, 1993.

agency based on it is modern too.[50] Furthermore, the scapegoat was not—as Franz Steiner makes clear—a stand-in for a legal culprit (someone who had himself failed to be adequately responsible), nor an expression of a primitive belief in *taboo*, but the ritual expulsion of evil from the renewed community.[51] The landlord is made responsible to society of which he is a member; the scapegoat's function is to be outside it. It is precisely the radicalized Protestant idea that "true religion" requires belief in "individual responsibility" and that ritual practices occupy the domain in which magic and superstition also flourish that gives us our oversimplified secular sense of the "scapegoat" as a person who is blamed for the misdeeds of others.

Like nineteenth-century anthropologists, Williams believes that the notion of "magical beliefs" (such as pollution caused by homicide) cannot be the basis of "moral agency." He is unlike them in thinking that the story of Oedipus is not essentially about primitive superstition but about what moderns would recognize as morality. However, he is like them in assuming that to justify this claim requires proof that the story contains a modern concept of responsibility, one divorced from superstition. "The whole of *Oedipus Tyrranus*, that dreadful machine, moves to the discovery of just one thing, that *he did it*," he writes. "Do we understand the terror of that discovery only because we residually share magical beliefs in blood-guilt, or archaic notions of responsibility? Certainly not: we understand it because we know that in the story of one's life there is an authority exercised by what one has done, not merely by what one has intentionally done" (p. 69). Williams would have us understand Oedipus as a familiar "human" individual, a character at once real and profound, whose moral status is independent of any *plot*. On that score there seems to be no essential difference for Williams between the way a fifth-century Athenian audience saw Oedipus and the way we are urged to see him. But the sense in this passage of the expression "there is an authority" is obscure. It allows one to evade the question of precisely when, how, and by whom the terror at the discovery that "he did it" comes to be construed as a recognition of one's "responsibility."

In the paradigm case of Oedipus it is not simply that he *unintentionally* offends against moral interdictions and only subsequently makes this terrible discovery. It is that he is, from his very birth, *destined* to do so.

---

50. See William Holdsworth, *A History of the English Law*, London, 1922–1952, vol. 8, p. 449.

51. See F. Steiner, *Taboo*, London: Cohen and West, 1958, Chapter 5.

Even his parents, Laius and Jocasta, contribute to that destiny by trying to evade it. And however much Oedipus tries to avoid it, he *unwittingly* acts in the way scripted for him. That plot is part of who he is. (Freud, famously, saw this plot as the working out of unconscious desires,[52] but we may also regard it as the story made up of the actions of many agents working together to produce a singular outcome.[53]) It is precisely the retrospective telling of this pre-scription that serves to define his present status as a moral agent—not because it liberates him from his past but because it traces his agency to his *habitus*, the ability to act sanely—albeit tragically— in accordance with his experience and situation. The authority of the past is *not* necessarily a sign of psychopathology, as Freud the modernist taught.

Paul Feyerabend once claimed that classical Greek tragedy was at once "a factual account of social conditions with a criticism of these conditions and the suggestion for an alternative."[54] But this statement does not allow for the possibility that tragedy (like pain itself) may be actively lived as a necessary form of life, one that no amount of social reform and individual therapy can eliminate forever. The tragedy of Oedipus does not illustrate "how institutions may paralyze action," as Feyerabend and others have put it. It shows how the past—whether secular or religious—constitutes agency. An "impossible choice" is a choice between terrible alternatives that have been pre-scripted for one—but it is still possible to choose, and to act on that choice. By this I do not mean of course that no reform of social arrangements depicted in the play is conceivable (of course it is, although the idea of reform is not equivalent to the secular ideas of history-making or self-empowerment). I mean simply that Oedipus *does* act, that he does so in a situation that was *not* his "responsibility," and that he can act creatively (to free his city) without aiming at self-empowerment. I mean further that reform cannot do away with pain—not merely because pain is always part of the vicissitudes of life, but because it is intrinsic to

52. Sigmund Freud, *The Interpretation of Dreams*, London: Penguin Books, 1975, pp. 362–66.

53. In this case humans and gods. Some classicists have seen Greek gods as persons, and others as powers. In his survey of recent scholarship, Jan Bremmer maintains that since the powers were personified the two interpretations are closer than it might at first appear (see Jan Bremmer, *Greek Religion*, Oxford: Oxford University Press, 1994, pp. 22–23).

54. Paul K. Feyerabend, *Three Dialogues on Knowledge*, Oxford: Blackwell, 1991, p. 97.

the Judeo-Christian-Islamic traditions of obligation, and to the secular tradition of attributing individual responsibility that has been formed out of the latter. The nature of *this* pain (punishment, repentance, discipline) is different from the one endured by Oedipus because it *is* rooted in the idea of responsibility, the idea that someone can be held accountable and blamable for a particular outcome. It implies that the acceptance of guilt and painful expiation opens the way back to a kind of just restoration.[55] For Oedipus such a return does not exist. The accumulation of events is not reversible. The future is not made, but encountered and suffered.

Concluding comment

It is essential, I think, to consider how, by whom, and in what context the concept of agency is defined and used if one is to get a better understanding of the ways "the religious" and "the secular" are continuously made and remade. Shifts in that concept, and in its connection with ideas of responsibility and consciousness, are crucial to revisions in our understanding of the religious—and therefore of the secular. What this calls for is not an abstract inquiry into mere changes in linguistic usage, but a response to questions about how the body lives pain and punishment, compassion and pleasure, hope and fear. It is with this in mind that I now turn in a general way to some secular attitudes to pain.

55. In *Oedipus and Job in West African Religion* (Cambridge: Cambridge University Press, 1959), Meyer Fortes attempts to show how the perspectives of Destiny and of Justice combine in Tallensi social thought and practice. A fascinating work that does not deserve the neglect it has encountered, even if in the end its conclusions are too sociologically reductive.

3

Reflections on Cruelty and Torture

A major motive of secularism has clearly been the desire to end cruelties—the deliberate infliction *in this world* of pain to the living body of others, and the causing of distress to their minds—that religion has so often initiated and justified. Only a secular legal constitution (so it is argued) can restrain, if not eliminate altogether, religious violence and intolerance toward religious minorities. This firm linking of institutional religion to cruelty has its roots in Western Europe's experience of religious wars and in the complex movement called the secular Enlightenment. But this perspective tends to overlook the devastatingly cruel powers of the twentieth century—Nazi Germany, Stalin's Russia, Imperial Japan, the Khmer Rouge, Mao's China—that were anything but religious, and the brutal conquests of African and Asian societies by European powers in the nineteenth century that had little to do with religion. Of course these instances of secular cruelty do not prove that institutional religion cannot generate cruelty and violence. But then religious movements have also preached (and practiced) compassion and forbearance. My simple point is that an equation of institutional religion with violence and fanaticism will not do.

In this chapter, however, I want to take a different approach to the problem. Instead of measuring the cruelty of religious regimes against secular ones I want to look at the way moral sensibilities about deliberately inflicted pain have been formed in modern secular society. I suggest that the idea of cruelty in modern discourse has distinctive characteristics, and that in describing them one is also identifying aspects of the secular. I propose therefore to begin by way of the rule stated in Article 5 of the *Universal Declaration of Human Rights* ("No one shall be subjected to torture or to cruel, inhuman or degrading treatment or punishment") that assumes the idea has a clear universal significance. In this statement the adjectives qualifying "treatment or punishment" seem to indicate forms of behavior that, if not quite equivalent to "torture," at least have a close affinity with it.

Moral and legal judgments that derive from this rule have an interesting history in the West, to which I shall advert in what follows. I want to advance the thesis that this universal rule covers a wide range of qualitatively different kinds of behavior. More precisely, I shall try to make four connected points: First, that the modern history of "torture" is not only a record of the progressive prohibition of cruel, inhuman, and degrading practices. It is also part of a secular story of how one becomes truly human. The second point is this: The phrase "torture or cruel, inhuman or degrading treatment" is intended to provide a cross-cultural criterion for making moral and legal judgments about pain and suffering. Yet it is given much of its operative sense historically and culturally. My third point is linked to the first two. It is that the new ways of conceptualizing *suffering* (which include "mental torture" and "degrading treatment") and *sufferer* (a term that now refers also to nonhumans and even to the natural environment) are increasingly universal in scope but particular in prescriptive content. The final point is that the modern dedication to eliminating pain and suffering often conflicts with other commitments and values: the right of individuals to choose, and the duty of the state to maintain its security.

Together, these four points aim at underscoring the unstable character of a central category deployed in modern, secular society. The instability relates, in brief, to the fact that the ideas of torture, cruelty, inhumanity, and degrading treatment are intended to measure what are often incommensurable standards of behavior. Perhaps most important, the idea of measured behavior is subverted by ideas of excess that come from other secular discourses.

Two histories of torture

I begin with a discussion of two books that together show very different ways of writing histories of cruelty. The first, by G. R. Scott, represents physical cruelty as a feature of barbaric societies—that is, societies that haven't yet been humanized. The other book is by D. Rejali. It makes a distinction between two kinds of physical cruelty, one appropriate to pre-modern and the other to modern societies, and describes that difference in the context of contemporary Iran.

Scott was a fellow of several British learned societies, including the Royal Anthropological Institute. His *History of Torture* is perhaps the first modern story of its kind.[1] It deals at length with "Savage and Primitive Races," ancient and early modern European peoples, and Asian "civilizations" (China, Japan, and India). On the one hand it tells a story of punishments now largely discontinued or suppressed; on the other it speaks of motives for inflicting suffering that are deep-rooted and pervasive. His indebtedness to Krafft-Ebing's ideas is evident not only in explicit form in his chapters on "Sadism" and "Masochism," but also in the general evolutionary scheme he employs according to which the primitive urge to inflict pain remains a latent possibility (sometimes realized) in civilized society.

Scott is somewhat unusual for his time in wanting to include the mistreatment of animals in his account of torture, and in describing their plight as a consequence of the nonrecognition of rights, for like other moderns he sees the extension of rights to be crucial for the elimination of cruelty. But in the course of arguing this thesis he hits on a profound and disturbing ambiguity. It is not entirely clear whether he thinks that human cruelty is merely an instance of bestial cruelty—that is, a working out of the supposedly universal instinct of stronger animals to hunt or attack the weaker. Or whether human cruelty is unique—not a characteristic of animal behavior at all—and that everyday human ruthlessness toward animals is essential for justifying the persecution of vulnerable people (defeated enemies, uninitiated children, and so on) on the ground that they are not fully human. In either case Scott disturbs liberal ideas of what it is to be truly human: humans are essentially no different from other animals, or they are different by virtue of their unique capacity for cruelty.

It is worth noting that the instances of physical pain Scott describes as "torture" belong sometimes to the involuntary submission to punishment and sometimes to the practices of personal discipline (for example, tests of endurance, ascetic techniques). He makes no distinction between the two: pain is regarded as an isolable experience, the visible reaction of a

1. *The History of Torture Throughout the Ages*, London: T. Werner Laurie, 1940.

mistreated body. If Scott had read Haller he would have understood him perfectly.

In the encounter between "Savage Races" and modern Euro-Americans, Scott has no doubt that "torture" is something the former do to the latter—perhaps because it is synonymous with "barbarity." At any rate the sufferings inflicted on Native Americans by white settlers and the expanding U.S. state has no place in his history of torture.

This is not to say that Scott asserts torture to be entirely absent in modern society. On the contrary, he is quite explicit about its use by the police to secure confession ("the third degree"). His position is that the story of modernity is in part a story of the progressive elimination of all morally shocking social behavior—including what is now described in international law as "cruel, inhuman and degrading treatment or punishment." Scott does not claim that that intention has been fully realized, only that progress has been made. In this story of progress, he tells us, the state's definition and defense of rights is the most effective protection against cruelty.

In his important book, the Iranian political scientist Darius Rejali makes the interesting argument that, far from being a barbaric survival in the modern state as Scott's story suggests, torture is in fact integral to it.[2] Although he classifies torture into two types, modern and premodern, he shares with Scott the view that the term "torture" has a fixed referent. More precisely, both of them take it that to speak of torture is to refer to a practice in which the agent *forcibly* inflicts pain on another—regardless of the place that the practice occupies within a larger moral economy.

Rejali offers a sophisticated account of the role of political punishments in Iran both before and after the inception of modernization in that country. Modern torture, he tells us, is a form of physical suffering that is an inseparable part of a disciplinary society. In Iran the practice of torture is as essential to the Islamic Republic today as it was to the Pahlevi regime it replaced. Both in their own way are modern disciplinary societies.

Rejali believes that his book refutes what Foucault had to say about torture in *Discipline and Punish*.[3] He maintains that torture does not give place to discipline in modern society, as Foucault claimed, but persists in a

2. D. M. Rejali, *Torture and Modernity: Self, Society, and State in Modern Iran*, Boulder, CO: Westview, 1994.

3. So also Page DuBois, *Torture and Truth*, New York: Routledge, 1991, pp. 153–57.

major way. But this belief arises from a misreading of Foucault, whose central concern was not with "torture" but with "power," and consequently with a contrast between sovereign power (which exhibits itself through theatrical displays of tortured bodies) and disciplinary power (which works through the normalization of bodies in everyday behavior).

Public rituals of torture are no longer deemed to be necessary to the maintenance of sovereign power (whether they were ever necessary to the maintenance of "social order" is, of course, another question). But Foucault's thesis about disciplinary power is not subverted by evidence of *surreptitious* torture in the modern state. On the contrary, when torture carried out in secret is intimately connected with the extraction of information, it becomes an aspect of policing. Policing presents itself as a governmental activity directed at defending a fundamental "interest of society": the ordinary and extraordinary security of the state and its citizens. It is also an institution in which knowledge and power depend upon each other. Much of it—and this point is curiously neglected by Rejali—circulating in secret.

Modern torture linked to policing is typically secret partly because inflicting physical pain on a prisoner is considered "uncivilized" and therefore illegal. It may also be secret because policing agents claim they do not wish to advertise what they learn from (tortured) prisoners—if and when they learn anything of significance. After all, the effectiveness of certain kinds of disciplinary knowledge is enhanced by its secrecy. The secret character of knowledge acquired in policing therefore relates at once to the uncertainty of outside critics as to whether, and if so how often, something illegal has been done by bureaucratic power to obtain it ("torture is intolerable in a civilized society"), and also to how, when, and where that power chooses to act given that it possesses secret information ("every society must protect itself against criminal and terrorist conspiracies").

Critics sometimes claim that "the extraction of information" is not the real goal of torture, but rather torture's justification. But I suggest that there is no such thing as "the *real* goal of torture." The motives (conscious and unconscious) of someone who carries out specific acts of torture are usually varied and mixed. The idea that specific acts of torture should be understood by the agent's motivation is either circular or based on the sentimental (and false) belief that only peculiar psychological types are capable of great cruelty.

My argument here is that "torture" as now used in the law is a form of cruelty that liberal societies do not approve of. That's the main reason why modern authorities typically generate a rhetoric of public denial—of disclaiming that "torture" has actually taken place within their domain of responsibility ("it was the unauthorized activity of undisciplined officials"), or of claiming that what appears to be "torture" is really something less reprehensible ("reasonable pressure"). This rhetoric is an important element in the public culture of modern liberalism, and it generates an air of secrecy around the subject—and therefore an air of "exposure" when incidents of torture are "made public." In premodern societies of the kind Foucault called Classical, "torture" was carried out unapologetically and in public. It was the object not of exposure but of display. From the point of view of the problem I pursue, the motives of those who carried out such theatrical torture are irrelevant—even if it were possible to determine them. What matters is that the public discourse on inflicting pain on a prisoner in the two cases (modern and premodern) is quite different. The rhetoric of denial, which is the other side of a rhetoric of accusation, is typical of modern *or* modernizing governments, and is linked to a liberal sensibility regarding pain.

Rejali's definition of torture as "sanguinary violence condoned by public authorities" slips uneasily between the legitimate and public practice of classical torture on the one hand, and, on the other hand, the *secretive* because "uncivilized" character of policing torture in modernizing states like Iran. Unfortunately, his argument doesn't address this difference. Modern torture, he insists at length, is integral to what Foucault called disciplinary society. It is, if not itself quite identical with discipline, then very close to it.

There are valuable insights in Rejali's book relating to the cruelty inflicted on people in the process of modernization, but I do not have the space to dwell on them. Here I mention only two objections that some readers might make to his argument. The first is that his main example (twentieth-century Iran) relates to what many readers will identify as a "modernizing" rather than a "fully modern" society. Whether all the transformations in Iran in the period covered by Rejali's book truly represent modernization in the sense of moral improvement is—these readers will say—an open question, but shocking evidence of blatant torture in that country does not prove that torture is integral to modernity; what it shows is that torture might occur in it, as Scott concedes. Rejali's argument at this point would have been stronger if he had referred to a modern society, like Nazi Germany, rather than a society merely on the way to being modernized. For although Nazi Germany was notoriously an *il*liberal state, it was certainly no less modern than any other.

The other objection is this: Rejali does not explain why, unlike discipline, *modern* state use of torture requires the rhetoric of denial. The brief answer to this question, surely, is that there is now a new sensibility regarding physical pain. Although it occurs frequently enough in our time, the modern conscience regards the inflicting of pain "without good reason" (to perform a medical operation, say, or to slaughter animals for meat) as reprehensible, and therefore as an object of moral condemnation. It is this attitude to pain that helps define the modern notion of cruelty.

The modern conscience is also a secular conscience, a category that subsumes moralized religion. (For Kant, "pure religion" is nothing more than conscience-based morality, and it stands apart from the dogmas of historical religion.)[4] Christianity, which was traditionally rooted in the doctrine of Christ's *passion*, consequently finds it difficult to make good sense of suffering today. Modern theologians have begun to concede that pain is essentially and entirely negative. "The secularist challenge," writes a modern Catholic theologian, "even though separating many aspects of life from the religious field, brings with it a more sound, interpretive equilibrium; the natural phenomena, even though sometimes difficult to understand, have their cause and roots in processes that can and must be recognized. It is a man's job, therefore, to enter into this cognitive analysis of the meaning of suffering, in order to be able to affront and conquer it. . . . Through his works, even before his words, Jesus of Nazareth proclaimed the goodness of life and of health, as the image of salvation. For Him pain is negativeness."[5]

The writer in this passage is clearly thinking of disease, but since pain can also be a consequence of human intention, it follows that such pain should be eliminated from the world of human interaction—even from re-

---

4. Immanuel Kant, *Religion within the Limits of Reason Alone*, New York: Harper and Row, 1960.

5. A. Autiero, "The Interpretation of Pain: The Point of View of Catholic Theology," in *Pain*, ed. J. Brihaye, F. Loew, H. W. Pia, Vienna/New York: Springer-Verlag, 1987, p. 124. Incidentally, there is a curious paradox in invoking a metaphor of military violence ("to affront and conquer") to describe the compassionate work of healing. But such paradoxes abound in Christian history, of course.

ligious disciplines, and from the enactment of martyrdom, where it once had an effective and honored place. The secular Christian must now abjure passion and choose action. Pain is not merely negativeness. It is, literally, a scandal.

Abolishing torture

Why has the infliction of physical pain now become scandalous? A well-known part of the answer is this progressivist story: two centuries ago critics of torture like Beccaria and Voltaire recognized how inhuman it was, and how unreliable as a way of ascertaining the truth in a trial. Thus they saw and articulated what others before them had (unaccountably) failed to see. Their powerful case against judicial torture shocked Enlightenment rulers into abolishing it. The theme of its intolerable cruelty emerged more clearly because the pain inflicted in judicial torture was declared to be *gratuitous*. Pain inflicted on prisoners to make them confess was immoral, it was argued, particularly because it was grossly *inefficient* in identifying their guilt or innocence.[6] (The Enlightenment reformers didn't necessarily condemn physical punishment as such, because it involved considerations other than simple instrumental ones, especially ideas of justice. Eventually, however, the evolution of modern ideas of justice were to contribute to growing hostility to punishment inflicted directly on the body.) But why was this gratuitous pain not condemned by critics earlier? What had prevented people from seeing the truth until the Enlightenment?

In his brilliant study *Torture and the Law of Proof,* John Langbein has provided a partial explanation. He demonstrates that torture was proscribed when the Roman canon law of proof—which required either confession or the testimony of two eyewitnesses to convict—declined in force in the seventeenth century. Increasing resort to circumstantial evidence secured convictions more easily and speedily. The abolition of judicial torture was thus in effect the proscription of an extremely cumbersome and

6. Thus Beccaria denounces "the barbarous and *useless* tortures multiplied with prodigal and *useless* severity for crimes that are either unproven or chimerical" (*On Crimes and Punishments,* ed. and trans. D. Young, Indianapolis: Hackett, 1986, p. 4, italics added). And Voltaire, with characteristic sarcasm, remarks that "On a dit souvent que la question [i.e., torture] etait un moyen de sauver un coupable robuste, et de perdre un innocent trop faible." (*Oeuvres complètes de Voltaire,* new edition, vol. 26, Paris, 1818, p. 314).

lengthy procedure that was now coming to be regarded as more or less redundant. Langbein implies that the moral truth about judicial torture was linked to the prior construction of a new concept of legal truth.[7]

When torture was the object of vigorous polemic in the eighteenth century, Jeremy Bentham came to the conclusion that the pain of torture applied for instrumental purposes is easier to justify than the suffering inflicted in the name of punishment. In the course of this justification he maintained, for example, that courts resorting to imprisonment in cases of contempt might find the application of physical pain, or even the threat of applying it, would secure obedience in a way "less penal" than prison: "A man may have been lingering in prison for a month or two before he would make answer to a question which at the worst with one stroke of the rack, and therefore almost always with only knowing that he might be made to suffer the rack, he would have answered in a moment; just as a man will linger on a Month with the Toothach [sic] which he might have saved himself from at the expense of a momentary pang."[8]

It is not Bentham's apparent refusal to distinguish between voluntary and involuntary subjection to pain that should be noted here. It is the more interesting idea that subjective experiences of pain can be objectively compared. This idea is crucial for the modern understanding of "cruel, inhuman and degrading treatment" in a cross-cultural context, although liberals today would strongly reject Bentham's view regarding the occasional preferability of torture to imprisonment. For it is precisely some notion of comparability in suffering that makes of long years in prison (including solitary confinement) a "humane" punishment and of flogging an "inhumane" one, even though *the experience* of imprisonment and of flogging are qualitatively quite different.

In *Discipline and Punish* Foucault notes that in the nineteenth century imprisonment was compared favorably to other forms of legal punishment mainly because it was regarded as the most egalitarian.[9] This was a consequence of the philosophical doctrine that freedom was the natural human condition. Penal reformers reasoned that since the desire for liberty

7. J. H. Langbein, *Torture and the Law of Proof: Europe and England in the Ancien Regime*, Chicago: University of Chicago Press, 1977.

8. See the two fragments first published as "Bentham on Torture" in *Bentham and Legal Theory*, ed. M. H. James, Belfast, 1973, p. 45.

9. See M. Foucault, *Discipline and Punish*, New York: Vintage Books, 1979, p. 232.

was implanted equally in every individual, depriving individuals of their liberty must be a way of striking at them equally—that is, regardless of their social status or physical constitution. For just as fines were easier for the rich to pay, so physical pain could be borne better by the more sturdy. No form of punishment accorded so precisely with our essential humanity, therefore, as imprisonment did. That legal incarceration was considered to be equitable contributed to the sense that physical punishment was gratuitous. For this reason although modern liberals must regard Bentham wrong in the conclusion he reached about torture, they must consider him right to have endorsed a quantitative comparison of very disparate kinds of suffering. It is not difficult to see how the utilitarian calculus of pleasure and pain has come to be central to cross-cultural judgment in modern thought and practice. For by a reductive operation the idea of a calculus has facilitated the comparative judgment of what would otherwise remain incommensurable qualities.[10]

Humanizing the world

The historical process of constructing a humane secular society, it is said, has aimed at eliminating cruelties. Thus it has often been claimed that European rule in colonial countries, although not itself democratic, brought about moral improvements in behavior—that is, the abandonment of practices that offend against the human.

Major instruments in this transformation were modern legal, administrative, and educational practices. And a central category deployed in them was the modern category of customary law. "Of all the restrictions upon the application of customary laws during the colonial period," writes James Read, "the test of repugnancy 'to justice or morality' was potentially the most sweeping: for customary laws could hardly be repugnant to the traditional sense of justice or morality of the community which still ac-

10. In *Classical Probability in the Enlightenment* (Princeton: Princeton University Press, 1988) Lorraine Daston has described how, over two centuries, Enlightenment mathematicians struggled to produce a model that would provide a moral calculus for "the reasonable man" in conditions of uncertainty. Although modern probability theory has become entirely divorced from this moral project since about 1840, the idea of a calculus continues to be powerful in liberal welfare discourse.

cepted them, and it is therefore clear that the justice or morality of the colonial power was to provide the standard to be applied." Read points out that the phrase "repugnant to justice and morality" does not have a precise legal meaning, and that early legislation in the colonies sometimes employed other expressions, such as "not opposed to natural morality and humanity," to perform the same revolutionary work.[11]

But moral and social progress in those countries has been uneven. Although Europeans tried to suppress cruel practices and forms of suffering that were previously taken for granted in the non-European world by making the practitioners legally culpable, the suppression was not always completely successful. Today the struggle to eliminate social suffering is taken up by the United Nations. Or so the story goes.

I want to propose, however, that in their attempt to outlaw customs the European rulers considered cruel it was not the concern with indigenous suffering that *dominated* their thinking, but the desire to impose what they considered civilized standards of justice and humanity on a subject population—that is, the desire to create new human subjects.[12] The anguish of subjects compelled under threat of punishment to abandon traditional practices—now legally branded as "repugnant to justice and moral-

11. See "Customary Law under Colonial Rule," in H. F. Morris and J. S. Read, eds., *Indirect Rule and the Search for Justice*, Oxford: Clarendon Press, 1972, p. 175.

12. Lord Milner, undersecretary for finance during the British occupation of Egypt that began in 1882, described Britain's imperial task in that country as follows: "This then, and no less than this, was meant by 'restoring order.' It meant reforming the Egyptian administration root and branch. Nay, it meant more. For what was the good of recasting the system, if it were left to be worked by officials of the old type, animated by the old spirit? 'Men, not measures,' is a good watchword anywhere, but to no country is it more profoundly applicable than to Egypt. Our task, therefore, included something more than new principles and new methods. *It ultimately involved new men.* It involved 'the education of the people to know, and therefore to expect, orderly and honest government—the education of a body of rulers capable of supplying it'" (*England in Egypt*, London: Edward Arnold, 1899, p. 23). Here Milner enunciates the government's need to create subjects (in both senses) as well as rulers informed by new standards of human behavior and political justice. That this would involve the application of some force and suffering was a secondary consideration. I stress that my point is not that colonial administrators like Milner lacked "humanitarian" motives, but that they were guided by a particular concept of "humanness."

ity" or as "opposed to natural morality and humanity," or even sometimes as "backward and childish"—could not therefore play a decisive part in the discourse of colonial reformers. On the contrary, as Lord Cromer put it with reference to the misery created among the Egyptian peasantry by legal reforms under British rule: "Civilisation must, unfortunately, have its victims."[13] In the process of learning to be "fully human" only some kinds of suffering were seen as an affront to humanity, and their elimination sought. This was distinguished from suffering that was *necessary* to the process of realizing one's humanity—that is, pain that was adequate to its end, not *wasteful* pain.

Inhuman suffering, typically associated with barbaric behavior, was a morally insufferable condition for which someone was therefore responsible; those requiring it (themselves inhuman enough to cause it to be inflicted) must be made to desist, and if necessary punished. That, at any rate, is the discourse of colonial reform. What individual administrators actually felt, thought, or did is another (though not entirely unrelated) matter. Most experienced administrators were prepared locally to tolerate various "uncivilized" practices for reasons of expediency, but all were no doubt aware of the dominant progressivist discourse rooted in "civilized" societies.

In an unpublished paper by Nicholas Dirks there is a nice example of just this discourse in late nineteenth-century British India. His account of the inquiry conducted by the colonial authorities into the ritual of hook-swinging[14] contains this sober judgment by the presiding British official: "It is, in my opinion, unnecessary at the end of the nineteenth century and, having regard to the level to which civilisation in India has attained, to consider the motives by which the performers themselves are actuated when taking part in hook swinging, walking through fire, and other barbarities. From their own moral standpoint, their motives may be good or they may be bad; they may indulge in self-torture in satisfaction of pious vows fervently made in all sincerity and for the most disinterested reasons; or they may indulge in it from the lowest motives of personal aggrandise-

13. "The Government of Subject Races," *Political and Literary Essays, 1908–1913*, London: Macmillan, 1913, p. 44.

14. Hookswinging involves a ceremony in which the celebrant swings from a crossbeam built for the purpose on a cart, suspended by two steel hooks thrust into the small of his back. See D. D. Kosambe, "Living Prehistory in India," *Scientific American*, vol. 216, no. 2, 1967.

ment, whether for the alms they might receive or for the personal distinction and local eclat that it may bring them; but the question is whether public opinion in this country is not opposed to the *external acts* of the performers, as being in fact repugnant to the dictates of humanity and demoralizing to themselves and to all who may witness their performances. I am of the opinion that the voice of India most entitled to be listened to with respect, that is to say, not only the voice of the advanced school that has received some of the advantages of western education and has been permeated with non-Oriental ideas, but also the voice of those whose views of life and propriety of conduct have been mainly derived from Asiatic philosophy, would gladly proclaim that the time had arrived for the Government in the interests of its people to effectively put down all degrading exhibitions of self-torture."[15]

The fact that the performers themselves declared that they felt no pain was irrelevant. So, too, was the plea that this was a religious rite. Such justifications were not acceptable. It was the offense given by the performance to a particular concept of being human that reduced qualitatively different kinds of behavior to a single standard. And it was the government's task to realize that standard here and now, not that of divinity to apply it in the afterlife.

Confirmation of the moral offensiveness of this behavior was obtained by listening to *some* colonized voices only. The latter included westernized Indians. But, more significantly, confirmation was provided also by those who accepted a westernized exegesis of their Asiatic philosophy.[16]

15. N. Dirks, "The Policing of Tradition: Colonialism and Anthropology in Southern India," unpublished manuscript. pp. 9–10.

16. In relation to the more celebrated British prohibition of *sati* (the self-immolation of the Hindu widow on the funeral pyre of her husband) in 1829, Lata Mani notes that "Rather than arguing for the outlawing of *sati* as a cruel and barbarous act, as one might expect of a true 'moderniser', officials in favour of abolition were at pains to illustrate that such a move was entirely consonant with the principle of upgrading indigenous tradition. Their strategy was to point to the questionable scriptural sanction for *sati* and to the fact that, for one reason or another, they believed its contemporary practice transgressed its original and therefore 'true' scriptural meaning" (L. Mani, "The Production of an Official Discourse on *Sati* in Early Nineteenth-Century Bengal," in F. Barker et al., eds., *Europe and Its Others*, Colchester: University of Essex, 1985, vol. 1, p. 107). Thus it was a modernized "Hinduism" that was made to yield the judgment that *sati* was a cruel and barbarous act.

From the point of view of moral progress, the voices of those who took up a "reactionary" position could not, of course, be attended to.

Clearly, then, in the cause of secular progress there was suffering and suffering. What is interesting, I think, is not merely that some forms of suffering were to be taken more seriously than others, but that "inhuman" suffering as opposed to "necessary" or "inevitable" suffering was regarded as being essentially *gratuitous*, and therefore legally punishable. Pain endured in the movement toward becoming "fully human," on the other hand, was necessary, in the sense that there were social or moral reasons why it had to be suffered. This view is of a piece with the post-Enlightenment concern to construct through judicial punishment the most efficient means of reforming offenders and of guarding society's interests.[17]

As the idea of progress became increasingly dominant in the affairs of Europe and the world, the need for measuring suffering was felt and responded to with greater sophistication.

Representing "torture," acting with deliberate cruelty

Pain is not always regarded as insufferable in modern Euro-American societies. In warfare, sport, scientific experimentation, and the death penalty—as well as in the domain of sexual pleasure—inflicting physical suffering is actively practiced and also legally condoned. The inflicting of pain on animals is a normal part of these societies, although there are statutes that prohibit "unnecessary" or "unjustifiable" pain and criminalize it as "cruelty."[18] This makes for contradictions that are exploited in public

17. "Reformative theory presented punishment to offenders as being 'in their best interests' while utilitarian theory cast it as an impartial act of social necessity. In rejecting retributive theory, the reformers sought, in effect, to take the anger out of punishment. As it was legitimized to the prisoner, punishment was no longer to be, in Bentham's words, 'an act of wrath or vengeance', but an act of calculation, disciplined by considerations of the social good and the offenders' needs" (M. Ignatieff, *A Just Measure of Pain*, Penguin Books, 1989, p. 75). This account fails to note, however, that vindictiveness can inhabit calculated anger.

18. Jerrold Tannenbaum demonstrates how difficult it is to define cruelty to animals in the law. However, he identifies a number of general criteria often used to determine whether "unnecessary" or "unjustifiable" pain has been inflicted in the case at hand: (1) The severity and duration of pain, (2) perceived legitimacy (by "society as a whole") of the particular activity involving animals, (3) avoidability of the pain given the activity or aim, (4) motivation of the defen-

debate. When transitive pain is described as "cruel and inhuman" it is often referred to as *torture*. And torture itself is condemned by public opinion and prohibited by international law.

It is hardly surprising, therefore, that the many liberal-democratic governments[19] that have employed torture have attempted to do so in secret. And sometimes they have been concerned to redefine legally the category of pain-producing treatment in an attempt to avoid the label "torture." Thus, "Torture is forbidden by Israeli law. Israeli authorities say that torture is not authorized or condoned in the occupied territories but acknowledge that abuses occur and state that they are investigated. In 1987 the Landau Judicial Commission specifically condemned 'torture' but allowed for 'moderate physical and psychological pressure' to be used to secure confessions and to obtain information; a classified annex to the report defining permissible pressure has never been made public."[20]

Needless to say, other governments in the region (for example, Egypt, Turkey, and Iran) have also condoned torture, and unlike Israel, which tortures only non-citizens, they have used it freely against their own citizens. But the remarkable feature of the Israeli case is the scrupulous concern of a liberal-democratic state with calibrating the amount of pain that is legally allowable. There is evidently a concern that *too much* pain should not be applied. (The thought "too much" relates here not to subjective experience, the unbearability of pain, but to objective means—to what is strictly necessary to secure the desired ends.) It is assumed that "moderate physical and psychological pressure" is at once necessary and sufficient to secure confession. Beyond that quantity, pressure is held to be excessive (gratuitous), and *therefore* presumably becomes "torture."[21] Other states in the Middle East are rarely so punctilious. Or so modern in their reasoning.

---

dant, (5) perceived value or moral status (by "society as a whole") of the animal or species (see Jerrold Tannenbaum, "Animals and the Law: Cruelty, Property, Rights . . . Or How the Law Makes Up in Common Sense What It May Lack in Metaphysics," *Social Research*, vol. 62, no. 3, 1995.

19. For example, France in Algeria, the United States in Vietnam, Israel in Gaza and the West Bank, Britain in Aden, Cyprus, and Northern Ireland.

20. U.S. Department of State, *Country Reports on Human Rights Practices for 1993*, p. 1204.

21. This is precisely Bentham's argument about the rationality of torture in comparison with punishment: "The purpose to which Torture is applied is such that whenever that purpose is actually attained it may plainly be seen to be at-

The use of torture by liberal-democratic states is part of their attempt to control populations of noncitizens. In such cases torture cannot be attributed to "primitive urges"—as Scott suggested. Nor to governmental techniques for disciplining citizens, as Rejali has argued. It is to be understood as a means used strategically for the maintenance of the nation-state's interests. Like warfare.

The category of torture is no longer limited to applications of physical pain: it now includes psychological coercion in which disorientation, isolation, and brainwashing are employed. Indeed "torture" in our day functions not only to denote behavior actually prohibited by law, but also desired to be so prohibited in accordance with changing concepts of "inhumane" treatment (for example, the public execution or flogging of criminals, and child abuse, as well as animal experiments, factory farming, and fox hunting).

This wider category of torture or cruelty could in theory be applied to the anguish and mental suffering experienced by people in societies obliged to give up their beliefs and act "humanly" (in the sense understood by Euro-Americans). But by a curious paradox it is a secular relativism that prevents such an application of the category. For that anguish is seen as the consequence of a passionate investment in the truth of beliefs that guide behavior. The modern *skeptical* posture, in contrast, regards such passionate conviction to be "uncivilized"—a perpetual source of danger to others and of pain to oneself. Beliefs should either have no direct connection to the way one lives, or be held so lightly that they can easily be changed. Otherwise secularism as a political arrangement cannot work very well.

One might be inclined to think that at least in humanizing societies more sorts of inflicted pain come to be considered morally unacceptable with the passage of time. In some cases, however, pain-producing behavior that was once shocking no longer shocks. Or if it does, then not in the way it did in the past. Putting large numbers of people in prison for more and more kinds of offense is one example. Inflicting new forms of suffering in battle is another.

Scarry has claimed that war is "the most obvious analogue to tor-

_____

tained; and as soon as ever it is seen to be attained it may immediately be made to cease. With punishment it is necessarily otherwise. Of punishment, in order to make sure of applying as much as is necessary you must commonly run a risque of applying considerably more: of Torture there need never be a grain more applied than what is necessary" (Bentham, p. 45).

ture."[22] However that may be, it is significant that the general concept of "cruel, inhuman and degrading treatment or punishment" is not applied to the *normal* conduct of war—although modern, technological warfare involves forms of suffering, in number and in kind, that are without precedent. The Geneva Convention, it is true, seeks to regulate conduct in war.[23] But paradoxically, this has the effect of legalizing most of the new kinds of suffering endured in modern war by combatants and noncombatants alike.

The military historian John Keegan wrote of the new practices of "deliberate cruelty" over two decades ago when he described some of the weaponry employed in twentieth-century warfare: "Weapons have never been kind to human flesh, but the directing principle behind their design has usually not been that of maximizing the pain and damage they can cause. Before the invention of explosives, the limits of muscle power in itself constrained their hurtfulness; but even for some time thereafter moral inhibitions, fuelled by a sense of the unfairness of adding mechanical and chemical increments to man's power to hurt his brother, served to restrain deliberate barbarities of design. Some of these inhibitions—against the use of poison gas and explosive bullets—were codified and given international force by the Hague Convention of 1899; but the rise of 'thing-killing' as opposed to man-killing weapons—heavy artillery is an example—which by their side-effects inflicted gross suffering and disfigurement, invalidated these restraints. As a result restraints were cast to the winds, and it is now a desired effect of many man-killing weapons that they inflict wounds as terrible and terrifying as possible. The claymore mine, for instance, is filled with metal cubes . . . , the cluster bomb with jagged metal fragments, in both cases because that shape of projectile tears and fractures more extensively than a smooth-bodied one. The HEAT and HESH rounds fired by anti-tank guns are designed to fill the interior of armoured vehicles with showers of metal splinters or streams of molten metal, so disabling the tank by disabling its crew. And napalm, disliked for ethical reasons even by

22. Scarry, p. 61.

23. It should not be forgotten, however, that medieval warfare also had its rules (see, for example, P. Contamine, *War in the Middle Ages*, Oxford: Blackwell, 1984). In one sense the moral regulation of conduct in warfare was even stricter in the early Middle Ages: killing and maiming, even in battle, was regarded as a sin for which the church demanded penance (see F. H. Russell, *The Just War in the Middle Ages*, Cambridge, 1975).

many tough minded soldiers, contains an ingredient which increases the adhesion of the burning petrol to human skin surfaces. Military surgeons, so successful over the past century in resuscitating wounded soldiers and repairing wounds of growing severity, have thus now to meet a challenge of wounding agents deliberately conceived to defeat their skills."[24] (Incidentally, the mushrooming or "dum-dum" bullet, invented in British India in 1897, is reported to have been "so vicious, for it tore great holes in the flesh, that Europeans thought it too cruel to inflict upon one another, and used it only against Asians and Africans."[25])

One might add to this that the manufacture, possession, and deployment of weapons of mass destruction (chemical, biological, and nuclear) must be counted as instances of declared governmental readiness to inflict cruel death upon civilian populations even when these weapons are not actually used. In brief, cruel modern technologies of destruction are integral to modern warfare, and modern warfare is an activity essential to the security and power of the modern state, on which the welfare and identity of its citizens depends. In war, the modern state demands from its citizens not only that they kill and maim others but also that they themselves suffer cruel pain and death.[26] Human life is sacred, but only in particular contexts that the state defines.

So how can the *calculated* cruelties of modern battle be reconciled with the modern sensibility regarding pain? Precisely by treating pain as *a quantifiable* essence. As in state torture, an attempt can be made to measure the physical suffering inflicted in modern warfare in accordance with the proportionality of means to ends. That is the principle supported by the Geneva Convention. The principle states that the human destruction inflicted should not outweigh the strategic advantage gained. Only *necessary* punishment of noncombatants should be used. But given the aim of ultimate victory the notion of "military necessity" can be extended indefi-

24. J. Keegan, *The Face of Battle*, Harmondsworth, UK: Penguin Books, 1978, pp. 329–330.

25. Daniel Headrick, "The Tools of Imperialism: Technology and the Expansion of European Colonial Empires in the Nineteenth Century," *Journal of Modern History*, vol. 51, 1979, p. 256.

26. The paradox here is that the modern citizen is a free individual and yet he is obliged to forgo the most important choice a free human being can make—that affecting his life or death. The modern state can send its citizens to their unwilling deaths in war and can forbid them from willingly ending their own lives in peace.

nitely. Any measure that is intended as a contribution to that aim, no matter how much suffering it creates, may be justified in terms of "military necessity." The standard of acceptability in such cases is set by public opinion, and that standard varies as the latter moves in response to contingent circumstances (for example, who the enemy is, how the war is going).

I want to stress that I am making no moral judgment here. My concern is simply to identify the paradoxes of modern thought and practice that relate to the deliberate infliction of pain in conflicts between states as well as within them. If I focus on state-condoned cruelty this is not because I assume that the state is its only source today, but because our moral discourse about cruel, inhuman, and degrading treatment or punishment is closely linked to legal concepts and political interventions.

In the instances discussed so far, I have tried to suggest that the instability of the concept of physical suffering is at one and the same time the source of ideological contradictions and of strategies available for evading them. I now shift my attention to the domain of interpersonal relations that the modern state defines as "private." Here we meet with a contradiction that has deeper roots, and one that cannot be resolved simply by, say, redefining the concept of torture as "moderate pressure" or by prohibiting excessive cruelty in military combat.

Subjecting oneself to "cruel and degrading treatment"

So while the category of "torture" has in recent times been expanded to include cases of induced suffering that are primarily or entirely psychological, it has also been narrowed to exclude some cases of the calculated infliction of physical pain. And this sometimes leads to contradictions. But there is another kind of contradiction that is characteristic of modern secular life.

It has always been recognized that there are situations in which a sharp separation cannot be made between the experience of pain and the experience of pleasure. Sadomasochism is disturbing to many people precisely because here they are confronted with suffering that is no longer simply painful. It is at once pain and not pain. And its object is *excess*. Two centuries of powerful criticism directed at the Utilitarian's calculus of pleasure versus pain has not destroyed the common view that these two experiences are mutually exclusive and that each can, in some sense, be measured. Yet in the eroticization of suffering the two are intimately linked, and it is actively sought by some.

Here is an extract from a sadomasochist *Handbook* published recently in New York: "Because I consider any attempt to define SM in a single concise phrase to be the ultimate exercise in futility—or masochism—I shall forego the temptation to add yet another version to the great discarded stack of unsuccessful, inadequate verbal garbage. Instead let me suggest a short list of characteristics I find to be present in most scenes which I would classify as SM:

1. A dominant-submissive relationship.
2. A giving and receiving of pain that is pleasurable to both parties.
3. Fantasy and/or role playing on the part of one or both partners.
4. A conscious humbling of one partner by the other (humiliation).
5. Some form of fetish involvement.
6. The acting out of one or more ritualized interactions (bondage, flagellation, etc)."[27]

Notice that this text speaks not about *representing* pain but about pain experienced and inflicted, in which both partners, the active and the passive, are jointly agents. So why is sadomasochism not rejected by all moderns who condemn pain as a negative experience?

One answer, according to some interpreters, is that not everyone "confuses the distinction between unbridled sadism and the social subculture of consensual fetishism. To argue that in consensual S/M the 'dominant' has power, and the slave has not, is to read theater for reality."[28]

However, the point of my question is not to dismiss the distinction between "unbridled sadism" and the "subculture of consensual fetishism." It is to ask what happens when individual self-fashioning embraces the difference between "pain" and "pleasure" within an aesthetic whole. We are sometimes told that the hybridization of categories, including those that organize our sensual experience, is a mode by which stable authority may be subverted in the name of liberty. But it is possible also that the eroti-

27. Larry Townsend, *The Leatherman's Handbook II*, New York: Carlyle Communications Ltd., 1989, p. 15.

28. A. McClintock, "Maid to Order: Commercial Fetishism and Gender Power," *Social Text*, no. 37, winter 1993, p. 87.

cization of pain is merely one of the ways in which the modern self attempts to secure its elusive foundation.

Recently, an article in a London newspaper gave the following account of a local performance by an American artist at the Institute of Contemporary Arts: "With his face set in a mask of concentration, Ron Athey allows his head to be pierced with a six-inch needle just above the eyebrow. You watch, transfixed, as the needle snakes along beneath the skin like water pulsing through an empty hosepipe. A droplet of blood wells up at the point where steel meets scalp. This is the first spike of Athey's crown of thorns—a body piercer's tribute to the power of Christian iconography, an ex-junkie's flirtation with the needle, and a gay man's defiance of infection with HIV.

"By the time the macabre 'sketch' is finished, Athey is encrusted with needles, garlanded with wire and oozing blood, in what appears to be a parody of the crucifixion. Ah, but is it a parody, defined in the dictionary as 'an imitation so poor as to seem a deliberate mockery of the original'? Or is it—as Athey's supporters would claim—an exploration of the nature of martyrdom, as manifest to a worldwide gay community in the era of Aids?"[29]

What is remarkable about these opening paragraphs is that the writer of this account finds herself having to put the familiar theatrical word "sketch" in quotation marks—but not so the equally familiar theological word *martyrdom*. The reader is given to understand that this is a *real* tribute to the power of Christian iconography, a *real* exploration of the nature of (Christian) martyrdom, but that it only "appears" to be a form of theater, an "imitation."[30] It is a mistake to see it as an illusion.

I stress that I am not here challenging this interpretation but underlining the writer's recognition that in the discourse of modern self-fashioning, the tension holding "real" and "theatrical" apart can collapse. It is especially in a modern culture, where the split between the real and its mere representation has become institutionalized, that it becomes necessary to

29. Claire Armistead, "Piercing Thoughts," *Guardian Weekly*, July 17, 1994, p. 26.

30. Cf. McClintock, op. cit., p. 106: "S/M is the most liturgical of forms, sharing with Christianity a theatrical iconography of punishment and expiation: washing rituals, bondage, flagellation, body-piercing, and symbolic torture." But why only *symbolic*? In traditional Christianity surely punishment, expiation, and suffering are very real.

assert from time to time that a given performance is *merely* theatrical, or that another performance is *not really* theater. My point here, however, is that it is the *difference* between "the real" and "the mimetic"—like the difference between "pain" and "pleasure"—that is available to modern self-fashioning. And that consequently the tension between "real" and "pretend" bondage is itself aestheticized, and the clarity with which consent can be distinguished from coercion becomes problematic.

Of course S/M as defined in the text I quoted earlier is different from this performance at the I.C.A. For one thing, in the latter there is a separation between performers and observers. No experience of giving and receiving pain binds the two together in mutual pleasure. We find only a one-sided representation (presentation?) of an evocative image of suffering, which is preceded by a painful construction of that image on the stage. Furthermore, its intention is not the production of private pleasure. We can't know whether the various members of Athey's audience respond primarily to the icon of Christ's last passion, or to the painful construction of that icon on the stage—or to both. Nor can we tell what difference it would make to those who would like to ban this performance if they were to be told that Athey suffers from a malfunctioning of the nervous system so that he actually feels no pain. Or—more tellingly—that like a religious virtuoso he has learnt to experience it *positively*.

Think of the Shi'a Muslim flagellants mourning the martyrdom of the Prophet's grandson Hussain annually every Muharram. That instance of self-inflicted pain is at once real *and* dramatic (not "theatrical"). It has even less to do with "pleasure" than does Athey's performance. It differs from the latter in being a collective rite of religious suffering and redemption. It is not a secular act that borrows a religious metaphor to make a statement about political prejudice. Nor is it premised on the right to self-fashioning and the autonomy of individual choice. Yet both strike against the modern sensibility that recoils from a willing, positive engagement with suffering. Because, in very different ways, for ascetics, as for sadomasochists, pain is not merely a means that can be measured and pronounced excessive or gratuitous in relation to an end. Pain is not calculated action but passionate engagement.

One of the earliest attempts to theorize *excess* as an element in the secular formation of modern subjectivity is Edmund Burke's notion of the sublime. In *A Philosophical Enquiry into the Origin of our Ideas of the Sublime and Beautiful* (1757), Burke argued that pain and pleasure are not opposites but different positive experiences, the latter to be distinguished from "delight." Pain, he says, is always the stronger, evoking greater passions—and even drawing us to it. We are drawn to the sight of disasters, Burke claims, by a delight: "there is no spectacle we so eagerly pursue, as that of some uncommon and grievous calamity; so that whether the misfortune is before our eyes, or whether they are turned back to it in history, it always touches with delight. This is not an unmixed delight, but blended with no small uneasiness."[31] Delight is distinguished from positive pleasure because it can be attached to pain and danger. The power that excites the mixture of pleasure and horror is Burke's "sublime," a power that can not be clearly defined (delimited). Hence infinite emptiness, darkness, and silence are all terrible, all manifestations of great obscurity and therefore of great terror. Sublime power is always imperial; it imposes itself on us, and has no utility.[32] Although Burke does not say this, we can see that this submission to the experience of horror-and-delight opens the way to a modern understanding of "the sacred" as well as to an aesthetics of excess. The implications of such an aesthetic for secular self-fashioning, both individual and national, are intriguing—especially in a culture whose moral and legal domains valorize measure and calculation.

These brief references to pain willingly endured in modern society help us to raise some questions at the transcultural level.

The interesting thing about the criteria enumerated in the S/M text I quoted above is that they come up against Article 5 of the *Universal Declaration of Human Rights*: "No one shall be subjected to torture or to cruel, inhuman or degrading treatment or punishment." This rule is not qualified by the phrase "unless the parties concerned are consenting adults." In the same way and for the same reason that one may not consent to sell oneself into slavery, even for a limited period. Not even if the parties concerned find the relationship of bondage erotic.

So, too, the liberalized Church strongly disapproves of monks being whipped at the command of their abbot for penalizable faults—even when the penance has a ritual closure and a dramatic character. And even if the

31. Part One, Section XIV.
32. "Whenever strength is only useful, and employed for our benefit or our pleasure, then it is never sublime; for nothing can act agreeably to us, that does not act in conformity to our will; but to act agreeably to our will, it must be subject to us; and therefore can never be the cause of a grand and commanding conception" (Part Two, Section V).

monks have taken monastic vows of obedience voluntarily. This disapproval follows from the modern rejection of physical pain in general, and of "gratuitous" suffering in particular. But it is more precise to put it this way: the modern hostility is not simply to pain, it is to pain that does not accord with a particular conception of being human—*and that is therefore in excess.* "Excess" is a concept of measure. An essential aspect of the modern attitude to pain rests on a calculus that defines rational (calculable) actions. But another aspect has to do precisely with the aesthetic pursuit of excess.

Needless to say nothing I have said so far is an argument against S/M. I am not denouncing a "dangerous" sexual practice.[33] Nor am I concerned to celebrate its "emancipatory" social potential.[34] These antagonistic positions seem to me to assume that "sadomasochism" has an essence. They are mirror images of each other. But the *essence* of what legal and moral discourse constructs, polices, and contests as "S/M" is not the object of my analysis. As in the field of "abnormal and unnatural" sexual practices generally, state power is, of course, directly and vitally involved—helping to define and regulate normality. My concern here, however, is with the structure of public debate over the valorization of painful experience in a secular culture that regards it negatively. In that debate argument is sharpened because on the one hand moderns disapprove of physical pain as "degrading." On the other hand they are committed to every individual's right to pursue unlimited physical pleasure "in private"—so long as that conforms to the legal principle of consenting adults and does not lead to death or serious injury. Thus one way that moderns attempt to resolve this contradiction is by defining cruelty in relation to the principle of individual autonomy, which is the necessary basis of free choice. However, if the concept of "cruel, inhuman and degrading treatment" cannot be consistently deployed without reference to the principle of individual freedom, it becomes relativized.

33. See for example R. R. Linden et al., eds., *Against Sadomasochism: A Radical Feminist Analysis*, San Francisco: Frog in the Well, 1982.

34. The radical social criticism allegedly expressed by S/M is eloquently argued for in McClintock's article, but the liberatory implications of S/M are explicitly retracted at the end. (See also the clever book by Angela Carter entitled *The Sadeian Woman*, London: Virago, 1979.) While such writings typically provide radical political decodings of S/M narratives, they also seem to be saying that, as a mode of obtaining orgasm, S/M is the product of socially distorted and sexually repressive relations.

This becomes clearer in the transcultural domain. For here it is not simply a matter of eliminating particular cruelties, but of imposing an entire secular discourse of "being human," central to which are its ideas about individualism and detachment from passionate belief. Thus while at home the principle of consenting adults within the bounds of the law works by invoking the idea of free choice based on individual autonomy, the presence of consenting adults abroad may often be taken to indicate mere "false consciousness"—a fanatical commitment to outmoded beliefs—which invites forcible correction.

Yet only the skeptical individual—always suspicious of his or her own beliefs as well as of others—can be truly free of fanatical convictions. And continuous suspicion introduces instability at another level: that of the secular, autonomous subject.

(In this connection it is worth noting that Jeremy Schneewind's magisterial survey of early modern moral philosophy—*The Invention of Autonomy* [Cambridge University Press, 1998]—contains virtually no mention of cruelty, except in passing in the few paragraphs on de Sade. In the writings discussed by Schneewind there are many arguments concerning the place of divine punishment in a system of sanctions—the fear of punishment and the hope of reward as motives for obeying God's natural law. In that sense the infliction and suffering of pain are part of a quasi-legal discourse—of morality construed on the analogy of law, and of "responsibility" as essential to it. De Sade, of course, had no interest in constructing a theory of morality. His concern was to disrupt civilized convention through the relentless pursuit of desire, to reject altogether the idea of "responsibility." The continuous experience of violent pain-pleasure was, for de Sade, the expression of an indifferent Nature that gave the lie to religious claims about reality.[35])

In the next chapter I explore further the autonomous subject that human rights seeks to redeem. In doing this I move directly to an aspect of secularism as a political doctrine.

35. See Octavio Paz, *An Erotic Beyond: Sade,* Harcourt Brace, 1998.

SECULARISM

4

Redeeming the "Human" Through
Human Rights

In the course of the UN intervention into Somalia some years ago, soldiers from Belgian and Canadian contingents were charged with torturing individual Somalis. At the same time U.S. forces carried out the destruction of entire city blocks and killed considerable numbers of civilians, as a consequence of the U.S. military doctrine of using overwhelming force (preferably from the air) in order to maintain minimal American casualties (preferably none).[1] It was noted at the time that this clear breach of the Geneva conventions was not followed up by the United States holding a public inquiry into those responsible for the breach in the way the Belgians and the Canadians pursued the torturers. "The reason," claims Alex de Waal, "is quite simple: orders for helicopter attacks came from higher authorities than the force commander in Mogadishu—they came from Centcom HQ in Florida and the White House itself. The charge sheet for any inquiry into Mogadishu war crimes might contain the names of some very high-ranking American individuals."[2] The point I want to make is not that the United States is powerful enough to flout international conventions with impunity. It is that while U.S. military doctrine makes breaches of the Geneva Convention more likely, it makes actual cases of *torture* less likely because and to the extent that a direct encounter between individual

1. This doctrine seems to be shared by other states too, as the Israeli army's response to the Palestinian resistance to occupation demonstrates.

2. Alex de Waal, "Dangers of Discretion," *London Review of Books*, January 21, 1999, p. 27.

soldiers and civilians is avoided. The use of excessive force against civilians through aerial bombardment is regarded differently from the use of violence perpetrated by particular officials against individual victims. It is not a matter of human rights abuse but of *collateral damage.*

But military action is not the only—or even the most important— form of intervention by powerful states in the affairs of others. Financial pressures can have effects that are more far-reaching than many military adventures. But the devastation these pressures can cause to social life, and the punishments they deliver to individual citizens of an economically weakened state, cannot be addressed as human rights violations.

For example: "In the early '90s, East Asian countries had liberalized their financial and capital markets—not because they needed to attract more funds (savings were already 30 percent or more) but because of international pressure, including some from the US Treasury Department. These changes provoked a flood of short-term capital—that is, the kind of capital that looks for the highest returns in the next day, week, or month, as opposed to long-term investment in things like factories. In Thailand, this short-term capital helped fuel an unsustainable real estate boom. . . . Just as suddenly as capital flowed in, it flowed out. . . . Output in some of the affected countries fell 16 percent or more. Half the businesses in Indonesia were in virtual bankruptcy or close to it. . . . Unemployment soared, increasing as much as tenfold, and real wages plummeted—in countries with basically no safety nets. Not only was the IMF not restoring economic confidence in East Asia, it was undermining the region's social fabric."[3] This account, which I have taken from Joseph Stiglitz (until recently vice-president and chief economist of the World Bank) can be replicated even more dramatically for Russia. In both cases, the ability of the affected states to uphold certain rights was directly compromised by IMF and U.S. policies aimed at liberalizing national economies throughout the world. But these interventions themselves cannot be regarded as instances of human rights violation; they are presented as the promotion of economic restructuring necessary for development.

The first part of Article 25 of *The Universal Declaration of Human Rights* states that "Everyone has the right to a standard of living adequate for the health and well-being of himself and his family, including food, clothing, housing and medical care and necessary social services, and the

3. Joseph Stiglitz, "The Insider," *The New Republic Online,* April 17, 2000.

right to security in the event of unemployment, sickness, disability, widowhood, old age or other lack of livelihood in circumstances beyond his control." But the responsibility for ensuring the conditions in which these rights can be realized is assigned solely to individual sovereign states, each of which is defined in part by its right to govern "the national economy." Damage done to the economy of another country (as in the case of the deliberate interventions I have mentioned) does not constitute a violation of human rights even if it causes immense suffering because in the final analysis the responsibility for the damage is borne only by the governors of "the national economy," and in any case it is considered a short-term cost of a long-term benefit.

I stress that my concern here is *not* to ascribe blame—to argue that Southeast Asian governments or Somali civilians were innocent victims of a conspiracy. In this chapter, unlike the previous one, my concern is not with cruelty as such but with how, in a secular system like human rights, responsibility is assigned for it. I point to a basic assumption about "the human" on which human rights stand: Nothing essential to a person's human essence is violated if he or she suffers as a consequence of military action or of market manipulation from beyond his own state when that is permitted by international law. In these cases, the suffering that the individual sustains as citizen—as *the national of a particular state*—is distinguished from the suffering he undergoes as *a human being*. Human rights are concerned with the individual only in the latter capacity, with his or her natural being and not civil status. If this is so, then we encounter an interesting paradox: the notion that inalienable rights define the human does not depend on the nation-state because the former relates to a state of nature, whereas the concept of citizen, including the rights a citizen holds, presupposes a state that Enlightenment theorists called political society. Human rights, including the moral rules that bind humans universally, are intrinsic to all persons irrespective of their "cultural" make-up. Yet the identification and application of human rights law has no meaning independent of the judicial institutions that belong to individual nation-states (or to several states bound together by treaty) and the remedies that these institutions supply—and therefore of the individual's civil status as a political subject.

A note on natural rights

The idea of a human being having rights independent of his civil status has a complicated history going back to the idea of natural law in Latin Christendom and its roots in readings of Roman law. The interesting thing about this story is how the essence of the human subject comes to be constituted in terms of inalienable *rights*, and how that informs the subject's secular status.

In his historical account of natural rights, Richard Tuck[4] employs a distinction, familiar to modern legal philosophy, between an *active right* (that is, inhering in the individual irrespective of his or her social relationships) and a *passive right* (that is, one that entails and is entailed by duties on other people). Only theories that use the former regard the idea of *liberty* as central. The essence of the human is quite different in the two cases—sovereignty in the one and dependence on a network of obligations in the other. The idea of a precivil state of nature, one in which man displays his natural rights independently of social and political institutions, fits more comfortably with theories using the notion of *active right*.

Medieval jurists talked about "property rights" in a state of nature, but they tended to do so in terms of *claims*, a notion that implied that every right entailed a reciprocal duty in accordance with objective (because divinely given) criteria.[5] In the later Middle Ages, however, the idea was introduced that a *property* right was *any* right that could be held against all other men, and that could be freely transferred by its possessor. In the sixteenth century there developed a debate between those for whom liberty itself was property (something *owned*), and therefore alienable in the same way and under the same terms as any other property; and those (like the Dominicans, for whom the welfare of humans rather than their essential liberty was what mattered) who held that liberty was not in that sense a property. In this way, a theory of rights sanctioned practices—such as slavery—that an antisubjectivist theory disallowed.[6]

4. Richard Tuck, *Natural Rights Theories: Their Origin and Development*, Cambridge: Cambridge University Press, 1979.

5. I am simplifying a fascinating debate between Franciscans (who sought to restore apostolic poverty) and Dominicans (of whom Aquinas was the most famous) on property as a natural right, because this is peripheral to the theme I pursue here.

6. Tuck points out that "this is a recurrent, perhaps *the* recurrent theme in the history of rights theories" (Tuck, p. 49).

It was no accident that the beginnings of modern rights theories are to be found in Portugal and the Netherlands, the main centers of the slave trade at that time. Thus according to the Portuguese theologian Molina, liberty as property could be traded. Man was pictured as a free being, capable of making his own economic and moral decisions, and of being bound by their consequences. Paradoxically, this picture of the individual as sovereign could be made to yield a defense of slavery and of absolutism. Similarly, Grotius's famous desire for peace was articulated through his rights theory: in the state of nature, man possessed active rights and the moral capacity to enter freely into contracts with others regarding his property. (The obligation to keep one's promise is a function of natural reason; it does not depend on prior divine law or social relations.) Even in the stage of civilization, conflicts between sovereign states and between sovereign individuals were caused by disputes over rights—the rights of the former and those of the latter being regarded as homologous, differing only in quantity.[7]

A major theme in the seventeenth-century debates about natural rights had to do with *obligation,* a concept that was typically linked to *punishment.* For as John Selden, an English follower of Grotius, put it, "The idea of a law carrying obligation irrespective of any punishment annexed to the violation of it . . . is no more comprehensible to the human mind than the idea of a father without a child."[8] A sharp distinction could thus be made between humans and animals. Only the former had an *awareness* that punishment was attached to the violation of a moral or legal rule—including an active right—hence only humans could have natural rights. Conversely, only subjects who possessed rights could be regarded as human.

It was Hobbes who famously merged the idea of *supernatural* punishment with the idea that all punishment was in a crucial sense *natural:* "Having thus briefly spoken of the natural kingdom of God, and his natural laws, I will add only to this chapter a short declaration of his natural punishments. There is no action of man in this life, that is not the beginning of so long a chain of consequences, as no human providence is high enough, to give a man a prospect to the end. And in this chain, there are

7. "The history of natural rights theories," observes Tuck, "is indeed a story of argument over precisely this issue: does a natural rights theory require a strongly individualistic psychology and ethical theory?" (ibid., p. 82).

8. Cited in ibid., p. 91.

linked together both pleasing and unpleasing events; in such a manner, as he that will do any thing for his pleasure, must engage himself to suffer all the pains annexed to it; and these pains, are the natural punishments of those actions, which are the beginning of more harm than good. And hereby it comes to pass, that intemperance is naturally punished with diseases, rashness, with mischances; injustice with the violence of enemies; pride, with ruin; cowardice, with oppression; negligent government of princes, with rebellion; and rebellion with slaughter. For seeing punishments are consequent to the breach of laws of nature; and therefore follow them as their natural, not arbitrary effects" (*Leviathan*, Everyman Edition, pp. 196–97). In this perspective moral obligation is reduced to prudential calculation, consistent with Hobbes's secular picture of natural rights— and so, too, of political obligation.

Later, Locke attempted to restore a religious foundation to both morality and civil government through the medieval idea of divine law: "The difference between moral and natural good and evil is only this; that we call that naturally good and evil, which, by the natural efficiency of the thing, produces pleasure or pain in us; and that is morally good or evil which, by the intervention of the will of an intelligent free agent, draws pleasure or pain after it, not by any natural consequence, but by the intervention of that power. Thus drinking to excess, when it produces the headache or sickness, is a natural evil; but as it is a transgression of law, by which a punishment is annexed to it, it is a moral evil. For rewards and punishments are the good and evil whereby superiors enforce the observance of their laws; it being impossible to set any other motive or restraint to the actions of a free understanding agent, but the consideration of good or evil; that is, pleasure or pain that will follow from it."[9] Laws might be sanctioned either by divine or by earthly power, but morality, according to Locke, depended *naturally* on the voluntary action of a sovereign subject— someone who, having chosen willingly in the knowledge of good and evil, would enjoy or suffer the consequences of his free action.

The Hobbesian thesis that natural rights could be given up to a political sovereign (the state) that could thereupon, as the total possessor of the collected rights of all those it now represented, end the war of all against all, depended on the idea of sovereign individuals in the state of nature. This view of transferable natural rights was challenged by radicals. No human being, they argued, could alienate the right of self-preservation, be-

9. Cited in ibid., pp. 168–69.

cause a natural right defined one's property and one's self, and therefore no rational man could have done so self-injurious a thing.[10]

But the Hobbesian thesis, resting as it did on the idea of active rights, was also attacked from a very different direction. For example Mathew Hale insisted that the state of nature was neither a civil society nor a war of all against all: "Altho' there was no instituted human government or lawes, but men were in that natural state wherein they were propagated into the world, yet even in that state there would be some things *justa honesta et decora*, and some things *injusta inhonesta et indecora*. Eveything would not be lawfull to every man; and that imaginary state of war; wherein every man might lawfully do what he thinks best without any law or controll, is but a phantasy; or if it be admitted, it must not, cannot be supposed the just state of nature, but as a disease disorder and corruption in it."[11] It was not necessary in this argument to prove that all humans had the same ideas of what was just, honest, and noble. What mattered was the claim that everyone *had* them independently of government and law—that is, in the state of nature.

The state of nature that these theories built on, and that became crucial in the later Enlightenment, was a secular condition in the sense that it did not presuppose the concept of God. But it did presuppose an argument from origins. In the modern era the quasi-historical "state of nature" is done away with as the essential foundation for human rights (except among theorists such as Canovan who reformulate it as "myth"[12]). Nevertheless, there is still an essence attributed to "the human"—the essence that the early European theorists of natural law recognized as *inalienable rights*. As Tuck puts it, this doctrine came to mean that "anything which it was reasonable to want, could now be construed as an inalienable right, the recovery of which was entirely justifiable: it was unlikely that any rational

10. According to Overton: "all iust *humaine powers* are but betrusted, confer'd and conveyed by ioynt and common consent, *for to every individual in nature, is given individuall propriety by nature, not to be invaded or usurped by any . . . for every one as he is himselfe hath a selfe propriety, else could not be himselfe*, and on this no second may presume without consent; and by natural birth, all men *are equall and alike borne to like propriety and freedome, every man by natural instinct aiming at his owne safety and weal.* . . . Now as no man by nature may abuse, beat, torment or afflict himself, so by nature no man may give that power to another, seeing he may not doe it himselfe . . . " (cited in ibid., p. 149).

11. Cited in ibid., p. 164.

12. See Chapter 1.

man would renounce his rights to such reasonable gratifications. The principle of interpretative charity had been stretched very wide, and we have here clearly the eighteenth-century notion of the inalienable rights of mankind."[13] One owed no allegiance that would compromise one's natural rights to any body—singular or collective. Natural rights were a necessary part of one's sovereignty, which the state acquired by delegation from the people (whence representative democracy). How was that individual sovereignty to be recognized and protected in a sovereign state? The doctrine of secularism—separating the individual right to (religious) belief from the authority of the state—was intended as an answer to that question.

Given that the subject was to be seen as an individual sovereign in a sovereign state, Tuck points to the dilemma that now faced liberal theory. Liberals, he writes, have usually distinguished between two principles of conduct: On the one hand, there are principles to which subjects have assented, whether directly or indirectly, and to which they therefore owe their political obligation. These include social custom, the law, and the constitution. On the other hand, there are principles of obligatory conduct that do not derive from consent. These are not many, and they form a "thin" account of morality—a minimum requirement of the kind of sociality in which individual autonomy is closely linked to collective violence. "However, a great deal of writing and talking about international affairs in our time supposes that there is an international community which polices its members and enforces quite a complex and contentious set of values upon them, and many people who are 'liberal' in domestic politics often favour such an idea. If what used to be the paradigm case of the liberal agent, the independent state, is now seen as inevitably enmeshed in complicated social settings; if sovereignty is widely treated (as it is in Europe, if not in North America) as an outdated and uninformative category for states; then that traditional cousin of the sovereign state, the sovereign individual, is going to be hard to conceptualize with the old vividness."[14]

The sovereign individual and the sovereign state

This leads to another point about the story of human rights that has to do not with the evolution of legal theories and the political power of

13. Tuck, p. 150.

14. Richard Tuck, *The Rights of War and Peace: Political Thought and the International Order from Grotius to Kant*, Oxford: Oxford University Press, 1999, p. 14.

those in a position to deploy them, but with the use of legal language itself. Thus it has been argued that because the massive growth of public debt in the seventeenth century increased the precariousness and volatility of property—especially the newer financial forms of property, distinct from the older, landed, "real" property—this development contributed to an intensified sense of the self's contingency among the middle and upper classes. If this argument is correct, then Locke's famous emphasis on natural right as a limit to arbitrary government may also be closely linked to the desire to stabilize the contingent character of the self through a legal concept of the person.[15] The essence of the human comes to be circumscribed by *legal* discourse: The human being is a *sovereign, self-owning agent—essentially suspicious of others—and* not merely a subject conscious of his or her own identity. It is on this basis that the secularist principle of the right to freedom of belief and expression was crafted.

Whatever its early history may be, today only a strong, secular state can enforce natural right and its successor as *the law*—whether that relates to the treatment of persons or of property. One does not have to subscribe to an Austinian definition of law in order to recognize that it is a matter of critical importance whether or not a state concedes that it has violated rights and restores them, or restores rights that have been violated within its own domain (or coerces a weaker state to the same end), or it legally endorses rights vindicated by other civil powers (trade unions, women's movements, ethnic groups, and so forth). Human rights depend, as Hannah Arendt long ago pointed out, on national rights—that is, rights that constitute, protect, *and punish* one as the citizen of a nation-state. This also means that the state has the power to use human rights discourse to coerce its own citizens—just as colonial rulers had the power to use it against their own subjects.[16] In defending its citizens' human rights it is only the state that can legally threaten to punish violators.

15. J. G. A. Pocock, "Modernity and Anti-Modernity," in *Patterns and Modernity*, vol. 1: *The West*, ed. S. N. Eisenstadt, London: Francis Pinter, 1987. These comments on Locke's invocation of natural rights should not be taken as a claim that it was really an ideological justification for early capitalism. For Locke, a faithful Christian, natural rights were at the center of a theological worldview (see Richard Ashcraft, "The Politics of Locke's *Two Treatises of Government*," in E. J. Harpham, ed., John Locke's *Two Treatises of Government*, Lawrence: University of Kansas Press, 1992).

16. In an article on human rights in Mexico, Shannon Speed and Jane Collier have described how the state government of Chiapas uses that discourse to undermine indigenous attempts at defending a measure of autonomy. They see this

In his influential account of the development of citizenship in Britain first published in 1950, T. H. Marshall traced the history of rights in that country since medieval times but stressed that the critical moments in their formation were—schematically—the seventeenth, eighteenth, and nineteenth centuries, that is, precisely when the modern state was being constructed.[17] He saw citizenship rights as being divided into *civil* ("liberty of the person, freedom of speech, thought and faith, the right to own property and to conclude valid contracts, and the right to justice"), *political* ("the right to participate in the exercise of political power, as a member of a body invested with political authority or as an elector of the members of such a body"), and *social* ("from the right to a modicum of economic welfare and security to the right to share to the full in the social heritage and to live the life of a civilized being according to the standards prevailing in the society").[18]

It is this classification, coming as it does out of the Anglo-American legal tradition and the Franco-American Revolutionary tradition, that makes its way in 1948 into *The Declaration of Human Rights*. Yet neither Marshall nor other political theorists who deal with the emergence of civil rights in Euro-America address the question of national rights on which

---

activity as being similar to the tactics of colonialist rulers: "The state government of Chiapas appears 'colonialist,' not just in imposing a literal interpretation of human rights documents on indigenous peoples, but, more importantly, in using the discourse of human rights to justify intervening in the affairs of indigenous communities whose leaders happen to displease the government. Just as colonial authorities in the past justified their right to intervene in the affairs of colonized peoples by claiming to eradicate practices that were 'repugnant' to 'civilized' sensibilities, so government officials in Chiapas are justifying their right to arrest indigenous leaders who (the government claims) have violated the human and constitutional rights of community members. The discourse of human rights, which was designed to protect individuals from arbitrary punishments by their governments, is thus having the opposite effect of rendering indigenous leaders vulnerable to state sanctions" ("Limiting Indigenous Autonomy in Chiapas, Mexico: The State Government's Use of Human Rights," *Human Rights Quarterly*, forthcoming).

17. T. H. Marshall, *Citizenship and Social Class*, London: Pluto Press, 1992 [1950].

18. Pierre Rosanvallon argues that although this scheme with its historical sequence may be roughly valid for England and America, it is not applicable to Germany and France (see *Le sacre du citoyen: Histoire du suffrage universel en France*, Paris: Gallimard, p. 16).

human rights inevitably depended. The constitutional structures of empire—of metropole, colonies, protectorates, mandates, and dominions—remain outside their theorization. The classification of rights thus moves from the context of a Euro-American state in which political struggles for the extension of rights are punctuated by *national* settlements, to the context of an abstraction sentimentalized as "the human family." This "family" is homogeneous and exclusive (it doesn't include animals or machines or gods), although real "families" are internally differentiated and they overlap with one another.

The Universal Declaration of Human Rights begins by asserting "the inherent dignity" and "the equal and inalienable rights of all members of *the human family*," and then turns immediately to the state. In doing so it implicitly accepts the fact that the universal character of the rights-bearing person is made the responsibility of sovereign states, each of which has exclusive jurisdiction over a limited group within the human family. This limited population is—as Foucault noted—at once the object of the state's care and a means of securing its own power.[19] In other words, although the individual does not have the right to decide his own fate, authorities of the state of which he is a citizen have the constitutional right to decide it for him. Thus when Kant wrote of "the Idea of the *dignity* of a rational being who obeys no law other than that which he at the same time enacts himself"[20] he referred not to the subject of the state (who is substitutable in war and always obliged to obey his country's laws) but to the rational, morally sovereign human being for whom there is no equivalent.[21]

However, the state has more than sovereign jurisdiction over all its subjects; it also seeks to create an exclusive national identity in each of its citizens. As Charles Taylor has rightly emphasized, the citizen of a modern secular state requires a healthy dose of nationalist sentiment that must be provided by its media. This renders the state the focus of intense emotions,

19. Foucault identified this seeming contradiction with the political principle of *raison d'état* (see especially "The Political Technology of Individuals," in *Technologies of the Self: A Seminar with Michel Foucault*, ed. L. H. Martin, H. Gutman, and P. H. Hutton, Amherst: University of Massachusetts Press, 1988.

20. Immanuel Kant, *Groundwork of the Metaphysical of Morals*, trans. H. J. Paton, New York: Harper Torchbook edition, 1964, p. 102 [p. 77].

21. "In the kingdom of ends everything has either a *price* or a *dignity*. If it has a price, something else can be put in its place as an *equivalent*; if it is exalted above all price and so admits of no equivalent, then it has a dignity" (ibid. [italics in original]).

which help to sustain national attachments and interests that are actually and potentially hostile to outsiders.

The Declaration states that unless human rights are "protected by the rule of law," subjects will be "compelled to have recourse, as a last resort, to rebellion against tyranny and oppression." It is not immediately clear whether this is to be read as a warning to rulers to be prudent or a recognition that the ruled are morally entitled to retrieve their natural rights. And yet *The Declaration* seems to justify rebellion only when it can be seen as a response to the government's violation of human rights *law*, although all infringements of the law (and their remedy) can be properly determined only by a court of law. There is no explicit recognition that what is allowed by the law may be unjust and therefore intolerable; there is only the statement that nothing contravening human rights can be lawful (which is either a tautology or untrue). In other words, *The Declaration* seems to assume a direct convergence of "the rule of law" (a notion that depends on the proper maintenance of rights by state institutions) with social justice (a vision of social life that logically presupposes *remedies* but not necessarily *rights*, and that is concerned more with questions of distribution and civility than with individual rights and liberties). If that is the case, *the rule called law* in effect usurps the entire universe of moral discourse.

There is an unresolved tension here between the moral invocation of "universal humanity" and the power of the state to identify, apply, and maintain the law. For not only does *The Declaration* equate law with justice, it also privileges the state's norm-defining function (or that of several states in association), thereby encouraging the thought that the authority of norms corresponds to the political force that supports them as law. Ironically, it was the moral revulsion against the legal atrocities of the Nazi state that led, after World War II, to a renewed interest in the old natural law tradition, and that contributed in a major way to the framing of *The Declaration*. (It was the Nuremberg War Crimes Tribunal that retrospectively introduced the notion of crimes against humanity into international law.) But the condemnation of a particular state's system of law and of its behavior in terms of norms entirely external to them led not to a recognition that nonstate norms have authority as such. They led instead to the formulation of sacred laws that must ultimately depend, *as laws*, on their recognition by states.[22] Of course there are now growing bodies of inter-

22. The Nazi atrocities are a favorite example used by advocates of universalism to underline the dangers of relativist thinking. However, the Nazis carried

national law that cover entire regions (such as the European Community, which also has its own Human Rights Charter) and that thus transcend the authority of individual states. But these regions also act as larger proto-states whose individual member-states retain considerable authority.

An aspect of the divergence between the moral authority of norms and the secular force of state laws may be illustrated by a recent example from Europe. As a consequence of Greece having joined the European Union, the Greek state was required by the European charter of human rights to remove any information on religious affiliation, family status, nationality, and thumb print in the identity cards issued to citizens. Popular opposition apparently saw this as a threat to collective religious identity. "We've got to fight for our right to be Christian Orthodox Greeks," one demonstrator put it. "It seems [Prime Minister Costas] Simitis is capable of selling everything that Greece stands for, for the sake of appearing European," observed another. But the protests and demonstrations have not shifted the government, which insists that the new cards must conform to the privacy law on personal data. The church has called for a referendum on the proposed change, but the government has rejected the idea on the grounds that "such methods cannot apply to issues of human rights." A compromise proposed by the church that the old form be retained on an optional basis has been dismissed by the government. The church, using the language of human rights to defend its authority, has charged that the new arrangement curtails the right of citizens to express their religious affiliation publicly if they so desire. The government, in its turn, has responded by issuing a judgment about religious belief: "The introduction of new identity cards poses no threat to the Greek Orthodox faith."[23] This is a *religious judgment* not in the sense of drawing on Orthodox theology (because it clearly doesn't do that) but in claiming to identify the essence of that faith.

Thus something more is indicated here than a case of bruised identities (which is how the foreign press represented it). It is also about the au-

---

out their policy of extermination not because there was no universal human rights charter at the time, but because Hitler's Germany had the organizational means and the ruthlessness to do it, and because the Allies could not or would not intervene to stop it. In general *The Universal Declaration of Human Rights* has been more useful for punishing criminals convicted of genocide than for preventing the crime.

23. *The Christian Science Monitor*, June 22, 2000.

thority of norms that the members of a social group may regard as vital to their *religious being* but which the government can constitutionally override, and do so by moving to an entirely different ideological terrain: the question of what does and what does not affect their freedom of *religious belief.*

The requirement that all citizens of European Union member states carry identity cards is not itself considered a violation of human rights but a general good. Identity cards have been integral to the way populations have been governed and cared for in modern European states. Britain, although a member of the European Union, has never had them (except during the Second World War) and is resisting their introduction on the grounds that they infringe the citizen's civil rights as understood historically in that country. Thus in Britain identity cards are thought of as a threat to the liberty of individual subjects (that is, *citizens*), and in the European Union states they are seen as a guarantee that a collective object (that is, the *population*) will be provided efficiently with equal welfare. The former focuses on liberty as an active right, the latter on welfare as a passive one. Each gives a different perspective on what is involved in being human in a secular state. And each contributes differentially to political discourses of justice.

Different legal-political traditions spell different ideas of guarantee and threat in relation to what is "human," and these are expressed in different languages that engage with the established power of the nation-state. The discourse of human rights is only one such language.

Redemption of the human

What assumptions of the human are involved in the languages of justice attached to different traditions? Do some ideas fit more comfortably with secularism than others? I now turn to discourses of redemption that I think may give some sort of answer because it is built around the concept of sovereign action. But first a caveat: It is important not to regard these discourses as merely legitimizing a priori positions of power, because languages of justice do not simply justify political acts, they help to shape political actors.

The U.S. government has been a major force behind the attempt to globalize human rights, especially since the collapse of the Soviet Union. It has also been central to the development of the idea of the human implicit in rights discourse since the end of the Cold War. Yet inside the United States the human rights language has had comparatively little purchase. I now take up the case of a modern American who invoked human rights but failed to mobilize public opinion behind him in that endeavor.

In a famous speech criticizing the American civil rights movement in the 1960s, Malcolm X urges his fellow African Americans to resort to human rights as a way of transcending the limitations of the American state. I quote at length the following passage with its powerful demotic style and its acute forensic intelligence. However, the transcendence Malcolm X seeks consists in a turn from the authority of one state to the collective authority of several other states—a fact indicating that one cannot escape from a world consisting of nation-states that are equal as sovereign entities but grossly unequal in power.

"We need to expand the civil-rights struggle to a higher level—to the level of human rights. Whenever you are in a civil-rights struggle, whether you know it or not, you are confining yourself to the jurisdiction of Uncle Sam. No one from the outside world can speak out in your behalf as long as your struggle is a civil-rights struggle. Civil-rights comes within the domestic affairs of this country. All of our African brothers and our Asian brothers and our Latin-American brothers cannot open their mouths and interfere in the domestic affairs of the United States. And as long as it's civil rights, this comes under the jurisdiction of Uncle Sam."

On the other hand, the United Nations has a charter of human rights, and that, says Malcolm X, opens up an opportunity for liberation. "You may wonder," he goes on, "why all of the atrocities that have been committed in Africa and in Hungary and in Latin America are brought before the UN, and the Negro problem is never brought before the UN. This is part of the conspiracy. This old, tricky, blue-eyed liberal who is supposed to be your and my friend, supposed to be in our corner, supposed to be subsidizing our struggle, and supposed to be acting in the capacity of an adviser, never tells you anything about human rights. They keep you wrapped up in civil rights. And you spend so much time barking up the civil-rights tree, you don't even know there's a human-rights tree on the same floor." So what should be done?

"When you expand the civil-rights struggle to the level of human rights, you can then take the case of the black man in this country before the nations in the UN. You can take it before the General Assembly. You can take Uncle Sam before a world court. But the only level you can do it on is the level of human rights. Civil-rights keeps you under his restrictions, under his jurisdiction. Civil rights keeps you in his pocket. Civil rights means you are asking Uncle Sam to treat you right. Human rights are something you were born with. Human rights are your God-given rights. Human rights are the rights that are recognized by all nations of this earth. And any time anyone violates your human rights you can take them to the world court. Uncle Sam's hands are dripping with blood, dripping with the blood of the black man in this country. He's the earth's number-one hypocrite. He has the audacity—yes, he has—imagine him posing as the leader of the free world. The free world!—and you over here singing 'We Shall Overcome.' Expand the civil-rights struggle to the level of human rights, take it into the United Nations, where our African brothers can throw their weight on our side, where our Asian brothers can throw their weight on our side, where our Latin-American brothers can throw their weight on our side, and where 800 million Chinamen are sitting there waiting to throw their weight on our side."[24]

Needless to say, the civil rights struggle was never expanded to what Malcolm X called the level of human rights. I don't want to dwell on the political reasons, both national and international, why this was so. I have quoted the passage at length because of its remarkable language. In it Malcolm X does three things: First, he diagnoses a profound crisis of justice in race-based America and claims that it cannot be resolved by a purely domestic maneuver—that is, by the state's formal extension of full citizenship to African Americans. Second, he defiantly asserts the humanity of African Americans quite independently of—in hostile opposition to—the American state and its political culture. Third, he proposes that justice consists in the legal conviction of America in an international court; justice is a matter of the law. This invocation of human rights by a black American citizen identifies America as the violator. The language of human rights invoked by him doesn't make a moral appeal—at any rate, not to those who are declared to be the violators of rights—it declares a state of war and gives reasons why this war is necessary. It thus reaffirms the connection of rights discourse with war and revolution. After all, the English Bill of Rights of 1699 came out of the seventeenth-century civil war, the War of Independence produced the American Bill of Rights, the French Revolution gave

24. "The Ballot or the Bullet," in *Malcolm X Speaks: Selected Speeches and Statements*, ed. G. Breitman, pp. 34–35.

birth to the Rights of Man and the Citizen, and the Universal Declaration of Human Rights of 1948 was a response to the destructive horrors of World War II. These bills and declarations not only came out of war, they carried the metaphor of warfare into the domain of social reform. And they sought to extend a specific legal culture beyond its original Euro-American location with the aim of emancipating the human individual throughout the world. Thus for Malcolm X the "human" is a subject born with certain inalienable rights, even though he or she often had to be freed through struggle in order to exercise those rights.

Hannah Arendt, writing at about the same time as Malcolm X gave his speech, observed that human rights depended essentially on being citizens of a nation-state: "The conception of human rights, based upon the assumed existence of a human being as such, broke down at the very moment when those who professed to believe in it were for the first time confronted with people who had indeed lost all other qualities and specific relationships—except that they were still human. The world found nothing sacred in the abstract nakedness of being human. And in view of objective political conditions, it is hard to say how the concepts of man upon which human rights are based—that he is created in the image of God (in the American formula), or that he is the representative of mankind, or that he harbors within himself the sacred demands of natural law (in the French formula)—could have helped to find a solution to the problem."[25] Arendt might have noted, however, that *sacredness* in the modern secular state is attributed not to real living persons but precisely to "the human" conceptualized abstractly, or imagined in a state of nature. Every *real* person who belongs to a particular nation-state is always subject to its institutional violence—including the violence of its law,[26] and liable to military conscription that can result in his death. It is only the abstract modern citizen

25. Hannah Arendt, *The Origins of Totalitarianism*, new edition, New York: Harcourt Brace Jovanovich, 1966, pp. 299–300. Arendt saw an important exception in the creation of Israel, but an exception that proved the rule that human rights depend on national rights: "Not only did loss of national rights in all instances entail the loss of human rights; the restoration of human rights, as the recent example of the State of Israel proves, has been achieved so far only through the restoration or the establishment of national rights" (ibid., p. 299).

26. See Robert Cover, "Violence and the Word," in M. Minow, M. Ryan, and A. Sarat, eds., *Narrative, Violence, and the Law: The Essays of Robert Cover*, University of Michigan Press, 1992.

who is sacred by virtue of his or her abstract participation in popular sovereignty.

Arendt is right, of course, in stressing the centrality of the state for securing individuals their rights. And although she was talking about European refugees immediately after the Second World War, her remarks are entirely applicable to African Americans. For it was precisely their humanness that was invoked by Malcolm X, not their ethnic origin or religious identity, and not their long residence in particular states of the Union virtually since their founding. The political failure of Malcolm X's use of the language of human rights should not be attributed to conspiracy. It can be explained by the fact that it ignored the power of the state in which he and other African Americans lived and turned to a collection of states that had neither the power nor the authority to intervene. The anomalous position of African Americans was that they were neither the bearers of national rights nor of human rights. Malcolm X had told his audience that "Human rights are something you were born with." However, African Americans were at once born American (with citizenship rights only in the United States), and they were human beings who happened to be black (to be a full human being in America one had to be white). One aspect of birth diminished the other, because citizenship and the status of being human, although connected, are not identical. So human rights were rendered purely notional.

But if the language of human rights made little impact, there were other languages in the United States in which social crises might be diagnosed, the weak defended, and substantial reform called for. And other ways of defining "the human."

An important language in the United States that overlaps in varying measure with rights language (not to be directly equated with human rights language) is its prophetic language. Unlike human rights discourse, American prophetic language not only draws its vocabulary and imagery from a particular scripture (the Old Testament), it is also deeply rooted in narratives of the founding of a particular nation (the American). Famously, there are two narratives—one anticipating, the other supplementing: First, the story of the seventeenth-century Puritan escape to religious freedom from persecution in England; and second, the story of the constitution of thirteen American colonies into a new sovereign state, signifying a repudiation of English despotism. In both cases freedom comes from a rejection of tradition. The power of prophetic language derives partly from its

Judeo-Christian origins but especially from a series of moral separations—from English tyranny, Amerindian paganism, and the subhumanity of African slaves. The class of humans remains intact when the tyrant, the pagan, and the slave are excluded from it. However offensive it might be to us today, the political definition on which that initial concept of the full human being was based is, in a sense, no less universal than others that succeeded it because it defines the class to which all who are "properly human," and only they, belong.

"In American political culture, the prophetic story of captivity, deliverance, and founding legacy, thus of decline from origins and redemption, has been especially important," writes George Shulman. "Americans have retold this story to authorize claims about rights, inequality, membership, history, and their meaning."[27] So this language allows, even encourages, the identification of social crises and the condemnation of social injustice, both by those who occupy the ideological center of American liberalism and by those who stand outside it as its critics. But it does so in terms of a particular, excluding origin. It guarantees the promise of freedom that needs to be redeemed or warns of the decline and corruption that threaten that promise, but it always demands the redemption of subjects if they are to vindicate their human status and join the universe of free, equal, and sovereign individuals.

This is the language that the leadership of the civil rights movement in America deployed to great effect. It is the language that Martin Luther King used when he proclaimed that "now is the time to make real the promise of democracy" thereby attaining "the goal of America [which is] freedom." Turning to fellow African Americans King declares: "Abused and scorned though we may be, our destiny is tied up with the destiny of America [because] the sacred heritage of our nation and the eternal will of God are embodied in our echoing demands." And he goes on to proclaim that "One day the South will know that when these disinherited children of God sat down at lunch counters they were in reality standing up for the best in the American dream and the most sacred values in our Judeo-Christian heritage, and thus carrying our whole nation back to the great wells of democracy, which were dug deep by the founding fathers in the formulation of the Constitution and Declaration of Indepen-

27. George Shulman, "American Political Culture, Prophetic Narration, and Toni Morrison's *Beloved,*" *Political Theory*, vol. 24, no. 2, 1996, p. 295.

dence."[28] Thus King's political discourse identifies the guilt of the white majority and urges their repentance, seeking thereby not merely an extension of civil rights to all American citizens irrespective of race but the regeneration of America itself. "Justice" for King is not primarily a secular legal concept, as it is for Malcolm X, but a religious one—the idea of redemption. To be redeemed and to redeem others was to restore an inheritance—the Judeo-Christian heritage in general and the American expression of it in particular. In this way the prophetic language of the Old Testament was fused with the salvationist language of the New. To the extent that the civil rights movement presented itself as an instrument of redemption, its project became the moral restoration of the white majority.

King's deeply Christian discourse stands in sharp contrast to the language of human rights used by Malcolm X. In its own way, it is neither less statist (it sought civil rights from the state) nor less universalist (it invoked universal brotherhood) than the discourse of Malcolm X—and yet, precisely because it was addressed to America (invoking its founding fathers and its dominant Judeo-Christian heritage) it mobilized American public opinion for change in a way that Malcolm X was never able to do. However, its discourse of redemption is not quite the same as the redemptive project of the American government.

The latter project of secular redemption explains, for example, Congress's passing and the president's signing the International Religious Freedom Act of 1998: It should come as no surprise that Section 2 (a) of that act, entitled "Findings," begins by defining the national identity of America in terms of the narrative of redemption: "(1) The right to freedom of religion undergirds the very origin and existence of the United States. Many of our Nation's founders fled religious persecution abroad, cherishing in their hearts and minds the ideal of religious freedom. They established in law, as a fundamental right and as a pillar of our Nation, the right to freedom of religion. From its birth to this day, the United States has prized this legacy of religious freedom and honored this heritage by standing for reli-

28. Cited in George Shulman, "Race and the Romance of American Nationalism in Martin Luther King, Norman Mailer, and James Baldwin" (unpublished typescript, p. 9). I am indebted for my understanding of the American prophetic language to Shulman's published and unpublished writings on the subject, as well as to personal conversations with him. Naturally, he is not responsible for the use to which I have put that understanding, and would certainly not agree with all of it.

gious freedom and offering refuge to those suffering religious persecution." The act then lays down the policy of the United States in this regard, requiring the president of the United States to enforce religious freedom globally by using economic sanctions wherever necessary, setting up a new office in the State Department to report annually on religious persecution in all foreign countries (that is, excluding the United States), and prescribing training in "religious freedom" for members of the U.S. Foreign Service, and so on.[29]

The significant feature of this project is not that it promotes "Christian values" but that it seeks to free people in this world, giving them the right to choose their religious beliefs, which in a secular world means everything that the modern state can afford to let go. And it is understandable that America, as the leader of Judeo-Christian civilization, must carry out this secular task—to free belief as it frees property, that is, as an object that can be negotiated and exchanged without any legal obstacles. The American secular language of redemption, for all its particularity, now works as a force in the field of foreign relations to globalize human rights. For that language does, after all, draw on the idea that "freedom" and "America" are virtually interchangeable—that American political culture is (as the Bible says of the Chosen People) "a light unto the nations." Hence "democracy," "human rights," and "being free" are integral to the universalizing moral project of the American nation-state—the project of humanizing the world—and an important part of the way very many Americans see themselves in contrast to their "evil" opponents. On the other hand, Martin Luther King's Christian discourse, being tied to the *practice of nonviolence* and eschewing the language of *evil enemies,* presupposes a readiness on the part of the civil rights activists in the South to suffer, a readiness that is not to be detected in the U.S. project of redeeming and humanizing the world. King extends the experience of pain—like Gandhi before him—from sympathy to compassion, and makes it relevant and effective within a particular secular state.

29. The act has its American critics, of course, who point, among other things, to its clear Christian bias as well as its sponsorship by evangelical organizations. The act was preceded in 1997 by an important report entitled "United States Policies in Support of Religious Freedom: Focus on Christians," which contained a foreword by Secretary of State Madeleine Albright. This total preoccupation with the persecution of Christians (to the exclusion of Muslims, for instance) is strongly reflected in the media. But this selectivity merely underlines that it is America's narrative of redemption that is being applied globally.

Human rights are often declared to be a "universal ideal" in opposition to "cultural relativism" and the latter regarded as little more than an excuse for condoning local cruelties. My discussion of Malcolm X and Martin Luther King is intended in part to show how closely intertwined the two languages—the culturally specific language of prophecy and the universalist language of human rights—have become in the global moral project of America. This needs to be stressed because pitting "relativism" against "universalism" is not, I think, helpful for understanding human rights. Of course everybody generally has an opinion about the customs and beliefs of other people ("other cultures"), regarding them as good, bad, or indifferent. But in my view that fact is less interesting than the question of the kind of violence (moral, legal, military) that *judgments* justify.

The self-owning "human"

I said earlier that the *Universal Declaration* does not define "the human" in "human rights" other than (tautologically) as the subject of human rights that were once theorized as natural rights. But what kind of human does human rights recognize *in practice*?

Those who formulate and implement Western policies often assume that there is a natural fit between the legal culture of "human rights" and the wider culture of "Western norms." This includes particular attitudes to the human body and to pain. In Chapter 3 I mentioned some post-Enlightenment views about measures of suffering that allowed imprisonment to be represented as humane as opposed to flogging. Here I want to pursue a slightly different point: attitudes to the body indicated by such moral preferences—why, for example, confinement, even solitary confinement, is an acceptable form of punishment while any punitive practice that directly impinges on the body is not.

High value is clearly given to the integrity of the body—which explains in part the particular horror in Euro-America at the widespread custom of female genital mutilation in some African regions.[30] I say "in part" because there is no comparable sense of horror at the custom of male genital mutilation. The latter is, of course, a quite familiar practice in the

30. It may be noted that while activists in this field often give the impression in the media that female circumcision is especially associated with Islamic societies, the overwhelming majority of Muslims in the world do not practice it, and large numbers (perhaps the majority) of those who do are non-Muslims.

Judeo-Christian West and the former is not. But there is more to it than that. There is the belief that female circumcision, unlike the male variety, interferes with the sexual pleasure of the woman. The enjoyment of sexual intercourse is a valued part of being human; anything that interferes with that enjoyment is in some powerful sense inhuman.[31] It therefore becomes a matter of a human right and its violation. So there is here both an offense against the physical integrity of the body and (so it is believed) an interference with the subject's ability to experience "full" sexual pleasure.[32] The human being owns his or her body and has the inalienable right to enjoy it.

In an impressive series of publications Martha Nussbaum has reopened the old question of human nature through the Aristotelian idea of human capabilities that she recognizes can also be linked to the concept of human rights. Her basic idea is that a list can be compiled of central human functional capabilities (for example, "Being able to use the senses, to imagine, think, and reason—and do these things in a 'truly human' way, a way informed and cultivated by an adequate education, including, but by no means limited to, literacy and basic mathematical and scientific training. Being able to use imagination and thought in connection with experiencing and producing self-expressive works and events of one's own choice, religious, literary, musical, and so forth").[33] The universal character of these

31. Martha Nussbaum cites "opportunities for sexual satisfaction" as an aspect of "Bodily Integrity," listed as one of the "central human functional capabilities" in her influential *Women and Human Development: The Capabilities Approach*, Cambridge: Cambridge University Press, 2000, p. 78. The assumption that "opportunities for sexual *satisfaction*" can be clearly identified and legally protected is intriguing.

32. This is not quite how human rights advocates put it. Thus in "Female Genital Mutilation—A Human Information Pack (1998)" Amnesty International states: "The Universal Declaration of Human Rights and a host of international standards that flow from it, underscore the obligation of states to respect and ensure respect for basic human rights, such as the right to physical and mental security, freedom from discrimination on the basis of gender, and the right to health. Governmental failure to take appropriate action to ensure the eradication of FGM violates these obligations" (www.amnesty.org/ailib/intcam/femgen/fgm4.htm). By linking it to security and gender discrimination, certain problematic aspects of this customary practice are glossed over, such as the fact that female circumcision is ritually performed by women on girls at the insistence of mothers and grandmothers. The tone in which government action is demanded in effect calls for criminalization and punishment rather than for persuasion.

33. Nussbaum, pp. 78–79.

capabilities, according to Nussbaum, can be found in the Rawlsian idea of "overlapping consensus," which I have discussed briefly in connection with Taylor's use of it in the Introduction. "By 'overlapping consensus' I mean what John Rawls means," she writes, "that people may sign on to this conception, without accepting any particular metaphysical view of the world, any particular comprehensive or ethical view, or even any particular view of the person or of human nature."[34] And yet, Nussbaum's idea of universal capabilities *does* express the emerging idea of "the human" in it. A subject possessing bodily integrity, able freely to express himself or herself, and entitled to choose for herself or himself what to believe and how to behave is not simply a "freestanding moral core of a political conception" to which people sign on. It is itself a thick account of what being human is—and one that underpins human rights.

As a view of human nature it follows that where these capabilities are not being exercised due to obstacles, their removal will allow humans either to exercise them spontaneously (and to rank them), or to freely choose not to do so. However, humans will have to be taught what *good* capabilities are and how to exercise them, and to be prevented from exercising vices that harm others. After all, humans are also capable of cruelty, greed, arrogance, treachery—indeed there is scarcely anything they are *not* capable of. So apart from being able to identify vices and their harmful social effects, someone must have the power to identify "obstacles," to remove them, and also to ensure—by force if necessary—that vices are not restored. *That* sovereign power is a human capability too, but not one that everyone may freely exercise simply on that account. When invested in the state, that juridical power becomes a precondition for the flourishing of human capabilities. According to Nussbaum, that state must, of course, be one committed to universal values. As such it would not only secure the same rights for all its citizens, but also their ability to experience the emotions of love, grief, justified anger—and even their ability to "use the senses, to imagine, think, and reason—and to do these things in a 'truly human' way."[35] One difficulty here is that the secular state now becomes the definer of "the truly human," and although Nussbaum attempts to distinguish between capability and functioning, assigning only the definition of the former to the state, it is not always possible to distinguish between them.

34. Ibid., p. 76.
35. Ibid., p. 78.

There are other well-known problems with this view that may be noted in passing. First, the ability to choose freely whether or not to exercise a capability sometimes encounters a contradiction: because certain choices are irrevocable, they themselves may constitute insurmountable obstacles to further choices (as an illiterate one cannot make an informed choice regarding literacy unless one has experienced it, but having become literate one cannot then change one's mind). Second, it is a notorious fact that human capabilities—and the conditions in which they are realized—are subject to conflicting interpretations. When "human capabilities" are legally enshrined the business of interpreting them is the privilege of judicial authorities and technical experts, and politics proper is excluded. In brief, it becomes a matter of domination rather than negotiation.

Who—in a world of nation-states—has the authority to interpret and the power to promote the conditions that facilitate human rights, and "the human" they sustain? At a meeting two years ago the U.S. Trade Representative negotiating China's entry into the World Trade Organization casually observed in response to a journalist's question that "democratic political reform and greater adherence to human rights are certainly encouraged by *an opening to the West and Western norms.*"[36] A direct connection is thus made between a free trade, human rights, and "Western norms." What might these norms be when viewed as styles of life relating to specific kinds of subjectivity?

In a recent article on American global power, Ignacio Ramonet, chief editor of *Le Monde Diplomatique*, recounts the scale of U.S. military, diplomatic, economic, and technological hegemony, and then goes on to ask why—given the liberal democratic ideology of equality and autonomy—there isn't more criticism of it? I quote his elegant answer in full:

"No doubt because US hegemony also embraces culture and ideology. It has long been the home of many fine, respected intellectuals and creative artists, rightly admired by everybody. Its mastery extends to the symbolic level, lending it what Max Weber calls charismatic domination. The US has taken control of vocabulary, concepts and meaning in many fields. *We have to formulate the problems it invents in the words it offers.* It provides the codes to decipher enigmas it created. It has set up many research centers and think-tanks just for this, employing thousands of analysts and experts. These eminent bodies produce reports on legal, social

36. Justin Brown, "After China Pact, a Diminished Role for Human Rights?" *Christian Science Monitor*, November 19, 1999, p. 4 (emphasis added).

and economic issues with a perspective that supports the ideal of the free market, the world of business and the global economy. Their lavishly funded work attracts media attention and is broadcast the world over. . . . Wielding the might of information and technology, the US establishes, with the passive complicity of the people it dominates, affable oppression or delightful despotism. And this is the more effective because the culture industries it controls capture our imagination. The US uses its know-how to people our dreams with media heroes, Trojan horses sent to invade our brains. Only 1% of the films shown in the US are foreign productions, while Hollywood floods the world. Close behind come television series, cartoons, videos and comics, fashion, urban development and food. The faithful gather to worship the new icons in malls—temples to the glory of consumption. All over the world these centers promote the same way of life, in a world of logos, stars, songs, idols, brands, gadgets, posters and celebrations (like the extraordinary spread of Halloween in France). All this is accompanied by the seductive rhetoric of freedom of choice and consumer liberty, backed by obsessive, omnipresent advertising (annual advertising expenditure in the US exceeds $200bn) that has as much to do with symbols as with goods. Marketing has become so sophisticated that it aims to sell not just a brand name or social sign, but an identity. It's all based on the principle that having is being. . . . The American empire has mastered symbols and seduction. Offering unlimited leisure and endless distraction, its hypnotic charm enters our minds and instils ideas that were not ours. America does not seek our submission by force, but by incantation. It has no need to issue orders, for we have given our consent. There is no need for threats, as it wins because of our thirst for pleasure."[37]

I do not present this statement as decisive evidence of what is going on in the world. Its interest lies in the explanation it offers of how, by having "to formulate the problems [America] invents in the words [America] offers," global society adapts to a stronger, more modern language—in which the equal right to pleasure can be articulated as America's project of secular redemption.[38] Ramonet's recognition that the desire to do as one

37. Ignacio Ramonet, "The Control of Pleasure," *Le Monde Diplomatique,* May 2000. I have collapsed the original paragraphing and supplied the italics.

38. But as the post-9/11 "war on terrorism" demonstrates, the United States does not simply seduce its opponents with pleasure. It is prepared to use devastating force. The war against Afghanistan was presented by the American media not only as the pursuit of terrorists but also as the liberation of Afghan women. See, in

pleases (to do what pleases one) evoked by marketing discourse is familiar enough—the normalization of consuming desire is a banal feature of contemporary capitalist society often noted by both supporters and critics. Familiar, too, is his suggestion that the human being assumed in modern market culture is an autonomous individual who seeks pleasure and avoids pain. For just as electoral democracy postulates the equivalence of citizens (each of whom counts as one and only one) within any given party, so market strategies assume the equivalence of buyers (each of whom counts as one) within any given niche. In both cases the choosing subject is a statistical object to be targeted, added to or separated from other individuals. It is this that explains the U.S. Trade Representative's claim that greater adherence to human rights is encouraged by the acquisition of "Western (that is, American) norms" in place of older ones, just as the opening up of free trade with the West and the blossoming of a market society will reinforce human rights.

My thought is not that this claim is arrogant, or otherwise morally tainted, but that it may be true.[39] "Cultures" are indeed fragmented and interdependent, as critics never tire of reminding us. But cultures are also *unequally displaced practices.* Whether cultural displacement is a means of ensuring political domination or merely its effect, whether it is a necessary stage in the growth of universal humanity or an instance of cultural takeover, is not the point here. What I want to stress is that cultures may

---

this connection, "Feminism, the Taliban, and Politics of Counter-Insurgency," by Charles Hirschkind and Saba Mahmood (to appear in *Anthropological Quarterly*, 2002).

39. Acquiring "Western norms" includes learning new verbal behavior. "The 200 students crammed into tight rows for 'Think in American English' class have mastered gerunds, prepositions, and past participles. But there's one skill keeping them from ultimate success: selling themselves verbally," reports Shai Oster from Beijing. The class teacher, Victor Wang, "recommends a little more American style assertiveness: In China using the first-person singular goes against the Confucian grain of modesty." Chinese students, Wang complains, "think you have to be Bill Gates to say you're outstanding." You own yourself, and should be proud of everything you own. But the newly assertive individual must also learn how to be less candid: The answer to the greeting "How are you doing?" they are told "is 'fine', no matter what you're feeling" (*Christian Science Monitor*, June 14, 2000). Of course not all Americans are assertive or calculating individualists, but the point is that this "Western norm" has come to be widely promoted as necessary to moral and social progress.

be conceived not only in *visual* terms ("clearly bounded," "interlaced," "fragmented," and so forth) but also in terms of the temporalities of power by which—rightly or wrongly—*practices* constituting particular forms of life are displaced, outlawed, and penalized, and by which conditions are created for the cultivation of different kinds of human.[40] Resentment on the part of the weak about being treated cruelly by the powerful is generally a spontaneous human reaction, but learning to see certain practices as insupportable that were not previously viewed as such, and organizing social opposition to them, are steps in the reconstruction of the human.

In an interdependent modern world, "traditional cultures" do not spontaneously grow or develop into "modern cultures." People are pushed, seduced, coerced, or persuaded into trying to change themselves into something else, something that allows them to be redeemed. It may not be possible to stop this process; it may be a wonderful thing that the process takes place as it does because people really are redeemed through it. I do not argue for or against such directed changes here. I merely emphasize that they are not possible without the exercise of political power that often presents itself as a force for redeeming "humanity" from "traditional cultures." Or—and this comes down in the end to the same thing—as the force for reclaiming rights that belong inalienably to man in a state of nature.

In the seventeenth century, so John Pocock proposed, the self was beginning to be seen as contingent. The anxiety that that provoked was the context in which Locke's political appeal to natural rights acquired added plausibility.[41] Legal discourses for defining the person gain added weight.

40. In a perceptive article on the new *fluid* anthropological notion of culture and its appeal to contemporary theorists of multiculturalism, David Scott poses a sharp question: "*for whom* is culture partial, unbounded, heterogeneous, hybrid, and so on, the anthropologist or the native? Whose claim is this, theory's or that of the discourse into which theory is inquiring?" (David Scott, "Culture in Political Theory," *Political Theory*, vol. 30, no. 4, 2002).

41. Stephen Greenblatt, among others, notes that in the sixteenth century "there appears to be an increased self-consciousness about the fashioning of human identity as a manipulable, artful process" and that this secular idea gradually replaced the previous Christian view on the subject: "Hands off yourself," Augustine declared. "Try to build up yourself and you build a ruin" (cited in *Renaissance Self-Fashioning*, Chicago: University of Chicago Press, 1980, p. 2). Pocock is concerned with the more unstable seventeenth century in which the conditions for self-fashioning become more precarious.

In an essay on flexible capitalism at the close of the twentieth century, Richard Sennett has argued that the highly unstable conditions of work in America are making a coherent narrative of the self—and therefore the realization of "character"—increasingly difficult.[42] It is possible (although this is not Sennett's argument) that this new stage in the growing anxiety about the private self is not unconnected to the increasing insistence on the redemptive quality of human rights at a global level. When the secularist ideological order separating public politics from private belief is seen to crumble, the new terrain is occupied by a discourse of human rights that can be taken as either sacred or profane. Canovan's appeal to myth to defend the liberal project of human rights (see Chapter 1), King's appeal to universal brotherhood and human dignity under God, the U.S. government's global project to free both belief and property, and Nussbaum's celebration of the capabilities of the sovereign human are all variations of this discourse.

Including and excluding subjects as "humans"

I look finally a little at how boundaries are established between the human and the nonhuman. This question has emerged challengingly in recent attempts to deal theoretically with the problem of animal suffering.

That animals have an *interest* in living free from human cruelty has long been recognized. But some people have gone further and asked: Why don't nonhuman animals have, like humans, all the rights of personhood? It is argued that the assumption that animals cannot have rights because they literally cannot claim their rights in a court of law is merely an arbitrary limitation in the meaning of "right"—to active right. What is required, it is said, is a radical reworking of attitudes and behaviors in which our modern concept of "the human" as the ultimately privileged being is embedded. For attempts to draw a radical separation between "human" and "animal" have been a continuous feature of modern thinking and practice. The criteria for constituting "the human" in contradistinction to "the animal" have been endlessly debated: Do animals possess real consciousness? Do they have language in the proper sense? Are they able to change their culture as humans are? Ultimately the aim behind this questioning seems to be to distinguish the subject of rights from the objects of

42. Richard Sennett, *The Corrosion of Character: The Personal Consequences of Work in the New Capitalism*, New York: Norton, 1998.

rights, the owner from the property owned. Although for a long time now the law has been concerned to penalize "unjustifiable" pain and distress to animals, there has been a strong reluctance to transform the way animals live in human company—except perhaps in allowing them to become subjects of biological and psychological experiments that aim at "knowledge for human benefit."

A new book by an animal rights activist and lawyer now argues that legal personhood—and consequently rights—be recognized for chimpanzees and bonobos who have been cruelly mistreated in Africa and in Euro-America. Should all life have rights? The prospect of an epidemic of rights appears daunting. But the book insists that "there are about 1 million species of animals [and that] many of them, say, beetles and ants, should never have these rights."[43] They are too different from us. However, chimpanzees and bonobos are like humans. We are told that their genes and brain structures are similar to ours, that they are conscious and self-conscious, that they understand relations of cause and effect, make tools, live in complex and fluid societies, that they deceive and empathize, use numbers, communicate with symbols, treat illnesses with medicinal plants. That is why "an increasing number of scientists demand they be tucked into the genus *Homo* with us,"[44] writes the author Steven M. Wise.

Wise wants the partition between humans and nonhumans to be flexible, but he cannot do without it. He does not employ the notion of overlapping and intrinsically differentiated networks because human rights law seems to require mutually exclusive categories (human/nonhuman, guilty/not guilty, legal person/nonperson). The assumption is that to qualify for rights "they" must be sufficiently like "us"—and conversely, that if they are too unlike us, they cannot be redeemed. Wise insists that the statement "Animals can't have human rights" seems like a scientific truth about the world but it is simply a formula for privileging humans over animals (or better, over "mere life"). However, Wise still needs to retain the idea that *some* nonhumans cannot claim to be legal persons.[45]

What counts as "being like us" (that is, who truly belongs in our privileged universe) is certainly a difficult question. But in modern, secu-

43. S. M. Wise, *Rattling the Cage: Toward Legal Rights for Animals*, Cambridge, Mass.: Perseus Books, 2000, p. 5.

44. Ibid., p. 6.

45. Snakes and frogs and beetles should never have rights. Transformed into a beetle, Gregor Samsa knew he had no right even to human compassion.

lar society it is regarded as a political and moral question and not a scientific or theological one. Even if it were the case that scientists and theologians never argued with one another about the significance of relevant evidence, the question for liberal democracies is what follows politically or morally from "the human," and about this there is no final appeal in a secular society to authorized experts. And yet when it is endowed with legal force, the abstract concept of "humanity" allows authorities to decide who, by virtue of being *not human*, can legitimately be treated "inhumanly" by the state and its citizens. Precisely because it is an inclusive category, "the human" belongs to an exclusive universe that does *not* contain mere life.

If historians of social thought are correct about the increasing salience of a language of "normality" in modern society,[46] perhaps we should look not to *scientific theories* of "human nature," but instead to the *political and economic practices* by which attempts are made to regulate "desirable conduct" in the world, both within the nation-state and beyond it, through the application of cost-benefit analysis. As human rights activists point out, it is not only state cruelty (and the cruelty of warring military factions in civil war) that they hold legally accountable; the customs of ordinary people that are intolerable are also objects of concern. This requires us to analyze human rights law as a mode of converting and regulating people, making them at once freer and more governable *in this world.* The employment of cost-benefit analysis derived from neoliberal economics has the advantage of defining "freedom" quantitatively ("objectively") for the consuming subject in terms of behavior. It also provides a pragmatic principle for deciding when and to what extent the government of a population requires the restriction or abrogation of particular individual "freedoms." The historical convergence between human rights and neoliberalism may not be purely accidental. For as Tuck has pointed out, while self-ownership and self-preservation are regarded as basic to a natural morality they are also a justification for realpolitik.

But while some historical developments may support human rights, others may undermine them. At any rate, we may get a further destabilization of the concept of the rights-bearing human subject, now not simply through the law that distinguishes "the human" from mere animal life, but as the result of interventions by genetic engineering and—more radically—by neuroscience. The reason for saying this is not simply that homi-

46. Ian Hacking, *The Taming of Chance*, Cambridge: Cambridge University Press, 1990.

noids and genetically engineered humans—including clones—are the product of human making (and are therefore "cultural" rather than "natural"). It is that we are now required to consider seriously what the human capabilities of machines are, and what genetic engineering does to the idea of responsibility. Because the modern concept of the *natural* is now being reconfigured, we may now have to rethink the *supernatural*.

More is involved here, however, than mere thought. Far-reaching political and moral consequences follow from the fact that *The Declaration of Human Rights* provides a guarantee to entrepreneurial property throughout the world. (See Article 17.) Corporations that have invested heavily in research and construction will have property rights in these hominoids, just as biotechnology firms will have rights in the genetic inheritance of "natural" humans. Because property rights are freely disposable in the market, hominoids (intelligent, emotional machines) will be bought and sold, and the superior genes of humans with privileged capabilities will be acquired and marketed by biocorporations.[47] (Such rights of disposition are, by the way, accompanied by the "commercial freedom of speech," which, so it is forcefully argued, is also guaranteed by human rights.[48]) The old juridically defined self, *the self-owning subject*, now becomes problematized. Who is to be counted as human, what the capabilities are of the human subject, will be decided through the global market in which property rights and cost-benefit analysis are central. Human rights become floating signifiers that can be attached to or detached from various subjects and classes constituted by the market principle and designated by the most powerful nation-states.

47. Jean-Claude Guillebaud argues that these developments may well provide renewed (scientific) legitimations for slavery and racism, practices only recently discredited (see Jean-Claude Guillebaud, *Le Principe d'humanité*, Paris: Seuil, 2001).

48. Consider the recent debate in Britain about relaxing the legal restrictions on television advertising. In support of this aim, the official spokesperson for the Advertising Association invokes human rights to promote an already expanding consumer culture. "The human rights act," she points out, "obliges public authorities to ensure that any prohibition on the advertising of a legal product or service can be justified under the act, which guarantees commercial freedom of speech" ("Is It Time to Relax Restrictions on T.V. Advertising?" *The Guardian*, May 13, 2000, p. 14).

5

Muslims as a "Religious Minority" in Europe

Muslims are clearly present in a secular Europe and yet in an important sense absent from it. The problem of understanding Islam in Europe is primarily, so I claim, a matter of understanding how "Europe" is conceptualized by Europeans. Europe (and the nation-states of which it is constituted) is ideologically constructed in such a way that Muslim immigrants cannot be satisfactorily represented in it. I argue that they are included within and excluded from Europe at one and the same time in a special way, and that this has less to do with the "absolutist Faith" of Muslims living in a secular environment and more with European notions of "culture" and "civilization" and "the secular state," "majority," and "minority."

I take it for granted that in Europe today Muslims are often misrepresented in the media and discriminated against by non-Muslims.[1] More interesting for my present argument is the anxiety expressed by the majority of West Europeans about the presence of Muslim communities and Islamic traditions within the borders of Europe. (In France, for example, a 1992 poll showed that two-thirds of the population feared the presence of Islam in that country.[2]) It's not merely that the full incorporation of Muslims into European society is thought to be especially hard for people who

1. See J. Wrench and J. Solomos, eds., *Racism and Migration in Western Europe*, Oxford: Berg, 1993, and especially the excellent contribution by S. Castles.

2. See A. Hargreaves, *Immigration, Race and Ethnicity in Contemporary France*, London: Routledge, 1995, p. 119.

have been brought up in an alien culture. It is their attachment to Islam that many believe commits Muslims to values that are an affront to the modern secular state.

Admittedly, there is no shortage of voices that respond to such anxieties with characteristic liberal optimism.[3] They speak of the diverse linguistic and ethnic origins of Muslim immigrants and of the considerable variation in individual attachments to old traditions. There is little to fear from most immigrants—liberals say—and much more from the consequences of the higher unemployment and greater prejudice to which they are subjected. Muslims in Europe can be assimilated into Western society. Liberals maintain that it is only the extreme right for whom the presence of Muslims and Islam in Europe represents a potential cultural disaster, and that right-wing xenophobia is rooted in the romantic nativism it espouses, and consequently in its rejection of the universalist principles of the Enlightenment. In this as in other matters liberals stand for tolerance and an open society.

All these claims may be true, but the liberal position is more layered than one might suppose. To begin with "the Islamic" disregard of the principle of secular republicanism (as symbolized by the *affaire du foulard*), and the "Islamic" attack against the principle of freedom of speech (as exemplified in the Rushdie affair) have angered liberals and the left no less than the extreme right. These events within Europe have been read as all of a piece with the Islamist resort to civil violence in North Africa and West Asia, and they have led even liberals to ask with growing skepticism whether the Islamic tradition (as distinct from its human carriers) can find a legitimate place in a modern Western society.

But I begin elsewhere. I focus not on liberal opposition to right-wing intolerance or dismay at the closed-mindedness of immigrants but with a larger question. Can contemporary European practices and discourses represent a culturally diverse society of which Muslim migrants (Pakistanis in Britain, Turks in Germany, North Africans in France) are now part? To answer this question I shall first address another: How is Europe represented by those who regard themselves as authentic Europeans?

3. Many of these voices are found in recent collections: B. Lewis and D. Schnapper, eds., *Muslims in Europe*, London: Pinter, 1994; S. Z. Abedin and Z. Sardar, eds., *Muslim Minorities in the West*, London: Grey Seal, 1995; G. Nonneman, T. Niblock, and B. Szajkowski, eds., *Muslim Communities in the New Europe*, London: Ithaca Press, 1996.

The general preoccupation in the social sciences with the idea of *identity* dates from after the Second World War. It marks a new sense of the word, highlighting the individual's social locations and psychological crises in an increasingly uncertain world.[4] "This is my name," we now declare, "I need you to recognize me by that name." More than ever before identity now depends on the other's *recognition* of the self. Previously the more common meaning of *identity* was "sameness," as in the statement that all Muslims do not have "identical interests," and attributively, as in "identity card." In Europe the newer twist in the sense of the word is almost certainly more recent than in America. Perhaps in both places the discourse of *identity* indicates not the rediscovery of ethnic loyalties so much as the undermining of old certainties. The site of that discourse is suppressed fear. The idea of European identity, I say, is not merely a matter of how legal rights and obligations can be reformulated. Nor is it simply a matter of how a more inclusive name can be made to claim loyalties that are attached to national or local ones. It concerns *exclusions* and the desire that those excluded recognize what is included in the name one has chosen for onself. The discourse of European identity is a symptom of anxieties about non-Europeans.

Muslims and the idea of Europe

What kind of identity, then, does Europe represent to Europeans? An empirical response would base itself on comprehensive research into literature, popular media, parliamentary debates, and local interviews. My primary interest, however, is in analyzing the grammar of a discourse—as articulated in some uses of the concept "Europe"—rather than in tracing its empirical spread. So I begin with a partial answer to the question. Consider this anecdote as reported in the 1992 *Time* magazine cover story on Turkey's attempt to become a member of the European Community: "However it may be expressed, there is a feeling in Western Europe, rarely stated explicitly, that Muslims whose roots lie in Asia do not belong in the Western family, some of whose members spent

4. Philip Gleason points out that the first edition of the *International Encyclopedia of the Social Sciences*, published in 1930–1935, carried no entry under that term, and that one appeared only in the 1968 edition. See "Identifying Identity: A Semantic History," *The Journal of American History*, vol. 69, no. 4, 1983.

centuries trying to drive the Turks out of a Europe they threatened to overwhelm. Turkish membership 'would dilute the E.C.'s Europeanness,' says one German diplomat."[5]

Clearly neither the genocide practiced by the Nazi state nor its attempt to overwhelm Europe have led to feelings in Western Europe that would cast doubt on where Germany belongs. I do not make this statement in a polemical spirit. On the contrary, I affirm that given the idea of Europe that exists, such violence does not dilute Germany's Europeanness because violence is—among other things—a complicated moral language. Far from being threatened by internal violence, European solidarity is strengthened by it.

Let me explain: Tony Judt powerfully argues that the idea of Europe stands as a convenient suppressor of collective memories of the widespread collaboration with Nazi crimes in East and West alike, as well as of mass brutalities and civil cruelties for which all states were directly or indirectly responsible.[6] His account has nothing to say, however, about violence perpetrated in this period by Europeans outside Europe—in colonial Africa, say, or in the Middle East. No mention is made even of Algeria, which was, after all, an internal department of France. I stress that my comment here is not moralistic but descriptive. It has to do with how the conceptual boundaries of moral and legal solidarity are actually traced. I do not object to Judt's leaving colonial violence out of his discussion. I merely point to what he thinks is important. I indicate that his discussion of collective culpability is limited in precisely the way that the "myth of Europe" defines the extent of its own solidarity. "The myth of Europe" does not simply suppress the collective memories of violence within Europe; the resurrection of those experiences as memories strengthens that myth. The moral failure displayed in these memories is considered particularly shameful because Europeans try to cover up their past cruelties in Europe to *other Europeans* instead of confronting that fact fully. The Turkish assault against Europe and the more recent European brutalization of non-Europeans have quite a different salience within the world of international law.

Historically, it was not Europe that the Turks threatened but Christendom, since Europe was not then distinct from Christendom. "For diplomats and men of affairs," writes Denys Hay, "the intrusion of the

5. *Time*, October 19, 1992, p. 31.
6. Tony Judt, "The Past Is Another Country: Myth and Memory in Postwar Europe," *Daedalus*, vol. 121, no. 4, 1992.

Turk was a fact which could not be ignored and the practical acceptance of a Moslem state into the field of diplomacy might well have produced an early rejection of Christendom in the field of international relations. . . . The language of diplomacy maintained the established terminology: 'the common enemy, the Christian republic, the Christian world, the provinces of Christendom' are found in the phraseology of a large number of sixteenth- and early seventeenth-century treaties. A similar attitude is to be found in the treatises of the international lawyers down to, and even beyond, Grotius. If the Turk was not different under natural law, he was certainly different under divine law: the Turk was not far short of a 'natural enemy' of Christians."[7]

Richard Tuck has traced some of the debates in the sixteenth and seventeenth centuries about the possibility of Christian sovereigns making binding treaties with infidels. He cites the Protestant theologian Peter Martyr who condemned the treaty between the king of France and the Turks as unlawful. Hugo Grotius, however, rejected Martyr's thesis that Christians could not enter into treaties with infidels because the latter lacked morality; instead, he maintained that infidels were *neighbors* and so should be the object of protection and love—as our Lord commanded. (According to Tuck, this argument was not unconnected with the fact that Grotius supported the Dutch move to establish trading treaties with the sultan of Johore in the East Indies at the expense of the Portuguese.) But to the lawfulness of treaties with infidels Grotius added new grounds for the lawfulness of wars against them by virtue of the right to punish those who violated the law of nature. "The idea that foreign rulers can punish tyrants, cannibals, pirates, those who kill settlers, and those who are inhuman to their parents neatly legitimated a great deal of European action against native peoples around the world. . . . The central reason why Grotius had developed his argument in this direction was, I think, that the Dutch had begun to change the character of their activity in the non-European world since his earlier works, and in particular had begun to annex territory."[8] Thus alliances could be made with the Turks on the grounds that they were human beings, but alliance does not mean solidar-

7. Denys Hay, *Europe. The Emergence of an Idea*, Edinburgh: Edinburgh University Press, 1957, pp. 113–14.

8. Richard Tuck, *The Rights of War and Peace; Political Thought and the International Order from Grotius to Kant*, Oxford: Oxford University Press, 1999, p. 103.

ity. On the contrary, many of their customs and practices constituted violations of natural law, and set them outside the pale of Christendom.

In the contemporary European suspicion of Turkey, Christian history, enshrined in the tradition of international law, is being re-invoked in secular language as the foundation of an ancient identity. The discourse of international law, and the practices it justified, are central to its relations with "non-Europe."

Consider another example: the 1995 interview with Tadeusz Mazowiecki on the subject of his principled resignation as the UN Special Rapporteur for the Commission on Human Rights in the Balkans. At one point the interviewers, Bernard Osser and Patrick Saint-Exupery,[9] pose the following question: "You are Polish and Christian. Is it strange to hear yourself defending Bosnians, many of whom are Muslims?" Some readers might wonder how it is that two French intellectuals, heirs to the secular Enlightenment, can formulate such a question in Europe today. But of course the aim of this leading question is to elicit the plea for tolerance that the interviewers know will be forthcoming. So I find it more significant that Mazowiecki expresses no surprise at the question itself. Instead, he responds as expected by urging tolerance. He assures his interviewers that the war in Bosnia is not a religious one, and that Bosnian Muslims are not a danger to Europe. "It bodes ill for us," he warns, "if, at the end of the twentieth century, Europe is still incapable of coexistence with a Muslim community."

Mazowiecki's assumption (accepted without comment by his French interlocutors) is that Bosnian Muslims may be *in* Europe but are not *of* it—and it is precisely for this reason that they should be accorded toleration. Even though they may not have migrated to Europe from Asia (indeed they are not racially distinguishable from other whites in Europe), and even though they may have adjusted to secular political institutions (insofar as this can be said of Balkan societies)[10] they cannot claim a Euro-

9. B. Osser and P. de Saint-Exupery, "The UN's Failure: An Interview with Tadeusz Mazowiecki," *New York Review of Books*, vol. XLII, no. 14, September 21, 1995.

10. "In its historical practice," writes François Thual, "Caucasian, Balkan, Greek, and Slav Orthodox Christianity has never known secularism based on the separation of Church and State" ("Dans le monde orthodoxie, la religion sacralise la nation, et la nation protège la religion," *Le Monde*, January 20, 1998, p. 13). It is a little known fact—and one very rarely publicized—that the Greek constitution is proclaimed in the name of the Holy Trinity, and that it affirms that "the dominant religion in Greece is that of the Eastern Orthodox Church of Christ."

peanness—as the inhabitants of Christian Europe can. It is precisely because Muslims are external to the essence of Europe that "coexistence" can be envisaged between "us" and "them."

For both liberals and the extreme right the representation of "Europe" takes the form of a narrative, one of whose effects is to exclude Islam. I don't mean by this that both sides are equally hostile toward Muslims living in Europe.[11] Nor do I assume that Muslim immigrants are in no way responsible for their practical predicament. I mean only that for liberals no less than for the extreme right, the narrative of Europe points to the idea of an unchangeable essence, and the argument between them concerns the kind of "toleration" that that essence calls for.

Islam and the narrative of Europe

Europe, we often read, is not merely a continent, but a civilization. The word "civilization" is no longer as fashionable in the West as it was at the turn of the nineteenth century, but it appears to be returning. Some still object that the term "civilization" should not be applied to Europe, while insisting that there is something that Europeans share. Thus Michael Wintle: "To talk in terms of a quintessential or single European culture, civilization, or identity leads quickly to unsustainable generalization, and to all manner of heady and evidently false claims for one's own continent. Nonetheless, if the triumphalism can be left to one side there is a long history of shared influences and experiences, a heritage, which has not touched all parts of Europe or all Europeans equally, and which is therefore hard and perhaps dangerous to define in single sentences or even para-

11. Although the hostility of secular liberals is often difficult to distinguish from that of the extreme right. In France, for example, when the headmaster suspended three Muslim schoolgirls for wearing head scarves on the grounds that they were in contravention of French laws of *laïcité*, the subsequent overturning of the headmaster's suspension order by the education minister produced a remarkable response. A group of leading intellectuals, including Regis Debray and Alain Finkelkraut, compared the minister's decision to the 1938 appeasement of Nazi Germany at Munich: "by implication," observes Hargreaves, "the Islamic bridgehead established by the three girls in Creil now represented a comparable threat to the future well-being of France." The form in which the issue was publicly represented helped the extreme right-wing Front National party to win a sweeping by-election victory near Paris, an event that in turn contributed to the adjustment of government policy on immigration (see Hargreaves, pp. 125–26).

graphs, but which is felt and experienced in varying ways and degrees by *those whose home is Europe*, and which is recognized—whether approvingly or disapprovingly—by many from outside."[12]

The key influences on European experience, Wintle continues, are the Roman Empire, Christianity, the Enlightenment, and industrialization. It is because these historical moments have not influenced Muslim immigrant experience that *they are not those whose home is Europe*. These moments are precisely what others have designated "European civilization," a notion that takes "Europe" to be a subject of civilization and not merely a natural territory.

Raymond Williams notes that the word "civilization" is used today in three senses: (1) a single universal development (as in "human civilization"); (2) the collective character of a people or a period that is different from and incommensurable with others (as in "the civilization of the Renaissance in Italy"); and (3) the culture of a particular population, which is rankable as higher or lower than another, and perhaps also capable of further development.[13] Although Williams does not say so, the three senses together articulate the essence of "European civilization": it aspires to a universal (because "human") status; it claims to be distinctive (it defines modernity as opposed to tradition); and it is, by quantifiable criteria, undoubtedly the most advanced—and knows itself to be so to the extent that it now includes North America. Taken together these senses require a narrative definition of "Europe."

The two journalistic examples I cited earlier both assume a historical definition of Europe as a civilization. But they do so in ways that are largely implicit. Hugh Trevor-Roper's *The Rise of Christian Europe*[14] is one of many academic texts that expresses the essence of European identity explicitly by means of a historical narrative. Trevor-Roper's book is interesting because it defines European civilization—and therefore European identity—as a narrative, or at least as the beginning of one whose proper

12. Michael Wintle, "Cultural Identity in Europe: Shared Experience," in M. Wintle, ed., *Culture and Identity in Europe*, Aldershot: Avebury, 1996, p. 13; emphasis added.

13. Raymond Williams, *Key Words*, London: Fontana, 1983.

14. H. Trevor-Roper, *The Rise of Christian Europe*, London: Thames and Hudson, 2nd ed., 1965. Described by a *Times Literary Supplement* reviewer as "One of the most brilliant works of historiography to be published in England in this century," it has been reprinted numerous times, most recently in 1989.

ending is already familiar. Like other texts with which it may be compared, it presents a twofold notion of history: the history of "the idea of Europe" and of "European history."[15] It also has an interesting historical location. It appeared in 1965, when British decolonization was more or less complete, and when the flood of non-European immigrants from the former colonies was stemmed by legislation—passed amidst charges of betrayal of its principles—by the Labour government. At the time a new role for Britain in its postimperial phase was being vigorously debated, in all sections of the political spectrum. The option of "joining Europe" politically was an important part of that debate.

When Trevor-Roper speaks of "European history" he does not mean narratives about the inhabitants of the European continent, which is why there is nothing in his book about Byzantium and Eastern Europe, or about northwestern Europe (other than brief references to the Viking's destructiveness), or about Jews (other than as victims), or about Muslim Spain (other than as an intrusive presence). "European history" is the narration of an identity many still derive from "European (or Western) civilization"—a narrative that seeks to represent homogeneous space and linear time.

What is the essence of that civilizational identity? Trevor-Roper reminds his readers that most of its ideas and many of its techniques entered European civilization from outside. The things that belong to European civilization, therefore, are those that were taken up and creatively worked on by "Europe." Productive elaboration becomes an essential characteristic of Europe as a civilization. This view makes sense, I would suggest, in the context of a particular Enlightenment theory about property first propounded by John Locke. Locke argued that a person's right to property comes from the mixing of labor with the common things of this world. "God gave the world to men in common, but since He gave it them for their benefit and the greatest conveniencies of life they were capable to draw from it, it cannot be supposed He meant it should always remain common and uncultivated. He gave it to the use of the industrious and rational (*and labor was to be his title to it*); not to the fancy or covetousness

15. For example, D. Hay, *Europe: The Emergence of an Idea*, Edinburgh: Edinburgh University Press, 1957; J.-B. Duroselle, *L'idée d'Europe dans l'histoire*, Paris: Denoel, 1963; R.H. Foerster, *Europa: Geschichte einer politischen Idee*, Munich: Nymphenburger, 1967; K. Wilson and J. Van der Dussen, eds., *The History of the Idea of Europe*, London: Routledge, 1995.

of the quarrelsome and contentious."[16] Applied to whole peoples, property was "European" to the extent that Europeans appropriated, cultivated, and then lawfully passed it on to generations of Europeans as their own inheritance.

"European history" thus becomes a history of continuously productive actions defining as well as defined by law. Property is central to that story not only in the sense familiar to political economy and jurisprudence, but in the sense of the particular character, nature, or essence of a person or thing. It is a story that can be narrated in terms of improvement and accumulation, in which the industrial revolution is merely one (albeit central) moment. According to this conception, "European civilization" is simply the sum of properties, all those material and moral acts that define European identity.

It follows from this view of Europe that real Europeans acquire their individual identities from the character of their civilization. Without that civilizational essence, individuals living within Europe are unstable and ambiguous. That is why not all inhabitants of the European continent are "really" or "fully" European. Russians are clearly marginal. Until just after World War II, European Jews were marginal too, but since that break the emerging discourse of a "Judeo-Christian tradition" has signaled a new integration of their status into Europe.[17] Completely external to "European history" is medieval Spain. Although Spain is now defined geographically as part of Europe, Arab Spain from the seventh to the fourteenth centuries is seen as being outside "Europe," in spite of the numerous intimate connections and exchanges in the Iberian peninsula during that period between Muslims, Christians, and Jews.

There is a problem for any historian constructing a categorical boundary for "European civilization" because the populations designated by the label "Islam" are, in great measure, the cultural heirs of the Hellenic world—the very world in which "Europe" claims to have its roots. "Islamic civilization" must therefore be denied a vital link to the properties that define so much of what is essential to "Europe" if a civilizational difference is to be postulated between them. There appear to be two moves by which this is done. First, by denying that it has an essence of its own, "Islam" can

16. J. Locke, *Two Treatises of Civil Government*, Book II, Chapter V, paragraph 34; emphasis added.

17. Of course anti-Semitism has not disappeared in Europe. But no one who aspires to respectability can now afford to be known publicly as an anti-Semite.

be represented as a *carrier civilization* that helped to bring important elements into Europe from outside, material and intellectual elements that were only contingently connected to Islam.[18] Then, to this carrier civilization is attributed an essence: an *ingrained* hostility to all non-Muslims. That attribution constitutes Islam as Europe's primary alter. This alleged antagonism to Christians then becomes crucial to the formation of European identity. In this, as in other historical narratives of Europe, this oppositional role gives "Islam" a quasi-civilizational identity.[19] One aspect of the identity of Islamic civilization is that it represents an early attempt to destroy Europe's civilization from outside; another is that it signifies the corrupting moral environment that Europe must continuously struggle to overcome from within.[20]

This construction of civilizational difference is not exclusive in any simple sense. The de-essentialization of Islam is paradigmatic for all thinking about the assimilation of non-European peoples to European civilization. The idea that people's historical experience is inessential to them, that it can be shed at will, makes it possible to argue more strongly for the Enlightenment's claim to universality: Muslims, as members of the abstract category "humans," can be assimilated or (as some recent theorists have put it) "translated" into a global ("European") civilization once they have divested themselves of what many of them regard (mistakenly) as essential to themselves. The belief that human beings can be separated from their histories and traditions makes it possible to urge a Europeanization of the

18. "The Arabs themselves . . . *had little of their own to offer.* . . . But as carriers, their services to Europe were enormous" (Trevor-Roper, p. 141).

19. In Trevor-Roper's picturesque language: "Out of this union [of ecclesiastical and feudal power], would come, in due time, the combined spiritual and material counter-attack of the enslaved West against its Moslem exploiters: the Crusades" (ibid., p. 100).

20. Hence, Trevor-Roper's account of the European Crusaders who established a principality in Jerusalem from the end of the eleventh century to the end of the twelfth: "The Christian kingdom of Jerusalem continued for less than a century. The Christian virtues, such as they were, evaporated in the East. The Christian dynasties ran out. . . . [T]he sons—or rather the successors, for there was a dearth of sons—settled down to a life of luxurious co-existence in which feudal bonds were rotted and oriental tastes indulged" (ibid., p. 104). By "Christian" Trevor-Roper refers of course only to those who originated in "Europe," because the Middle East at the time was largely inhabited by indigenous Christians who were major contributors to "Islamic civilization."

Islamic world. And by the same logic, it underlies the belief that the *assimilation* to Europe's civilization of Muslim immigrants who are—for good or for ill—already in European states is necessary and desirable.

The motive of "European history" in this representation is the story of Europe's active power to reconstruct the world (within Europe and beyond) in its own Faustian image.[21] Europe's colonial past is not merely an epoch of overseas power that is now decisively over. It is the beginning of an irreversible global transformation that remains an intrinsic part of "European experience," and is part of the reason that Europe has become what it is today. It is not possible for Europe to be represented without evoking this history and the way in which its active power has continually constructed its own exclusive boundary—and transgressed it.

The shifting borders of modern Europe?

It is often conceded that several peoples and cultures inhabit the European continent, but it is also believed that there is a single history that articulates European civilization—and therefore European identity. The official EC slogan expresses this thought as "unity in diversity." But determining the boundaries of that unity continues to be an urgent problem for anyone concerned with the civilizational basis of the European Community. Perry Anderson has noted some of the difficulties about boundaries encountered in recent discourse: "Since the late Eighties, publicists and politicians in Hungary, the Czech lands, Poland and more recently Slovenia and even Croatia have set out to persuade the world that these countries belong to Central Europe that has a natural affinity to Western Europe, and is fundamentally distinct from Eastern Europe. The geographical stretching involved in these definitions can be extreme. Vilnius is described by Czeslaw Milosz, for example, as a Central European city. But if Poland—let alone Lithuania—is really in the center of Europe, what is the east? Logically, one would imagine, the answer must be Russia. But since many of the same writers—Milan Kundera is another example—deny that Russia has ever belonged to European civilization at

21. On Europe's "Faustian" identity, see Agnes Heller, "Europe: An Epilogue?" in B. Nelson, D. Roberts, and W. Veit, eds., *The Idea of Europe: Problems of National and Transnational Identity*, Oxford: Berg, 1992.

all, we are left with the conundrum of a space proclaiming itself center and border at the same time."[22]

Anderson's witty account highlights the illogicality of recent definitions of Europe. Yet it is precisely the politics of civilizational identity that is at work in the discourse of Europe's extent. For Poles, Czechs, and Hungarians it is a matter not only of participating in the European common market, but of distancing themselves from a socialist history. Where Europe's borders are to be drawn is also a matter of representing what European civilization is. These borders involve more than a confused geography. They reflect a history whose unconfused purpose is to separate Europe from alien times ("communism," "Islam") as well as from alien places ("Islamdom," "Russia").

J. G. A. Pocock has spelled out another aspect of this politics of civilization: "'Europe'—both with and without the North America whose addition turns it from 'Europe' into 'Western Civilization'—is once again an empire in the sense of a civilized and stabilized zone which must decide whether to extend or refuse its political power over violent cultures along its borders but not within its system."[23] In Pocock's separation between a "civilized zone" and "violent cultures," we sense that Europe's borders at once protect and threaten its unity, define its authority and engage with external powers that have entered its domain. The "inside" cannot contain the "outside," violent cultures cannot inhabit a civil one—Europe cannot contain non-Europe. Certainly immigrants in the grip of Islamic passions and ideas cannot live comfortably in the civilized institutions of secular Europe. And yet Europe must try to contain, subdue, or incorporate what lies beyond it, and what consequently comes to be within it. European strategic and economic interests cannot be confined to the European continent. Nor its desire to morally redeem the world—although that desire has now seized the extension of Europe we know as the United States of America.

The representation of Europe's borders is, of course, symbolic. But the signs and symbols have a history. Like the borders of its constituent states, the European Community's boundaries are inscribed in treaties according to the conventions of international law—the cumulative result of

22. P. Anderson, "The Europe to Come," *London Review of Books*, January 25, 1996.

23. J. G. A. Pocock, "Deconstructing Europe," *London Review of Books*, December 19, 1991.

earlier narratives of Europe. The status of individual borders as well as the very institution of international law that regulates today's worldwide society of nation-states have been constituted by narratives of Europe.

Adam Watson summarizes the story: "The expansion of Europe was neither uniform nor systematic. It occurred over several centuries, for a number of reasons, and assumed many different forms. Chronologically we can distinguish in retrospect four main phases. First came the medieval crusades into Iberia and round the Baltic. The second phase covered three centuries of competitive maritime exploration and expansion and the parallel evolution of a European international society. Thirdly in the nineteenth century the industrial revolution enabled the European Concert to encompass the entire globe and to administer most of it. Lastly in our own century the tide of European dominion ebbed, and was replaced by a world-wide society based on the European model but in which Europeans now play only a modest role."[24] What this story misses is that Europe did not simply expand overseas; it made itself through that expansion. It also underemphasizes the role that Europeans—especially those who inhabit the United States—still play in regulating "world-wide society," a role that is by no means "modest." The borders of political Europe have varied not only over time, but also according to the European model governing global relations.

Can Muslims be represented in Europe? As members of states that form part of what Watson and others call European international society Muslims have, of course, long been represented (and regulated) in it. But representing Muslims in European liberal democracies is a different matter. It raises a question that does not apply to the international system: how can a European state represent its "minorities"?

European liberal democracy and minority representation

So far I have explored the idea that Islam is excluded from representations of Europe and the narratives through which the representations are constituted. I now approach the question from another angle: What are the possibilities of representing Muslim minorities in secular European states?

24. A. Watson, "European International Society and Its Expansion," in H. Bull and A. Watson, eds., *The Expansion of International Society*, Oxford: Clarendon Press, 1985, p. 32.

I begin with what many readers will consider an outrageous statement: The ideology of political representation in liberal democracies makes it difficult if not impossible to represent Muslims as Muslims. Why? Because in theory the citizens who constitute a democratic state belong to a class that is defined only by what is common to all its members and its members only. What is common is the abstract equality of individual citizens to one another, so that each counts as one. Marie Swabey has stated the issue succinctly: "The notion of equality central to democracy is clearly a logical and mathematical conception. . . . [O]nce equality is admitted, the notions of number, per capita enumeration, and determination by the greater number are not far to seek. . . . Citizens are to be taken as so many equivalent units and issues are to be decided by the summation of them. . . . Once we conceive the whole (the state) as composed of parts (the citizens) which are formally distinct but without relevant qualitative differences, we are applying the notion in its essentials. Involved here is the assumption not only that the whole is authoritative over any of its parts, but that what there is *more of* has *ipso facto* greater weight than that which differs from it merely by being less. In the democratic state this idea is expressed as the postulate that the opinion of the people as a whole, or of the greater part of them, is authoritative over that of any lesser group."[25] It follows, Swabey goes on, that the opinion of a majority "is more likely to represent approximately the opinion of the whole body than any other part." In this conception representative government is assimilated to the notion of an outcome that is statistically representative of "the whole body" of citizens. The same principle applies to segments of "the whole (the state)" according to which representatives of geographically demarcated constituencies represent aggregates of individual voters. It is no accident that the statistical concept of representativeness emerged in close connection with the construction of the welfare state (a process that began toward the end of the nineteenth century) and the centralization of national statistics.[26] Both in the history of statistical thinking and in the evolution of democratic politics, these developments were especially important—demography, social security legislation, market research, and national election polls.

In principle, therefore, nothing should distinguish Muslims from

25. Marie Collins Swabey, *The Theory of the Democratic State*, Cambridge: Harvard University Press, 1939, pp. 18–20; emphasis in original.

26. See Alain Desrosières, *The Politics of Large Numbers: A History of Statistical Reasoning*, Cambridge: Harvard University Press, 1998.

non-Muslims as citizens of a European democratic state other than their fewer numbers. But "a minority" is not a purely quantitative concept of the kind stipulated by Swabey, not an outcome of probability theory applied to determine the opinion of a corporate body—"the people as a whole." The concept of minority arises from a specific Christian history: from the dissolution of the bond that was formed immediately after the Reformation between the established Church and the early modern state. *This* notion of minority sits uncomfortably with the secular Enlightenment concept of the abstract citizen.

The post-Reformation doctrine that it was the state's business to secure religious uniformity within the polity—or at least to exclude Dissenters from important rights—was crucial to the formation of the early modern state. By contrast, the secular Enlightenment theory that the political community consists of an abstract collection of equal citizens was propounded as a criticism of the religious inequality characterizing the absolutist state. The most famous document embodying that theory was the "Declaration of the Rights of Man and the Citizen." The theory was criticized almost from the moment it was first stated—notably by Burke for the license it gave to destructive passions, and by Marx for disguising bourgeois self-interest. However, the decisive movements that helped to break the alliance of church and state seem to have been religious rather than secular—Tractarianism in England, and Ultramontanism in France and Europe generally. The arguments they deployed most effectively were strictly theological and were aimed at securing the freedom of Christ's church from the constraints of an earthly power.[27] An important consequence of abandoning the total union of church and state was the eventual emergence of "minority rights" as a central theme of national politics. Members of minorities became at once equal to all other citizens, members of the body politic ("the people as a whole"), and, as a minor body, unequal to the majority, requiring special protection.

The political inclusion of minorities has meant the acceptance of groups formed by specific (often conflicting) historical narratives, and the embodied memories, feelings, and desires that the narratives have helped to shape. The rights that minorities claim include the right to maintain

27. Joseph Heim, "The Demise of the Confessional State and the Rise of the Idea of a Legitimate Minority," in J. W. Chapman and A. Wertheimer, eds., *Majorities and Minorities*, New York: New York University Press, 1990.

and perpetuate themselves as groups. "Minority rights" are not derivable from general theories of citizenship: status is connected to membership in a specific *historical* group, not in the abstract class of citizens. In that sense minorities are no different from majorities, also a historically constituted group. The fact that they are usually smaller in number is an accidental feature. Minorities may be numerically much larger than the body of equal citizens from whom they are excluded. In the British empire vast numbers of colonial subjects were ruled by a democratic state of citizens far smaller in number through a variety of constitutional devices—which rendered them legally and ideologically minorities.[28] Because minorities are defined as minorities only in hierarchical structures of power.

Take the case of France. Religious Muslims who reside in France are similar to the Christian (and post-Christian) inhabitants of that country in this regard: each group has constituted itself *as a group* through its own narratives. These narratives, and the practices they authorize, help to define what is essential to each group. To insist in this context that Muslim groups must not be defined in terms they regard as essential to themselves is in effect to demand that they can and should shed the narratives and practices they take to be necessary to their lives as Muslims. The crucial difference between the "majority" and the "minorities" is, of course, that the majority effectively claims the French state as its national state. In other words, to the extent that "France" embodies the Jacobin narrative, it *essentially* represents the Christian and post-Christian citizens who are constituted by it.

Thus Jean Le Pen's insistence in the early 1980s on the right of the majority ("the French in France") to protect its distinctive character against the influence of minority difference is not only an extension of the left slogan "the right to difference." It is a claim that the majority's right to be French "in their own country" precludes the right of minorities to equal treatment in this regard. "We not only have the right but the duty to defend our national personality," Le Pen declares, "and we too have our right

28. "Colonies, protectorates, mandates, intervention treaties, and similar forms of dependence make it possible today for a democracy to govern a heterogeneous population without making them citizens, making them dependent upon a democratic state, and at the same time held apart from the state. This is the political and constitutional meaning of the nice formula 'the colonies are foreign in public law, but domestic in international law'" (Carl Schmitt, *The Crisis of Parliamentary Democracy*, Cambridge, Mass.: MIT Press, 1985 [1926], p. 10).

to be different."[29] Given the existence of a French national personality of which the Jacobin republic—secular and rational—is claimed to be the embodiment, and given that the majority is its representative, Le Pen can argue that only those immigrants able and willing to join them (thereby ceasing to belong to a minority) have the right to remain in France as French citizens. It follows that the "inassimilable" ones (North African Muslims) should be encouraged to leave when their labor is no longer required by France. This may be an intolerant position but it is not illogical.[30] To be a French citizen is to reflect, as an individual, the collective personality that was founded in the French Revolution and embodied in the laws and conventional practices of the French Republic, and that is recounted in its national story. Although that personality may not be regarded as eternal and unchangeable, it represents a precondition of French citizenship. As even liberals concede, the individual citizen cannot make with the state any contract he or she chooses independently of that personality. In brief, the narratives that define "being French," and the practices they authorize, cannot be regarded as inessential. *French citizens, carriers of a secular heritage, cannot be de-essentialized.* This view, shared by left, center, and right, rejects the notion that the citizen is identical only with himself or herself, that he or she therefore essentially represents an abstract quantity that can be separated from his or her social identity, added up and then divided into groups that have only numerical value. It should not be surprising that Le Pen has been able to push the greater part of the majority toward endorsing reforms of the Nationality Code in the direction de-

29. "Nous croyons que la France est notre patrie, que les Français y ont des devoirs mais aussi des droits supérieurs à tous autres, et que nous avons non seulement le droit mais le devoir de défendre notre personnalité nationale et nous aussi notre droit à la différence" (*Le Monde*, September 21, 1982, cited in part, and in English translation, by Miriam Feldblum, "Re-Visions of Citizenship: The Politics of Nation and Immigration in France, 1981–1989," Ph.D. diss., Yale University, 1991, p. 48. My translation of the original is slightly different from Feldblum's).

30. Feldblum argues that the immigration politics of the extreme right are better described as "nativist" than as "racist," because the latter term does not explain why many of the nonracist left also share certain crucial elements of the same position. While Feldblum's study as a whole is valuable for understanding developments in recent French ideas of national identity, she does not discuss the contradictions inherent in liberal ideas of citizenship. Her use of the pejorative term "nativism" to denote populist denunciation of "foreign influences" deflects her from an adequate consideration of liberal forms of exclusivism and intolerance.

manded by the extreme right.[31] The very existence of the French Jacobin narrative permits the extreme right to occupy the ideological center in contemporary French immigration politics.

Liberals are generally dismayed at the resurgence of the right, but the notion of primordial intolerance will not explain it. Many critics have observed that part of the problem resides in the identification of national boundaries with those of the state. Some of them have sought a solution in the radical claim that all boundaries are indeterminate and ambiguous. William Connolly has recently theorized the matter more perceptively. He asks, pointedly, "whether it is possible to prize the indispensability of boundaries to social life while resisting overdetermined drives to *overcode* a particular set." He goes on to question the assumption that "the boundaries of a state must correspond to those of a nation, both of these to a final site of citizen political allegiance, and all three of those to the parameters of a democratic ethos."[32]

The problem of representing Islam (or any other "minority" religion) in European liberal democracies cannot be addressed adequately unless such questioning is taken seriously. With America especially in mind, Connolly urges a shift in the prevalent idea of pluralism "from a majority nation presiding over numerous minorities in a democratic state to a democratic state of multiple minorities contending and collaborating with a general ethos of forbearance and critical responsiveness."[33] The decentered pluralism he advocates in place of liberal doctrines of multiculturalism requires a continuous readiness to deconstruct historical narratives constituting identities and their boundaries (which, he argues, have a tendency to become sacralized and fundamentalized) in order to "open up space through which *care* is cultivated for the abundance of life."[34]

To what extent and how often historical narratives that constitute identities can be politically deconstructed remains a difficult question. Thus I have been arguing on the one hand that Europe's historical narrative of itself needs to be questioned, and on the other that the historical narratives produced by so-called "minorities" need to be respected. This

31. See Hargreaves, op. cit., pp. 169–76.

32. W. E. Connolly, "Pluralism, Multiculturalism and the Nation-State: Rethinking the Connections," *Journal of Political Ideologies*, vol. 1, no. 1, 1996, p. 58; emphasis in original.

33. Ibid., p. 61.

34. Ibid., p. 70; emphasis in original.

apparent inconsistency is dictated partly by a liberal concern that time and place should be made for weaker groups within spaces and times commanded by a dominant one. Muslims in Europe, I have implied, should be able to find institutional representation as a minority in a democratic state that consists only of minorities. For where there are only minorities the possibilities of forging alliances between them will be greater than in a state with a majority presiding over several competing minorities. To what extent the realities of power (especially disparities in wealth and information) and of habitus obstruct such possibilities is of course an important consideration.

But my comments also reflect an unresolved tension: how can respect for individuals be ensured *and* conditions be fostered that nurture collective "ways of life"? This concern is not merely a matter of "recognition"—of the demand that one should be able to name oneself as a group and be confirmed by others as the bearer of that name, and thereby have one's anxieties allayed. It is also a matter of embodied memories and practices that are articulated by traditions, and of political institutions through which these traditions can be fully represented. (The constituency represented does not have to be geographically continuous or univocal.) Our attention needs to be directed not so much at how identities are negotiated and recognized (for example through exploratory and constructive dialogue, as Charles Taylor has advocated).[35] Rather, the focus should be on what it takes to live particular ways of life continuously, co-operatively, and unselfconsciously.

John Milbank's arguments for decentering are different from Connolly's, and they are linked to a specifically medieval historical experience. His contrast between what he calls "enlightenment simple space" and "gothic complex space" has implications for a Europe of nation-states: "complex space has a certain natural, ontological priority, simple space remains by comparison merely an abstracting, idealizing project. . . . This is the case because there is no such thing as absolute non-interference; no action can be perfectly self-contained, but always impinges upon other people, so that spaces will always in some degree 'complexly' overlap, jurisdictions always in some measure be competing, loyalties remain (perhaps benignly) divided."[36]

35. See Charles Taylor, *Multiculturalism and "The Politics of Recognition,"* Princeton: Princeton University Press, 1992.

36. J. Milbank, "Against the Resignations of the Age," in F. P. McHugh and S. M. Natale, eds., *Things Old and New: Catholic Social Teaching Revisited,* New York: University Press of America, 1993, p. 19.

One consequence of this fact is that the sovereign state cannot (never could) contain all the practices, relations, and loyalties of its citizens.

The idea of complex space (in contrast to the discourse of a border-less world[37]) is in my view a fruitful way of thinking about the intersecting boundaries and heterogeneous activities of individuals as well as of groups related to traditions. Unlike the modern, secular world of nation-states, medieval Christendom and Islam recognized a multiplicity of overlapping bonds and identities. People were not always expected to subject themselves to one sovereign authority, nor were they themselves sovereign moral subjects.

But in addition to complex space we need to think also of heterogeneous time: of embodied practices rooted in multiple traditions, of the differences between horizons of expectation and spaces of experience—differences that continually dislocate the present from the past, the world experienced from the world anticipated, and call for their revision and reconnection. These simultaneous temporalities embrace both individuals and groups in complexities that imply more than a simple process of secular time.

Complex space and complex time reduce the scope for "national politics" with its exclusive boundaries and homogeneous temporality. The question here is not simply one of devolution or of regional integration, the question now being debated in the European Community, but of how overlapping patterns of territory, authority, and time collide with the idea of the imagined national community. The scope of national politics is reduced in part for the well-known reason that the forces of global capitalism often undermine attempts to manage the national economy—although it is necessary to stress that this is truer of some national economies than of others. And it is reduced also because networks that straddle national boundaries mobilize variable populations for diverse tasks that have unpredictable consequences.

But there is something else: because the temporalities of many tradition-rooted practices (that is, the time each embodied practice requires to complete and to perfect itself, the past into which it reaches, that it reencounters, reimagines, and extends) cannot be translated into the homogeneous time of national politics. The body's memories, feelings, and desires necessarily escape the rational/instrumental orienta-

37. Kenichi Ohmae, *The Borderless World: Power and Strategy in the Interlinked Economy*, New York: HarperCollins, 1990.

tion of such politics. (This is not properly understood by those well-wishing critics who urge Asian immigrants to abandon their traditions, to regard some of their collective memories and desires as not essentially their own, and to embrace instead the more modern conception of self-determination underlying the European nation-state in which they now live.[38]) For many Muslim minorities (though by no means all) being Muslim is more than simply belonging to an individual faith whose private integrity needs to be publicly respected by the force of law, and being able to participate in the public domain as equal citizens. It is more, certainly, than a cultural identity recognized by the liberal democratic state. It is being able to live as autonomous individuals in a collective life that extends beyond national borders. One question for them (although not necessarily asked by all of them) is: What kind of conditions can be developed in secular Europe—and beyond—in which *everyone* may live as a minority among minorities?

I conclude with another question because decisive answers on this subject are difficult to secure. If Europe cannot be articulated in terms of complex space and complex time that allow for multiple ways of life (and not merely multiple *identities*) to flourish, it may be fated to be no more than the common market of an imperial civilization,[39] always anxious about (Muslim) exiles within its gates and (Muslim) barbarians beyond. In such an embattled modern space—a space of abundant consumer choice, optional life styles, and slogans about the virtues of secularism—is it possible for Muslims (or any other immigrants, for that matter) to be represented as themselves?

38. As in Homi Bhabha's "where once we could believe in the comforts and continuities of Tradition, today we must face the responsibilities of cultural Translation," written in a spirit of friendly advice to Muslim immigrants in Britain during the Rushdie affair (*New Statesman and Society,* March 3, 1989). Yet how innocent is the assumption that Muslim "Tradition" carries no responsibilities, and that "cultural Translation" to a British lifestyle in Britain is without any comforts.

39. "Europe is again an empire concerned for the security of its *limites*—the new barbarians being those populations who do not achieve the sophistication without which the global market has little for them and less need of them" (J. G. A. Pocock. There remains, however, a periodic need for barbarian labor *within* Europe).

6

Secularism, Nation-State, Religion

I have tried to follow aspects of the secular indirectly—through ideas of myth and the sacred, through concepts of moral agency, pain, and cruelty—and also more directly through the notion of human rights as well as the idea of religious minorities in European states that claim to govern themselves according to secularist principles. In this chapter I examine the secularization thesis with particular reference to the formation of modern nationalism.

Volumes have been written on the idea of secularization and its alleged centrality for modernity. Is it worth saving? The secularization thesis in its entirety has always been at once descriptive and normative. In his impressive book on the subject,[1] José Casanova points to three elements in that thesis, all of which have been taken—at least since Weber—to be essential to the development of modernity: (1) increasing structural differentiation of social spaces resulting in the separation of religion from politics, economy, science, and so forth; (2) the privatization of religion within its own sphere; and (3) the declining social significance of religious belief, commitment, and institutions. Casanova holds that only elements (1) and (3) are viable.

Many contemporary observers have maintained that the worldwide explosion of politicized religion in modern and modernizing societies proves that the thesis is false. Defenders of the thesis have in general re-

1. José Casanova, *Public Religions in the Modern World*, Chicago: University of Chicago Press, 1994.

torted that the phenomenon merely indicates the existence of a widespread revolt against modernity and a failure of the modernization process. This response saves the secularization thesis by making it normative: in order for a society to be modern it has to be secular and for it to be secular it has to relegate religion to nonpolitical spaces because that arrangement is essential to modern society. Casanova's book attempts to break out of this tautology in an interesting way. It argues that the deprivatization of religion is not a refutation of the thesis if it occurs in ways that are consistent with the basic requirements of modern society, including democratic government. In other words, although the privatization of religion within its own sphere is part of what has been meant by secularization, it is not essential to modernity.

The argument is that whether religious deprivatization threatens modernity or not depends on *how* religion becomes public. If it furthers the construction of civil society (as in Poland) or promotes public debate around liberal values (as in the United States), then political religion is entirely consistent with modernity. If, on the other hand, it seeks to undermine civil society (as in Egypt) or individual liberties (as in Iran) then political religion is indeed a rebellion against modernity and the universal values of Enlightenment.

This is certainly an original position, but not, I would submit, an entirely coherent one. For if the legitimate role for deprivatized religion is carried out effectively, what happens to the allegedly viable part of the secularization thesis as stated by Casanova? Elements (1) and (3) are, I suggest, both undermined.

When religion becomes an integral part of modern politics, it is not indifferent to debates about how the economy should be run, or which scientific projects should be publicly funded, or what the broader aims of a national education system should be. The legitimate entry of religion into these debates results in the creation of modern "hybrids": the principle of structural differentiation—according to which religion, economy, education, and science are located in autonomous social spaces—no longer holds. Hence element (1) of the secularization thesis falls. Furthermore, given the entry of religion into political debates issuing in effective policies, and the passionate commitments these debates engender, it makes little sense to measure the social significance of religion only in terms of such indices as church attendance. Hence element (3) of the secularization thesis falls. Since element (2) has already been abandoned, it seems that nothing retrievable remains of the secularization thesis.

However, this doesn't mean that the secularization thesis must either be accepted in its original form or dismissed as nonsense. Its numerous critics are right to attack it, but they have generally missed something vital. I'll try to outline what that is later on. For the moment I simply assert that neither the supporters nor the critics of the secularization thesis pay enough attention to the concept of "the secular," which emerged historically in a particular way and was assigned specific practical tasks.

I begin by examining *the kind* of religion that enlightened intellectuals like Casanova see as compatible with modernity. For when it is proposed that religion can play a positive political role in modern society, it is not intended that this apply to *any* religion whatever, but only to those religions that are able and willing to enter the public sphere for the purpose of rational debate with opponents who are to be persuaded rather than coerced. Only religions that have accepted the assumptions of liberal discourse are being commended, in which tolerance is sought on the basis of a distinctive relation between law and morality.

Ever since Habermas drew attention to the central importance of the public sphere for modern liberal society, critics have pointed out that it systematically excludes various kinds of people, or types of claim, from serious consideration. From the beginning the liberal public sphere excluded certain kinds of people: women, subjects without property, and members of religious minorities.[2] This point about exclusions resembles the objection made many years ago by critics of pluralist theories of liberal democracy.[3] For these critics the public domain is not simply a forum for rational

2. See, for example, Mary P. Ryan, "Gender and Public Access: Women's Politics in Nineteenth-Century America," and Geoff Eley, "Nations, Publics, and Political Cultures: Placing Habermas in the Nineteenth Century," both in Craig Calhoun, ed., *Habermas and the Public Sphere*, Cambridge, Mass.: MIT Press, 1992.

3. Robert Wolff, for example, wrote in 1965: "There is a very sharp distinction in the public domain between legitimate interests and those which are absolutely beyond the pale. If a group or interest is within the framework of acceptability, then it can be sure of winning some measure of what it seeks, for the process of national politics is distributive and compromising. On the other hand, if an interest falls *outside* the circle of the acceptable, it receives no attention whatsoever and its proponents are treated as crackpots, extremists, or foreign agents" (R. P. Wolff, "Beyond Tolerance," in *A Critique of Pure Tolerance*, by R. P. Wolff,

debate but an exclusionary space. It isn't enough to respond to this criticism, as is sometimes done, by saying that although the public sphere is less than perfect as an actual forum for rational debate, it is still an ideal worth striving for. The point here is that the public sphere is a space *necessarily* (not just contingently) articulated by power. And everyone who enters it must address power's disposition of people and things, the dependence of some on the goodwill of others.

Another way of putting it is this. The enjoyment of free speech presupposes not merely the physical ability to speak but *to be heard,* a condition without which speaking to some effect is not possible. If one's speech has no effect whatever it can hardly be said to be in the public sphere, no matter how loudly one shouts. *To make others listen* even if they would prefer not to hear, to speak to some consequence so that something in the political world is affected, to come to a conclusion, to have the authority to make practical decisions on the basis of that conclusion—these are all presupposed in the idea of free public debate as a liberal virtue. But these performatives are not open equally to everyone because the domain of free speech is always shaped by preestablished limits. These include formal legal limitations to free speech in liberal democracies (libel, slander, copyright, patent, and so forth), as well as conventional practices of secrecy (confidentiality) without which politics, business, and morality would collapse in any society. But these examples do not exhaust the limits I have in mind. The limits to free speech aren't merely those imposed by law and convention—that is, by an external power. They are also intrinsic to the time and space it takes to build and demonstrate a particular argument, to understand a particular experience—and more broadly, to become particular speaking and listening subjects. The investment people have in particular arguments is not simply a matter of abstract, timeless logic. It relates to the kind of person one has become, and wants to continue to be. In other words, *there is no public sphere of free speech at an instant.*

Three questions follow. First: Given that historical forces shape elements of "the public" differently, particular appeals can be made successfully only to some sections of the public and not to others. If the perform-

---

B. Moore Jr., and H. Marcuse, London: Cape, 1969 [U.S. edition 1965], p. 52; emphasis in original). William Connolly has pushed this criticism in new and more interesting directions in his *The Ethos of Pluralism,* Minneapolis: University of Minnesota Press, 1995.

ance of free speech is dependent on free listening, its effectiveness depends on the kind of listener who can engage appropriately with what is said, as well as the time and space he or she has to live in. How have different conceptions and practices of religion helped to form the ability of listeners to be publicly responsive? This last question applies not only to persons who consider themselves religious but to those for whom religion is distasteful or dangerous. For the *experience* of religion in the "private" spaces of home and school is crucial to the formation of subjects who will eventually inhabit a particular public culture.[4] It determines not only the "background" by which shared principles of that culture are interpreted, but also what is to count as interpretive "background" as against "foreground" political principles.

My second question is this. If the adherents of a religion enter the public sphere, can their entry leave the preexisting discursive structure intact? The public sphere is not an empty space for carrying out debates. It is constituted by the sensibilities—memories and aspirations, fears and hopes—of speakers and listeners. And also by the manner in which they exist (and are made to exist) for each other, and by their propensity to act or react in distinctive ways. Thus the introduction of new discourses may result in the disruption of established assumptions structuring debates in the public sphere. More strongly: they may *have* to disrupt existing assumptions to be heard. Far from having to prove to existing authority that it is no threat to dominant values, a religion that enters political debate *on its own terms* may on the contrary have to threaten the authority of existing assumptions. And if that is the case, what is meant by demanding that any resulting change must be carried out by moral suasion and negotiation and never by force? After all, "force" includes not only degrees of subtle intimidation but also the dislocation of the moral world people inhabit.

This brings me to a question about the law. Secularists are alarmed at the thought that religion should be allowed to *invade* the domain of our personal choices—although the process of speaking and listening *freely* im-

4. An example of this was made dramatically evident in Turkey early in the summer of 1997, when the secularist army forced the resignation of the coalition government led by the pro-Islamic Welfare Party. The military-backed government that succeeded it has instituted major reforms in an effort to contain the growing resurgence of Islam in the population. A crucial part of these reforms is the formal extension of compulsory secular education for children from five to eight years, a measure designed to stop the growth of Islamic sentiment in the formation of schoolchildren.

plies precisely that our thoughts and actions should be opened up to change by our interlocutors. Besides, secularists accept that in modern society the political increasingly penetrates the personal. At any rate, they accept that politics, through the law, has profound consequences for life in the private sphere. So why the fear of religious intrusion into private life? This partiality may be explained by the doctrine that while secular law permits the essential self to make and defend itself ("our rights constitute us as modern subjects"), religious prescriptions only confine and dominate it. Yet even if we take as unproblematic the assumption that there exists a priori a secular self to be made, the question of coercion in such a constructive task can't easily be brushed aside. For the juridification of all interpersonal relations constrains the scope for moral suasion in public culture. In that context, far from becoming a source of moral values that can enrich public debate, deprivatized religion (where religion has already been defined essentially as a matter of belief) becomes a site of conflict over nonnegotiable rights—for example, the parent's right to determine his or her child's upbringing, or the pregnant woman's right to dispose of her fetus.

One old argument about the need to separate religion from politics is that because the former essentially belongs to the domain of faith and passion, rational argument and interest-guided action can have no place in it. The secularist concedes that religious beliefs and sentiments might be acceptable at a personal and private level, but insists that organized religion, being founded on authority and constraint, has always posed a danger to the freedom of the self as well as to the freedom of others. That may be why some enlightened intellectuals are prepared to allow deprivatized religion entry into the public sphere for the purpose of addressing "the moral conscience" of its audience—but on condition that it leave its coercive powers outside the door and rely only on its powers of persuasion. In a liberal democratic society, as Charles Taylor puts it in his discussion of modes of secularism, citizens belonging to different religious traditions (or to none) will try to persuade one another to accept their view, or to negotiate their values with one another.

The public, however, is notoriously diverse. Modern citizens don't subscribe to a unitary moral system—moral heterogeneity is said to be one of modern society's defining characteristics (even if the modern state does promote a particular ethical outlook). The puzzle here is how a deprivatized religion can appeal effectively to the consciences of those who don't accept its values. And the possibility of negotiation depends on the prior agreement of the parties concerned that the values in question are in fact negotiable. In a modern society such agreement does not extend to all values. The only option religious spokespersons have in that situation is to act as secular politicians do in liberal democracy. Where the latter cannot persuade others to negotiate, they seek to manipulate the conditions in which others act or refrain from acting. And in order to win the votes of constituents they employ a variety of communicative devices to target their desires and anxieties. I will return to the idea that deprivatized religion in a secularized society cannot be any different.

My conclusion so far is that those who advocate the view that the deprivatization of religion is compatible with modernity do not always make it clear precisely what this implies. Is the assumption that by appealing to the conscience of the nation religious spokespersons can evoke its moral sensibilities? The difficulty here is that given the moral heterogeneity of modern society referred to above, nothing can be identified as a national conscience or a collective moral sensibility. So is the assumption then that religious spokespersons can at least enrich public argument by joining in political debates? But even liberal politicians don't merely engage in public talk for the sake of "enriching" it. As members of a government and as parliamentarians they possess the authority to take decisions that are implemented in national policies. What authority do religious spokespersons have in this matter?

Should nationalism be understood as secularized religion?

Is nationalism, with its affirmation of collective solidarity, already a religion of the nation-state? Is that how religious spokespersons can derive their authority in the public sphere, by invoking the national community as though it were also a religious one? There is certainly a long and interesting tradition that suggests nationalism *is* a religion. Thus as far back as 1926 Carlton Hayes remarked that "Nationalism has a large number of particularly quarrelsome sects, but as a whole it is the latest and nearest approach to a world-religion."[5]

Julian Huxley, writing in 1940, maintained that "humanist religion"

5. C. J. H. Hayes, *Essays on Nationalism*, New York, 1926, cited in John Wolffe, *God and Greater Britain: Religion and National Life in Britain and Ireland, 1843–1945*, London and New York: Routledge, 1994, p. 16.

was destined to replace traditional theological religion, and that social movements of a religious nature like Nazism and Communism were evidence of this supersession. Their cruel and repulsive character, he went on to suggest, merely reflected their youthfulness in relation to evolutionary development: "Just as many of these early manifestations of theistic religion were crude and horrible . . . so these early humanist and social religions are crude and horrible."[6] Although Huxley doesn't address the question of nationalism directly, the idea of nationalism as the highest stage of religion conceived within an evolutionary framework is not hard to discern in his text.

More recently, Margaret Jacob has made an argument about the historical connection between secular rituals and the formation of modern political values. She describes how a new pattern of sentiments, beliefs, and ceremonial activities—a "new religiosity"—came to be associated with eighteenth-century Freemasonry, and how it contributed to the emergence of liberal society.[7] "Reason" and "civil society," she proposes, were thus sacralized in the life of early West European nations—and (in her view) a good thing too.

Among anthropologists, Clifford Geertz is famous for having identified the centrality of sacred symbols springing from religious impulses to all forms of political life, nationalist as well as prenationalist, in societies both modern and premodern. The symbolic activities that take place in the center, Geertz suggests, give it "its aura of being not merely important but in some odd fashion connected with the way the world is built." This is why "The gravity of high politics and the solemnity of high worship" are akin.[8] Since Geertz there has been a spate of writing by anthropologists that describe "the deification" of the supreme leader, the promotion of national "icons" and "pilgrimage sites," the solemnity of state "ritual," and so on.

6. Julian Huxley, *Religion without Revelation*, abridged edition, London: Watts and Co., 1941, p. viii.

7. See Margaret C. Jacob, *Living the Enlightenment: Freemasonry and Politics in Eighteenth-Century Europe*, New York: Oxford University Press, 1992, and especially her "Private Beliefs in Public Temples: The New Religiosity of the Eighteenth Century," *Social Research*, vol. 59, no. 1, 1992.

8. Clifford Geertz, *Local Knowledge: Further Essays in Interpretive Anthropology*, New York: Basic Books, 1983, p. 124. See also Robert Bellah, "Civil Religion in America," in *Beyond Belief: Essays on Religion in a Post-Traditional World*, New York: Harper and Row, 1970.

However, I am not persuaded that because national political life depends on ceremonial and on symbols of the sacred, it should be represented as a kind of religion—that it is enough to point to certain parallels with what we intuitively recognize as religion. One problem with this position is that it takes as unproblematic the entire business of defining religion. It does not ask why *particular* elements of "religion" as a concept should be picked out as definitive, and therefore fails to consider the discursive roles they play in different situations. (This kind of definition is what Steiner criticized in his book *Taboo*, mentioned earlier.)

Of course notions of sacredness, spirituality, and communal solidarity are invoked in a variety of ways to claim authority in national politics (sovereignty, the law, national glories and sufferings, the rights of the citizen, and so forth). Critics often point to the words in which these notions are conveyed as signs of "religion." But this evidence is not decisive. I suggest that we need to attend more closely to the historical grammar of concepts and not to what we take as signs of an essential phenomenon. In the first chapter I tried to do this—albeit far too briefly—by looking at "the sacred," "myth," and "the supernatural."

A writer who appears to do the same is Carl Schmitt. Schmitt argues that many theological and political concepts share a common structure. "All significant concepts of the modern theory of the state are secularized theological concepts," he writes, "not only because of their historical development—in which they were transferred from theology to the theory of the state, whereby, for example, the omnipotent God became the omnipotent lawgiver—but also because of their systematic structure, the recognition of which is necessary for a sociological consideration of these concepts. The exception in jurisprudence is analogous to the miracle in theology. Only by being aware of this analogy can we appreciate the manner in which the philosophical ideas of the state developed in the last centuries."[9] Although Schmitt's thesis about the secularization of religious concepts is not about nationalism as such, it does have implications for the way we see it. For if we accept that religious ideas can be "secularized," that secularized concepts retain *a religious essence*, we might be induced to accept that nationalism has a religious origin.

However, my view is that we should focus on the differential results rather than on the corresponding forms in the process referred to as "secu-

9. Carl Schmitt, *Political Theology*, Cambridge, Mass.: MIT Press, 1985 [original, 1934], p. 36.

larization." For example, when it is pointed out that in the latter part of the nineteenth century Tractarianism in England and Ultramontanism in France (and in Europe generally) helped to break the post-Reformation alliance between church and state,[10] and that this was done by deploying religious arguments aimed at securing the freedom of Christ's church from the constraints of an earthly power, we should regard this development as significant not because of the essentialized ("religious") agency by which it was initiated, but because of the difference the outcome yielded. That outcome not only included the development of different moral and political disciplines, such as those that Foucault identified as governmentality.[11] It involved a redefinition of the essence of "religion" as well as of "national politics."

By way of contrast: in later eighteenth-century England, supporters of the established church regarded it as a representative institution reflecting popular sentiment and public opinion. It would not be right to say that religion was then being used for political purposes or influencing state policy. The established church, which was an integral part of the state, made the coherence and continuity of the English national community possible. We should not say that the English nation was *shaped or influenced* by religion: we should see the established church (called "Anglican" only in the nineteenth century) as its *necessary condition*. Nor, given that it was a necessary condition of the nation-state, should we speak of the *social location* of religion in the eighteenth century being different from the one it came to occupy in the late nineteenth and beyond. Rather, the very essence of religion was differently defined, that's to say, in each of the two historical moments different conditions of "religion's" existence were in play. What

10. The constitutional privilege accorded the Church of England in the British state today is largely a formality—and to the extent that it still has material consequences, it is often cited as evidence of Britain's "incompletely modernized" state. See Tom Nairn, *The Break Up of Britain*, London: New Left Books, 1977.

11. Strictly speaking, Foucault doesn't think of discipline as being intrinsic to governmentality but only as something "in tension with it." That's why he speaks of "a triangle, sovereignty-discipline-government, which has as its primary target the population and as its essential mechanism the apparatus of security" (see "Governmentality," in *The Foucault Effect*, ed. G. Burchell, C. Gordon, and P. Miller, Chicago: University of Chicago Press, 1991). I'm not persuaded, however, that discipline can be conceptually separated from governmentality, whose raison-d'être is the management of target populations within nation societies.

we now retrospectively call *the social,* that all-inclusive secular space that we distinguish conceptually from variables like "religion," "state," "national economy," and so forth, *and on which the latter can be constructed, reformed, and plotted,* didn't exist prior to the nineteenth century.[12] Yet it was precisely the emergence of *society* as an organizable secular space that made it possible for the state to oversee and facilitate an original task by redefining religion's competence: the unceasing material and moral transformation of its *entire* national population regardless of their diverse "religious" allegiances. In short, it is not enough to point to the structural analogies between premodern theological concepts and those deployed in secular constitutional discourse, as Schmitt does, because the practices these concepts facilitate and organize differ according to the historical formations in which they occur.[13]

I am arguing that "the secular" should not be thought of as the space in which *real* human life gradually emancipates itself from the controlling power of "religion" and thus achieves the latter's relocation.[14] It is this assumption that allows us to think of religion as "infecting" the secular domain or as replicating within it the structure of theological concepts. The concept of "the secular" today is part of a doctrine called secularism. Secularism doesn't simply insist that religious practice and belief be confined to a space where they cannot threaten political stability or the liberties of "free-thinking" citizens. Secularism builds on a particular conception of the world ("natural" and "social") and of the problems generated by that

12. Mary Poovey notes that "By 1776, the phrase *body politic* had begun to compete with another metaphor, *the great body of the people.* . . . By the early nineteenth century, both of these phrases were joined by the image of the social body" (*Making A Social Body: British Cultural Formation,* Chicago: University of Chicago Press, 1995, p. 7). See also the second chapter, "The Production of Abstract Space."

13. Hans Blumenberg criticizes Schmitt for not taking into account the way theological metaphors are selected and used within particular historical contexts, and therefore for mistaking analogies for transformations. See *The Legitimacy of the Modern Age,* Cambridge, Mass.: MIT Press, 1983 (original, 1973–1976), part I, chapter 8. This point—as also his more extensive critique of Karl Löwith's thesis about the essentially Christian character of the secular idea of progress—is well taken. But I find Blumenberg's delineation and defense of "secularism" rooted firmly as it is in a conventional history-of-ideas approach unconvincing. His relative neglect of *practice* is also remarkable given the nature of his criticism of Schmitt.

14. For an illuminating discussion of this point, see John Milbank's *Theology and Social Theory,* Oxford: Blackwell, 1990.

world. In the context of early modern Europe these problems were perceived as the need to control the increasingly mobile poor in city and countryside, to govern mutually hostile Christian sects within a sovereign territory, and to regulate the commercial, military, and colonizing expansion of Europe overseas.[15]

The genealogy of secularism has to be traced through the concept of the secular—in part to the Renaissance doctrine of humanism, in part to the Enlightenment concept of nature, and in part to Hegel's philosophy of history. It will be recalled that Hegel—an early secularization theorist—saw the movement of world history culminating in the Truth and Freedom of what he called "the modern period." Like later secularists, he held that from the Reformation to Enlightenment and Revolution, there emerged at last a harmony between the objective and subjective conditions of human life resulting from "the painful struggles of History," a harmony based on "the recognition of the Secular as capable of being an embodiment of Truth; whereas it had been formerly regarded as evil only, as incapable of Good—the latter being essentially ultramundane."[16]

In fact the historical process of secularization effects a remarkable ideological inversion, though not quite in the way that Hegel claimed in the sentence just cited. For at one time "the secular" was part of a theological discourse (*saeculum*). "Secularization" (*saecularisatio*) at first denoted a legal transition from monastic life (*regularis*) to the life of canons (*saecularis*)—and then, after the Reformation, it signified the transfer of ecclesiastical real property to laypersons, that is, to the "freeing" of property from church hands into the hands of private owners, and thence into market circulation.[17] In the discourse of modernity "the secular" presents itself as the ground from which theological discourse was generated (as a form of false consciousness) and from which it gradually emancipated itself in its march to freedom. On that ground humans appear as the self-conscious makers of History (in which calendrical time provides a measure and direction for

15. Cf. James Tully, "Governing Conduct," in E. Leites, ed., *Conscience and Casuistry in Early Modern Europe*, Cambridge: Cambridge University Press, 1988. This work is an attempt to apply a Foucauldian perspective to the intellectual history of early modern Europe.

16. G. W. F. Hegel, *The Philosophy of History*, trans. J. Sibree, Buffalo, NY: Prometheus Books, 1991, p. 422.

17. See "Säkularisation, Säkularisierung," in *Geschichtliche Grundbegriffe*, ed. O. Brunner, W. Conze, and R. Koselleck, Stuttgart: E. Klett, 1972–1997, vol. V, pp. 789–830.

human events), and as the unshakable foundation of universally valid knowledge about nature and society. The human as agent is now responsible—answerable—not only for acts he or she has performed (or refrained from performing). Responsibility is now held for events he or she was unaware of—or falsely conscious of. The domain in which acts of God (accidents) occur without human responsibility is increasingly restricted. Chance is now considered to be tamable. The world is disenchanted.

The interesting thing about this view is that although religion is regarded as alien to the secular, the latter is also seen to have generated religion. Historians of progress relate that in the premodern past secular life created superstitious and oppressive religion, and in the modern present secularism has produced enlightened and tolerant religion. Thus the insistence on a sharp separation between the religious and the secular goes with the paradoxical claim that the latter continually produces the former.

Nationalism, with its vision of a universe of national *societies* (the state being thought of as necessary to their full articulation) in which individual humans live their worldly existence requires the concept of the secular to make sense. The loyalty that the individual nationalist owes is directly and exclusively to the nation. Even when the nation is said to be "under God," it has its being only in "this world"—a special kind of world. The men and women of each national society make and *own* their history. "Nature" and "culture" (that famous duality accompanying the rise of nationalism) together form the conditions in which the nation uses and enjoys the world. Mankind dominates nature and each person fashions his or her individuality in the freedom regulated by the nation-state.

One should not take this to mean that the worldliness of the secular members of modern nations is an expression of the truth revealed through the human senses, since senses themselves have a history. However unworldly medieval Christian monks and nuns may have been, they too lived in the world (where else?), but they lived differently in it from laypersons. Allegiance demanded of them was solely to Christ and through him to other Christians. Benedict Anderson quite rightly represents the worldliness of secular nationalism as a specific ideological construct (no less ideological than the one it replaces) that includes in the present an imagined realm of the nation as a community with a "worldly past." And he makes an important point when he draws our attention to the fact that nationalism employs highly abstract concepts of time and space to tell a particular story—even though that story is presented as commonsensical, that is, as accessible to all in the nation—a story about the nation as a natural and self-evident unity whose members share a common experience. This construct is no less real for being ideological; it articulates a world of actual objects and subjects within which the secular nationalist lives. What needs to be emphasized beyond Anderson's famous thesis is that the complex medieval Christian universe, with its interlinked times (eternity and its moving image, and the irruptions of the former into the latter: Creation, Fall, Christ's life and death, Judgment Day) and hierarchy of spaces (the heavens, the earth, purgatory, hell), is broken down by the modern doctrine of secularism into a duality: a world of self-authenticating things in which we *really* live as social beings and a religious world that exists only in our imagination.

To insist that nationalism should be seen as religion, or even as having been "shaped" by religion is, in my view, to miss the nature and consequence of the revolution brought about by modern doctrines and practices of the secular in the structure of collective representations. Of course modern nationalism draws on preexisting languages and practices—including those that we call, anachronistically, "religious." How could it be otherwise? Yet it doesn't follow from this that religion forms nationalism.

We should not accept the mechanical idea of causality always and without question. Thus if we take cause to be about the way an event is "felt" in subsequent events, we will tend to look for the continuity of religious causes in nonreligious effects. But searching in this way for the origin of elements or for the "influence" of events on one another is, I would submit, of limited value here: what requires explaining (how nationalism contains a religious influence) is being used innocently as the means of explanation (religion as at once both cause and effect). If instead we were to attend to an older sense of cause (cause is that which answers to the question "Why?") we would ask about the reformation of historical elements in order to understand why their meaning is no longer what it was. After all, religion consists not only of particular ideas, attitudes, and practices, but of followers. To discover how these followers instantiate, repeat, alter, adapt, argue over, and diversify them (to trace their tradition) must surely be a major task. And so too with secularism. We have to discover what people do with and to ideas and practices before we can understand what is involved in the secularization of theological concepts in different times and places.

Or should Islamism be regarded as nationalism?

Let us take for granted that nationalism is essentially secular (in the sense that it is rooted in human history and society). Can we now argue from the opposite direction and say that some apparently religious movements should be viewed as nationalist, and that they are therefore really secular? Many observers of political Islam have adopted this argument, although in doing so they are in effect simply reversing the terms of the secularization thesis.

To represent the contemporary Islamic revival (known by those who approve of it in the Arab world as *as-sahwa*, "the awakening") as a form of crypto-nationalism,[18] to refer to it explicitly by the term "cultural nationalism,"[19] is to propose that it is best understood as a continuation of the familiar story of Third World nationalism. That proposal renders the claim by Muslim activists to be part of a historical Islamic tradition specious because, as cultural nationalists, they must be seen as part of something essentially (though distortedly) "modern." However, the fact that those active in the revival are usually highly critical of "traditional" teachers and practices does not prove that they are really rejecting tradition. Belonging to a tradition doesn't preclude involvement in vigorous debate over the meanings of its formative texts (even over which texts *are* formative) and over the need for radical reform of the tradition. The selectivity with which people approach their tradition doesn't necessarily undermine their claim to its integrity. Nor does the attempt to adapt the older concerns of a tradition's followers to their new predicament in itself dissolve the coherence of that tradition—indeed that is precisely the object of argument among those who claim to be upholding the essence of the tradition.

All of this is not to say that there is nothing in common between the

18. For example A. Ayalon, "From Fitna to Thawra," *Studia Islamica*, vol. 66, 1987; and N. Keddie, "Islamic Revival as Third Worldism," in J. P. Digard, ed., *Le Cuisinier et le Philosophe: Hommage à Maxime Rodinson*, Paris: Maisonneuve et Larose, 1982.

19. Luciani, reviewing the effect of the Islamic resurgence on modern Middle Eastern politics, observes that "modern Islamic thinking, in avowedly different ways, offers radical answers to contemporary issues. These answers are, in a sense, a form of cultural nationalism, in which religion gives more substance to the rejection of Western domination" (G. Luciani, ed., *The Arab State*, Berkeley: University of California Press, 1990, p. xxx).

motives of Islamists and of Arab nationalists. There are overlaps between the two, notably in their similar stance of opposition against "the West," which has been experienced in the Middle East in the form of predatory nationalisms of the great powers. Because, as individuals, Islamists and nationalists share this position they are sometimes led to seek a common alliance—as happened at the Khartoum international conference of Islamists and Arab nationalists in the aftermath of the Gulf War.[20] However pragmatic and brittle such alliances turn out to be, they presuppose differences that the would-be allies believe should be bridged.

The differences spring from the Islamist project of regulating conduct in the world in accordance with "the principles of religion" (*usul uddin*), and from the fact that the community to be constructed stands counter to many of the values of modern Western life that Arab nationalism endorses. Both these conditions define what one might call contemporary Islamic worldliness. The basic thrust of Arab nationalist ideology is of course supra-denominational (despite its invocations of Islamic history and its concessions to Islamic popular sentiment), and it is committed to the doctrine of separating law and citizenship from religious affiliation and of confining the latter to the private domain. In brief, "religion" is what secular Arabism specifies and tries to set in its proper social place.

For nationalism the history of Islam is important because it reflects the early unification and triumph of the Arab nation; in that discourse the "Arabian Prophet" is regarded as its spiritual hero.[21] This is an inversion of the classical theological view according to which the Prophet is not the ob-

20. The delegates were mostly from countries that had opposed the U.S.-led invasion of Kuwait and Iraq, including Islamist and Marxist currents within the PLO, but oppositional elements from Muslim states that had supported the Americans—such as Egypt and Turkey—also participated (see Majdi Ahmad Husain, "al-mu'tamar ash-sha'bi al-'arabi al-islami: al-fikra, al-mumarasa, ath-thamara," *ash-Sha'b*, May 7, 1991, p. 3).

21. A Christian Arab nationalist writes with admiration of the personality of the Prophet Muhammad, of his strength of conviction and firmness of belief, and concludes: "This is the spiritual message contained in the anniversary of the Arabian Prophet's birth which is addressed to our present national life. It is for this, in spite of their different tendencies and their diverse religions and sects, that the Arab nationalists must honor the memory of Muhammad b. Abdallah, the Prophet of Islam, the unifier of the Arabs, the man of principle and conviction" (Qustantin Zuraiq, *al-wa'i al-qaumi*, Beirut, 1949, cited in S. G. Haim, ed., *Arab Nationalism: An Anthology*, Berkeley: University of California Press, 1962, p. 171).

ject of national inspiration for an imagined community, but the subject of divine inspiration, a messenger of God to mankind and a model for virtuous conduct (*sunna*) that each Muslim, within a Muslim community, must seek to embody in his or her life, and the foundation, together with the Qur'an, of *din* (now translated as "religion"). Nor is Islamic history in the classical view an account of the Arab nation's rise and decline. Classical Islamic chronicles are not "history" in the sense that nationalism claims "it has a history." They grow out of *hadith* accounts (records of the sayings and doings of the Prophet) on which the *sunna* is based, and they articulate a Qur'anic world view as expressed in the political and theological conflicts among the faithful. At any rate it is easy to see that while the "Arab nation" is inconceivable without its history, the Islamic *umma* presupposes only the Qur'an and *sunna*.

The Islamic *umma* in the classical theological view is thus not an imagined community on a par with the Arab nation waiting to be politically unified but a theologically defined space enabling Muslims to practice the disciplines of *din* in the world. Of course the word *umma* does also have the sense of "a people"—and "a community"—in the Qur'an. But the members of every community imagine it to have a particular character, and relate to one another by virtue of it. The crucial point therefore is not that it is imagined but that what is imagined predicates distinctive modes of being and acting. The Islamic *umma* presupposes individuals who are self-governing but not autonomous. The *shari'a*, a system of practical reason morally binding on each faithful individual, exists independently of him or her. At the same time every Muslim has the psychological ability to discover its rules and to conform to them.

The fact that the expression *umma 'arabiyya* is used today to denote the "Arab nation" represents a major conceptual transformation by which *umma* is cut off from the theological predicates that gave it its universalizing power, and is made to stand for an imagined community that is equivalent to a total political society, limited and sovereign like other limited and sovereign nations in a secular (social) world.[22] The *ummatu-l-muslimīn* (the Islamic *umma*) is ideologically not "a society" onto which *state, economy*, and *religion* can be mapped. It is neither limited nor sovereign, for un-

22. The reference here is to Benedict Anderson's definition of the nation: "it is an imagined political community—imagined as both inherently limited and sovereign" (*Imagined Communities: Reflections on the Origin and Spread of Nationalism*, London: Verso, 1983, p. 15).

like Arab nationalism's notion of *al-umma al-'arabiyya*, it can and eventually should embrace all of humanity. It is therefore a mistake to regard it as an "archaic" (because "religious") community that predates the modern nation.[23] The two are grammatically quite different.

I do not mean to imply that the classical theological view is held in all its specificity by individual Islamists. All Muslims today inhabit a different world from the one their medieval forebears lived in, so it cannot be said of any of them that they hold the classical theological view. Even the most conservative Muslim draws on experiences in the contemporary world to give relevance and credibility to his or her theological interpretations. As I indicated above, people who have been called "Islamists" are in many ways close to nationalists even though nationalism had no meaning in the doctrines of the classical theologians. Yet it is evident that "Islamists," as they have been called by observers (to themselves they are simply proper Muslims), relate themselves to the classical theological tradition by translating it into their contemporary political predicament. Of course this relationship isn't articulated identically in different countries, or even within the same country. But the very fact that they must interpret a millennium-old discursive tradition—and, in interpreting it, inevitably disagree with one another—marks them off from Arab nationalists with their Western-derived discourse. For example, the right of the individual to the pursuit of happiness and self-creation, a doctrine easily assimilable by secular nationalist thought, is countered by Islamists (as in classical Islamic theology) by the duty of the Muslim to worship God as laid down in the *shari'a*.

Both Arab nationalism (whether of the "liberal" or the "socialist" variety) and Islamism share a concern with the modernizing state that was put in place by Westernizing power—a state directed at the unceasing material and moral transformation of entire populations only recently organized as "societies."[24] In other words, Islamism takes for granted and seeks to work through the nation-state, which is so central to the predicament of all Muslims. It is this *statist* project and not the fusion of religious and po-

23. Cf. Anderson, p. 40.

24. It's worth noting that the modern Arabic word for "society"—*mujtama'*—gained currency only in the 1930s. (See Jaroslav Stetkevych, *The Modern Arabic Literary Language*, Chicago: University of Chicago Press, 1970, p. 25.) Lane's *Lexicon*, compiled in the mid-nineteenth century, gives only the classical meaning of *mujtama'*: "a meeting place."

litical ideas that gives Islamism a "nationalist" cast. Although Islamism has virtually always succeeded Arab nationalism in the contemporary history of the Middle East, and addressed itself directly to the nation-state, it should not be regarded as a form of nationalism.[25] The "real" motives of Islamists, of whether or not individuals are "using religion for political ends," is not a relevant question here. (The motives of political actors are, in any case, usually plural and often fluctuating.) The important question is what circumstances oblige "Islamism" to emerge publicly as a political discourse, and whether, and if so in what way, it challenges the deep structures of secularism, including its connection with nationalist discourse.

From the point of view of secularism, religion has the option either of confining itself to private belief and worship or of engaging in public talk that makes no demands on life. In either case such religion is seen by secularism to take the form it should properly have. Each is equally the condition of its legitimacy. But this requirement is made difficult for those who wish to reform life given the ambition of the secular state itself. Because the modern nation-state seeks to regulate all aspects of individual life—even the most intimate, such as birth and death—no one, whether religious or otherwise, can avoid encountering its ambitious powers. It's not only that the state intervenes directly in the social body for purposes of reform; it's that all social activity requires the consent of the law, and therefore of the nation-state. The way social spaces are defined, ordered, and regulated makes them all equally "political." So the attempt by Muslim activists to ameliorate social conditions—through, say, the establishment of clinics or schools in underserviced areas—must seriously risk provoking the charge of political illegitimacy and being classified *Islamist*. The call by Muslim movements to reform the social body through the authority of popular majorities in the national parliament will be opposed as "antidemocratic," as in Algeria in 1992 and in Turkey in 1997. Such cases of deprivatized religion are intolerable to secularists primarily because of the *motives* imputed to their opponents rather than to anything the latter have actually done. The motives signal the potential entry of religion into space already occupied by the secular. It is the nationalist secularists themselves,

25. Arguably, the idea of an Islamic state is not identifiable at the beginnings of Islamic history (see my comments on the subject in "Europa contra Islam: De Islam in Europa," in *Nexus*, no. 10, 1994; the English version has been published in *The Muslim World*, vol. 87, no. 2, 1997).

one might say, who stoutly reject the secularization of religious concepts and practices here.

The main point I underline is that Islamism's preoccupation with state power is the result not of its commitment to nationalist ideas but of the modern nation-state's enforced claim to constitute legitimate social identities and arenas. No movement that aspires to more than mere belief or inconsequential talk in public can remain indifferent to state power in a secular world. Even though Islamism is situated in a secular world—a world that is presupposed by, among other things, the universal space of *the social* that sustains the nation-state—Islamism cannot be reduced to nationalism. Many individuals actively involved in Islamist movements *within the Arab world* may regard Arab nationalism as *compatible* with it, and employ its discourse too. But such a stance has in fact been considered inconsistent by many Islamists—especially (but not only) outside the Arab world.[26]

Some outstanding questions

In conclusion, I want to suggest that if the secularization thesis seems increasingly implausible to some of us this is not simply because religion is now playing a vibrant part in the modern world of nations. In a sense what many would anachronistically call "religion" was *always* involved in the world of power. If the secularization thesis no longer carries the conviction it once did, this is because the categories of "politics" and "religion" turn out to implicate each other more profoundly than we thought, a discovery that has accompanied our growing understanding of the powers of the modern nation-state. The concept of the secular cannot do without the idea of religion.

True, the "proper domain of religion" is distinguished from and sep-

26. Thus when a delegate from Jordan at the conference (mentioned in note 20) maintained that disagreements between the aims of the Islamic movement and those of Arab nationalism were relatively minor, and that it was certain that "any movement that is to prevail in our Arab world must be either a nationalist movement incorporating the Islamic perspective with a commitment to democracy and social justice, or an Islamic movement incorporating nationalist perspectives" (Husain, ibid.), his assertion was strongly contested, especially—but not only—by delegates from non-Arab countries who insisted that the only bond between Muslims at present divided among nation-states was Islam.

arated by the state in modern secular constitutions.[27] But formal constitutions never give the whole story. On the one hand objects, sites, practices, words, representations—even the minds and bodies of worshipers—cannot be confined within the exclusive space of what secularists *name* "religion." They have their own ways of being. The historical elements of what come to be conceptualized as religion have disparate trajectories. On the other hand the nation-state requires clearly demarcated spaces that it can classify and regulate: religion, education, health, leisure, work, income, justice, and war. The space that religion may properly occupy in society has to be continually redefined by the law because the reproduction of secular life within and beyond the nation-state continually affects the discursive clarity of that space. The unceasing pursuit of the new in productive effort, aesthetic experience, and claims to knowledge, as well as the unending struggle to extend individual self-creation, undermines the stability of established boundaries.

I do not deny that religion, in the vernacular sense of that word, is and historically has been important for national politics in Euro-America as well as in the rest of the world. Recognition of this fact will no doubt continue to prompt useful work. But there are questions that need to be systematically addressed beyond this obvious fact. How, when, and by whom are the categories of religion and the secular defined? What assumptions are presupposed in the acts that define them? Does the shift from a religious political order to one that is governed by a secular state simply involve the setting aside of divine authority in favor of human law? In the chapter that follows, I try to address this latter question in relation to a particular place and a particular time.

27. Although whether it should be so is contested even in the paradigmatic case of the United States. Thus it is pointed out that the phrase "separation of church and state" is not found in the Constitution, but represents the Supreme Court's interpretation of the founders' intention. See David Barton, *The Myth of Separation*, Aledo, Texas: Wallbuilder Press, 1992.

SECULARIZATION

7

Reconfigurations of Law and Ethics
in Colonial Egypt

At the beginning of this study I proposed that the modern idea of a secular society included a distinctive relation between state law and personal morality, such that religion became essentially a matter of (private) belief—a society presupposing a range of personal sensibilities and public discourses that emerged in Western Europe at different points in time together with the formation of the modern state. Another way of putting this is that the idea of religious toleration that helps to define a state as secular begins with the premise that because belief cannot be coerced, religion should be regarded by the political authorities with indifference as long as it remains within the private domain. The individual's ability to believe what he or she chooses is translated into a legal right to express one's beliefs freely and to exercise one's religion without hindrance—so "religion" is brought back into the public domain. This freedom is qualified, however. The public expression of religious belief and performance of religious ritual must not be a probable cause of a breach of the peace, nor should it be construable as a symbolic affront to the state's personality. Perhaps the most famous examples of this have occurred in recent years in France (see Chapter 5). This indicates that the secular state, like others, is conceived of as a person who can be morally threatened.

In this final chapter I begin with two questions: How did Muslims think about secularism prior to modernity? What do Muslims today make of the idea of the secular? In contemporary polemics about the proper place of religion in Egypt several writers have claimed that secular life was always central in the past, and seen to be such, because religious law (that is, the *shari'a*) always occupied a restricted space in the government of society.[1] But the issue here is not an empirical one. It will not be resolved simply by more intensive archival research, just as understanding the place of the secular today requires more than mere ethnographic fieldwork, and more than a vigorous defense of its value for the political world we inhabit. A careful analysis is needed of culturally distinctive concepts and their articulation with one another. So in what follows I shall focus on Egypt in the late nineteenth and early twentieth century, a period in which significant shifts occurred in the relations between law, religion, and morality. So in spite of the questions with which I begin, I shall refer to premodern concepts and contemporary discourses briefly—and then only in order to draw certain contrasts.

One clue to how the secular was thought before the involvement of Egyptian history with the history of the modern West is found in nineteenth-century attempts to translate the term "secular" and its cognates into Arabic. The commonest word used today for the adjectives "secular" and "lay" as well as for "secularist" and "layman" is *'almāniyy*.[2] This latter word, now the most commonly used, was invented in the latter part of the nineteenth century. (There is no entry for it or for any of its cognates in Lane's *Arabic-English Lexicon* compiled in Egypt in the first half of the nineteenth century.) The word yields the abstract noun *'almāniyyah* to mean "secularism" or "laicism."

1. See, e.g., Muhammad Nur Farhat, *al-Mujtama' wa al-shari'a wa al-qānūn*, Cairo: Al-Hilal 1986, p. 39.

2. The only relevant entry in *Muhīt al-Muhīt* (the first modern Arabic-Arabic dictionary, published in Beirut in 1870) is *'almāniyy*, which it renders as nonclerical and which it derives from *al-'ālam*, the world. Thus the Arabic-English *Al-Mawrid* (8th edition, 1996) gives the following: "secular, lay, laic(al); secularist; layman" for *'almāniyy*; "secularism, laicism" for *'almāniyyah*; "to secularize, laicize" for *'almana*; and "secularization, laicization" for *'almanah* [the nominal form derived from the invented verb]. *'Almanah* is also equated with *'almāniyyah*. The relative recency of this concept is also reflected in the fact that *The Oxford English-Arabic Dictionary of Current Usage* (1972) gives *'ilmāniyy* and not the now standard *'almāniyy* for "secular." The former is still used conversationally—often provoking pedantic attempts at correction—and its popularity may in part be due to the implicit suggestion that the concept of "secularism" is related to *'ilm*, meaning "knowledge" and "science," in contrast to "religion." Indeed Ahmad Hatum in his "'ilmaniyyah bi-kasr al-'ayn la bi-fathiha" (*al-Nāqid*, vol. 44, no. 20, 1990) distinguishes interestingly between the two forms.

Badger's *English-Arabic Lexicon*, published in 1881, gives two words for "secular" in the sense of "lay, not clerical": *'almāniyy* and *'āmmiyy*. But the latter carries the senses of "common," "vulgar," "popular," and "ordinary." Badger also renders "secular," in the sense of "worldly," as *dunyāwiyy* (and *dunyawiyy*). It has no entry for "secularism," but under "secularity" it gives *hubbu al-'ālam* (literally, "love of the world") as well as *dunyāwiyyah* (the abstract noun from the word for "worldly"), and *'ālamiyyah*, on the same pattern, derived from the word *'ālam*, meaning "world" or "logical universe." The latter occurs in the familiar Qur'anic epithet for God, *rabb al-'ālamīn*, "Lord of the two worlds" (namely, the world of men and the world of jinns [spirits]). But *'ālamiyyah* also signified "the state of knowledge," that is to say of Islam, as opposed to *jāhiliyya*, "the state of ignorance" or "paganism.[3] In contemporary usage *'ālamiyyah* signifies "internationalism" not "secularism" or "secularity," although the adjectival form *'ālamiyy* does also carry the sense of "worldly" and "secular."

The response of Egyptians to the concept of secularism, their attempt to further it or attack it, was mediated by this work of translation. Thus in the nineteenth century the verbal form "to secularize" had no single Arabic equivalent. It is only very recently that the verb *'almana* was invented by working backward from the abstract noun *'almāniyyah*. (The normal procedure in Arabic is for the verbal root form to yield qualifiers and substantives.) More interesting is the fact that the verbal form was restricted to a legal sense indicating transfer of property—as in the Reformation sense of *saecularisatio* (secularization) mentioned in Chapter 5. Thus the process of "secularization" was rendered *tahwīl al-awqāf wa al-amlāk al-mukhtassa bi al-'ibāda wa al-diyāna ila al-aghrād 'ālamiyyah*[4]—literally, "the transfer to worldly purposes of endowments and properties pertaining to worship and religion." One problem with that was that a *waqf* (normally translated as a "religious endowment") might have a "religious or devotional purpose" (if it was a mosque, say), but more often than not it had no such purpose (as in the case of agricultural lands), or, more commonly, several purposes, "religious" and "nonreligious" (hospitals and schools, for example). *Waqf* (plural *awqāf*) was simply the sole form of inalienable property in the *sharī'a*, described by Max Weber and others as "sacred law." The Hanafi school

3. See Kazimirski's *Dictionnaire Arabe-Français*, revised and corrected by Ibed Gallab, volume 3, Cairo, 1875.

4. Badger, *English-Arabic Lexicon*, p. 937.

of law, followed in Egypt, defines the endowment of a *waqf* as (1) the extinction of the founder's right and the transfer of ownership to God, (2) that therefore becomes perpetual and irrevocable, and (3) which is devoted to the benefit of mankind.

In Europe, the word "secularism" denoting the doctrine that morality, national education, the state itself, should not be based on religious principles, dates from the middle of the nineteenth century[5]—as does the French "laïcisme" ("the doctrine that gives institutions a non-religious character").[6] The French expression "laïcisme" draws on the Jacobin experience, one that authorizes a stronger, more aggressive secularism (including hostility toward the presence of some "religious symbols" in state institutions) than the British equivalent does. There are therefore significant national differences in the way "secularism" is understood in Europe corresponding to different political histories. But by and large these are family differences: they articulate particular struggles over whether religious doctrines and communal morality—in their historical variety—should be allowed to affect the formation of public policy. So although both the concept and word were available in nineteenth-century Western Europe— used in connection with different institutions and politics—no attempt was made at that time to supply an Arabic word. Of course, this verbal lack does not in itself prove that Egyptians in the nineteenth century had no conception of "secularism." It does indicate, however, that political discourse in Arabic did not need to deal directly with it as it has since then. In this sense, secularism did not exist in Egypt prior to modernity.

What made its existence possible? In this chapter I try to trace some changes in the concept of the law in colonial Egypt that helped to make secularism thinkable as a practical proposition. I focus on some of the ways that legal institutions, ethics, and religious authority became transformed, my purpose being to identify the emergence of social spaces within which "secularism" could grow. I start by recounting the well-known story of the gradual narrowing of *sharīʿa* jurisdiction (that is, a restriction of the scope of "religious law") and the simultaneous importation of European legal codes. This process has been represented by historians as the triumph of the rule of law, or as the facilitation of capitalist exploitation, or as the complex struggle for power between different kinds of agent—especially

5. See *The Oxford English Dictionary*.
6. See *Dictionnaire alphabétique et analogique de la langue française*.

colonizing Europeans and resisting Egyptians. Each of these perspectives may have something to be said for it, but my concern here is with something else: with exploring precisely what is involved when conceptual changes in a particular country make "secularism" thinkable.

I therefore look briefly at the wider context of cultural change and Islamic reform, and I point to the importance of the modern state for these developments. In this context the state is not a cause but an articulation of secularization. I stress that I do not aim at a total history of legal reform, although my focus is on the reform of the *shariʿa*, regarded by would-be reformers as a religious law that is largely inappropriate for a modern society. So I do a reading of a report on the reform of the *shariʿa* court system written by the highly influential Islamic reformer Muhammad Abduh in 1899 to examine the ways in which it reflects the new spaces of a modernizing state. I then do the same for Qasim Amin's famous book on the legal emancipation of women, and for the writings of the lawyer Ahmad Safwat who, as early as the second decade of the twentieth century, proposed principles for the reform of the *shariʿa* crucial to the constitution of a secular state. Safwat is not as well known or influential a figure as Abduh—or even Abduh's friend Amin. Indeed, his work is little known today. But his attempt to think through separate domains for state-administered law and religiously derived morality is highly instructive for understanding a space necessary to the secularizing impulse. The separation presupposes a very different conception of ethics from the one embedded in the classical *shariʿa*. That is why my reading of Safwat's texts is followed by a discussion of the relation between law and ethics in classical Islamic jurisprudence (*fiqh*). And why I return from this digression into classical thought to an analysis of connections between ritual worship (*ʿibādāt*)—as stipulated in the rules of the *shariʿa*—and the authority of the religious law. This returns me to another aspect of Muhammad Abduh's discourse.

My interest in the texts I deal with is not in the influence they may have had on social and legal reform but in the arguments they display. I claim that the shifts in these texts reflect reconfigurations of law, ethics, and religious authority in a particular Muslim society that have been ignored by both secularists and Islamists.

The story of law reform

Egypt in the nineteenth century was formally part of the Ottoman empire but it possessed a large measure of political autonomy.[7] Internal order in the Ottoman empire during the nineteenth century was maintained by a variety of institutions—the police, inspectors of markets, the ruler's court of complaints, and so on. *Shari'a* courts had primary jurisdiction over urban Muslims,[8] rural tribes followed customary rules and procedures (*'urf*),[9] and *milliyya* courts were regulated by and for the various sects of Christians and Jews.[10] Hence *shari'a* courts were by no means the only form of law administration.[11] Indeed, the ruler had his own body of administrative law (*qanūn*) that did not draw its authority from the *shari'a*. From the mid-nineteenth century on, a series of progressive legal reforms was carried out in the empire under the rubric of the *tanzīmāt* (the Commercial Code was issued in 1850, the Penal Code in 1858, the Commercial Procedure Code in 1861, and the Maritime Commerce Code in 1863) that involved the wholesale adoption of European codes. The first attempt in the Ottoman empire to codify the *shari'a*, known as the *majalla*, was pub-

7. For a standard Western account of nineteenth-century legal changes, see J. N. D. Anderson, *Islamic Law in the Modern World*, London: Stevens & Sons, 1959. For a recent sketch, see Rudolph Peters, "Islamic and Secular Criminal Law in Nineteenth-Century Egypt: The Role and Function of the Qadi," *Islamic Law and Society*, vol. 4, no. 1, 1997.

8. See Muhammad Nur Farahat, *al-Tārikh al-ijtimā'i li al-qānūn fi misr al-hadītha*, Cairo, 1993.

9. See *'URF* in *Encyclopaedia of Islam*.

10. See George N. Sfeir, "The Abolition of Confessional Jurisdiction in Egypt: The Non-Muslim Courts," *Middle East Journal*, vol. 10, no. 3, 1956.

11. Recent research into eighteenth- and nineteenth-century Ottoman archives seems to show that the administration of justice for non-Muslims was much more fluid and complicated than previously thought. On the one hand, evidence for the existence of full-fledged communal courts is exiguous; on the other hand there is copious evidence of Christians and Jews resorting voluntarily to *shari'a* courts. This was strikingly the case for non-Muslim women who turned to these courts in matters relating to marriage, divorce, and inheritance, because there the *shari'a* was often more favorable to them than the rules followed in their own religious communities. See Najwa al-Qattan, "Dhimmis in the Muslim Court: Legal Autonomy and Religious Discrimination," *International Journal of Middle East Studies*, vol. 31, 1999.

lished over a period of seven years, from 1870 to 1877. Officially it had jurisdiction throughout the empire, but in fact it was never effective in Egypt.[12] There the formal control of Egypt's national budget by the European powers, to whom it had become heavily indebted, very quickly led (in 1876) to the introduction of a civil code for the Mixed Courts of Egypt—an autonomous institution administered by European judges by which European residents (over one percent of the population at the end of the nineteenth century) were legally governed in all matters including their interactions with Egyptians (thus disputes between natives and Europeans always fell under the jurisdiction of the Mixed Courts). A code for *sharīʿa* courts was promulgated in 1880 and substantially amended in 1887. In 1883, a year after the British Occupation of Egypt, a modified version of the code used in the Mixed Courts was compiled for the National (*ahliyya*) Courts, both codes being based mainly on the Napoleonic Code. On the other hand, courts administering *sharīʿa* law, often described by European historians as "religious courts," were deprived of jurisdiction over criminal and commercial cases and confined to administering family law and pious endowments (*awqāf*). The so-called "secular courts" (both Mixed and National) had jurisdiction over the rest.[13] The bureaucratization of the *sharīʿa* courts (that is, the introduction of an appellate system, a new emphasis on documentation in judicial procedure as well as the authorization of written codes) drew on Western principles and incorporated the *sharīʿa* into the modernizing state. The march from premodern chaos to modern order was initiated by Europeans and overseen at first by them and later by Europeanized Egyptians.[14] Law began to disentangle itself from the dictates of

12. See S. S. Onar, "The Majalla," in *Law in the Middle East*, ed., M. Khadduri and H. J. Liebesny, Washington, D.C.: The Middle East Institute, 1955. In *al-Sharīʿa al-islāmiyya wa al-qanūn al-wadʿi*, Cairo: Dar al-Sharuq, 1996, p. 15, Tariq al-Bishri mentions that there were attempts to codify the *sharīʿa* in the sixteenth and seventeenth centuries.

13. It may be noted, incidentally, that Fathi Zaghlul, in his influential history of the legal profession in the nineteenth century entitled *al-Muhāmā* (Cairo, 1900), does not write of *al-mahākim al-dīniyya wa al-ʿalmāniyya* but of *mahākim al-sharʿiyya wa al-madaniyya*—that is, not "religious and secular courts" but "*sharīʿa* and civil courts." By the time we get to the 1930s we find the term *mahākim zamaniyya* (literally "temporal" courts) being used explicitly, as by Hamid Zaki (see note 17).

14. A summary statement of "the progress made in the administration of justice" in Egypt under British tutelage is contained in John Scott, "Judicial Re-

religion, becoming thereby both more modern and more secular. In 1955, under Jamal Abdul Nasir, the dual structure of the courts was finally abolished.[15] This unification and extension of state power, and the accompanying triumph of European-derived codification, have together been seen as part of Egypt's secularization and its progress toward "the rule of law."

Why *this* reform?

The story historians tell is of course more complex, deals with particular times and places, and has resort to the motives (declared or inferred) of actors in a changing political field. But what interests me are the categories used in the story, and the attempts to explain aspects of it through them—such as "agency," "tradition," "subjectivity," "ethics," "freedom."

The massive process of Westernization is not in dispute among historians of modern Egypt. A question that is in some dispute, however, is why the reformers looked to Europe rather than build on preexisting *shari'a* traditions. The Egyptian jurist Tariq al-Bishri contends that what he calls the mimicry of the West was the outcome of a combination of circumstances, chief among them European coercion and the Egyptian elites' infatuation with European ways.[16] Bishri seems to me to have a better

---

form in Egypt," *Journal of the Society of Comparative Legislation*, no. 2, July 1899. Sir John Scott, who was charged by Lord Cromer, the British consul-general, with overseeing these reforms, repeats the colonial notion that "until recently there was no such thing as native justice" (p. 240). This view was then taken up by Egyptian progressivists as well

15. John Anderson writes that "In Egypt the reason given for the abolition of both the *Shari'a* courts and the community courts of the various Christian and Jewish sects was the unsatisfactory nature of some of their judgments and procedure; but there can be little doubt that behind this lay—naturally enough—a general predilection for bureaucratic unification" (J. N. D. Anderson, "Modern Trends in Islam: Legal Reform and Modernisation in the Middle East," *International and Comparative Law Quarterly*, vol. 20, 1971, p. 17).

16. "When we look at the closing years of the nineteenth century and the opening years of the twentieth, we are struck by names applied to what they do not mean. Thus altering legal organizations so as to accommodate them to the West was called 'reform', although 'reform' means the removal of corruption, that is, continuity together with improvement. It does not mean radical change and substitution. Thus taking from the old (*al-qadim*) was called 'imitation' (*taqlid*),

sense of the contingent character of the changes brought about by the encounter with Europeans than many historians, Western and Egyptian, who narrate Europeanization as the story of true civilization.[17]

So how is one to understand the Egyptian elites' adoption of European models of law? Sa'id Ashmawi, ex-judge of the Appeal Court, writes that the assumption of a foreign law having been imported into Egypt is wrong. Roman law, he explains, was a synthesis of various customs, conventions, and laws prevailing in the empire (including Rome itself of course, as well as West Asia and North Africa) that was codified in the Institutes of Justinian in 533 C.E. Thus Roman law, says Ashmawi, has a great deal in common with Islamic law and jurisprudence (*fiqh*) because it provided a foundation for the latter.[18] When Napoleon Bonaparte charged the lawmakers of France to draw up a civil code they turned naturally to the Institutes of Justinian to devise what came to be known as the Napoleonic Code. And when the Egyptian lawmakers intended in 1883 to modernize the judicial system and legal style, they noticed that Islamic jurisprudence was not properly organized and categorized, and that legal procedure and judgment lacked adequate method and system. So they translated French compilations into Arabic, and with some slight modifications this became Egyptian law.[19] "But Egyptian law is neither French nor Roman," insists Ashmawi, "meaning that it does not contain principles foreign to Egyptian society or remote from the Islamic *shari'a*, or it would have been impossible to apply it so successfully for more than a century, implanting the principles of justice and ensuring social peace and security."[20] Even if these generalizations regarding the Roman origins of both the Napoleonic Code

---

while taking from the West was called 'renewal' (*tajdīd*) and innovation (*ibdā'*)— despite the fact that it was precisely taking from the West that was mere mimicry (*al-muhākā*). For when someone mimics he doesn't mimic himself but another, so that the term 'imitation' is applied more appropriately to taking over something from another" (Tariq al-Bishri, *al-Hiwār al-islāmi al-'almāni*, Cairo: Dar al-Sharuq, 1996, p. 9).

17. Thus the lawyer Hamid Zaki, in arguing for the reform of personal status law, refers repeatedly to European societies as "civilized countries," implying perhaps that Egypt was not quite one of them yet ("*al-Mahākim al-ahliyya wa al-ahwāl al-shakhsiyya*," *Majallat al-qānūn wa al-iqtisād*, December 1934).

18. Sa'id al-'Ashmawi, *al-Sharī'a al-islāmiyya wa al-qānūn al misrī*, Cairo: Maktabat Madbuli al-Saghir, 1996, pp. 32–33.

19. Ibid., p. 36.

20. Ibid., p. 37.

and the *shari'a* were correct, this denial of *difference* makes it impossible to understand the specific implications of importing modern European codes into nineteenth-century Egypt for law and morality. This is crucial, in my view, for understanding secularism, a doctrine that is not Roman but modern.

Nathan Brown, the author of an excellent history of law in the modern Arab world, has complained that "much recent scholarship continues to assert that the basic contours of legal systems were laid by the metropole, local imperial officials, and expatriate populations. . . . This view, centered as it is on the motives and actions of the imperial power, should cause some discomfort because it risks writing the population of much of the world out of its own history."[21] Thus Brown argues that contrary to the repeated nationalist claim that the Mixed Courts were imposed because of the capitulations, the Mixed Courts were in fact a means by which a partially independent Egyptian government sought to limit the capitulations.[22] *This* motivation, he says, should be attributed to the entire movement of legal reform along European lines because the latter can be seen as a tool for resisting direct European penetration.[23]

But the motives were surely more diverse—especially in different periods. For example, when Muhammad Ali initiated certain penal reforms on the European model in the first few decades of the nineteenth century, he was not doing this to resist European penetration but to consolidate his own control over the country's administration of justice: "Europeans are people who conduct their affairs properly," he noted, "and they have found an easy way of solving every matter of concern, so we must emulate them (*wa nahnū majbūrīn al-iqtidā bihim*)."[24] By the time of his grandson Ismail, this utilitarian reason for imitating Europeans is joined by others: "Our parliament is a school," declares Nubar Pasha proudly in Paris, "by means of which the government, being more advanced than the popula-

21. Nathan Brown, "Law and Imperialism: Egypt in Comparative Perspective," *Law and Society Review*, vol. 29, no. 1, 1995, pp. 104–5.

22. See also Byron Cannon, *Politics of Law and the Courts in Nineteenth Century Egypt*, Salt Lake City: University of Utah Press, 1988, pp. 37–61.

23. Brown, p. 115. But Rudolph Peters disagrees: "The wholesale reception of foreign law in Egypt beginning in 1883 must . . . be attributed to strong foreign pressure" (R. Peters, "Islamic and Secular Criminal Law in Nineteenth-Century Egypt: The Role and Function of the Qadi," *Islamic Law and Society*, vol. 4, no. 1, 1997, p. 78).

24. Cited in Fathi Zaghlul, *al-Muhāmā*, p. 183.

tion, instructs and civilizes that population."[25] The attempt at explaining major social changes in terms of motives is always a doubtful business.

In 1882, immediately after the British Occupation, Husayn Fakhri Pasha, the new minister of justice, wrote a memorandum arguing that a *sharīʿa*-based code would not be consistent with the arrangements to which Egyptians were accustomed, and urged that the laws then being applied in the Mixed Courts should be adopted by the National Courts.[26] The notion that such laws would be more suitable for Egyptians than anything that might be based on the *sharīʿa* represents an aspiration for a Westernized future rather than for a reformed continuity of the recent past. As a supporter of the importation of European codes, Fakhri knows that the function of law is not merely to reflect social life but also to reconstruct it—if necessary by force and against all opposition. For all his talk about making the law conform to the prevailing conditions of society, he knows that European law will help to create the modern conditions to which Islamic law must then adapt itself. Whether that knowledge was central to what motivated him is another matter. For whatever the *motives* impelling him and others to draw on European codes, the result was to help create new spaces for Islamic religion and morality.

25. In order to impress the European powers, who were also his creditors, Ismail convened an advisory chamber of delegates (the Majlis Shura al-Nuwwab) in 1866. While this "was meant to ensure Egypt a place among the 'civilized' countries, within Egypt it was intended as a 'civilizing' instrument. Nubar [Ismail's foreign minister] declared to the French Foreign Minister in December 1866 that 'notre parlement est une école au moyen de laquelle le gouvernement, plus avance que la population, instruit et civilise cette population.'" (A. Schölch, *Egypt for the Egyptians! The socio-political crisis in Egypt, 1878–82*, London: Ithaca, 1981, p. 15). It was Nubar who originated the idea of the Mixed Courts (see J. Y. Brinton, *The Mixed Courts of Egypt*, rev. ed., New Haven: Yale University Press, 1968, chapter 1).

26. Fakhri's implicit reference is to the previous minister of justice, Muhammad Qadri Pasha, who had attempted to codify the *sharīʿa*. "Is it really possible," Fakhri writes, "to apply [the *sharīʿa*] on the inhabitants [of this country] given that their customs and their dealings at present with one another or with Europeans are governed by the Civil Code that settles disputes over sale, rent, ownership, and the like?" ("*Mudhakkirāt hussayn fakhrī bāshā nāzir al-haqqāniyya li majlis al-nuzzār*," in *Al-kitāb al-dhahabi li al-mahākim al-ahliyya*, vol. 1 [1883–1933], Cairo: Bulaq Press, 1937, p. 112). In effect, Fakhri's argument in the memorandum is that legal changes in Egypt have gone too far to talk of "returning" to a reformed *sharīʿa*—and anyway, the European codes are superior.

The notion of resistance is attractive to historians and anthropologists who wish to give subordinated peoples what they think of as "their own agency." (See Chapter 2.) In the context of Egypt's colonial history the notion allows for the argument that European reforms were not imposed on helpless agents but used by them. However, the notion we are presented with is obscure, for sometimes resistance to the reforms is described as "rigidity and reaction," at other times it is attributed to the fear that material interests are being threatened.[27] How good are such explanations? Talk of reactionaries merely invokes a metaphysic of teleological progress and as such is no explanation at all. Reference to the resisters' material motives is in principle an explanation, although a reductive one. It does not account for opposition to the reform by those who had nothing material to lose by it. More generally, it raises problems that all explanations in terms of attributed motives encounter, but fails to address them.

What is frequently missed in such attempted explanations, however, is that since the idea of "resistance" implies the presence of intrusive power, proper attention must be paid to what that power consists of, what intrusive power seeks when it seeks "improvement"—in short, one must ask what acts one is confronted with and how they are fitted into a larger figure. If "imperialism" is thought of as the term for an actor contingently connected to acts, for a player calculating what his next move should be in a game whose stakes are familiar to all participants, and whose rules are accepted by them, then one may talk of agents seeking to strategize and of others resisting that strategy. If, on the other hand, imperialism is regarded not as an already constituted agent who acts in a determinate way but as the totality of forces that converge to create (largely contingently) a new moral landscape that defines different kinds of act, then one should certainly not say, as some now do, that "imperialism was a far weaker force for legal reform than has generally been assumed to be the case."[28] The basic question here, in my view, is not the determination of "oppressors" and "oppressed," of whether the elites or the popular masses were the agents in

27. Farhat Ziadeh mentions resistance on the part of advocates in the 1930s: "In controversies that pertained to religious or quasi-religious matters *shari'ah* advocates tended to rigidity and reaction." Furthermore, "Appeals to religion were sometimes utilized in fighting the inroads into jurisdiction of the *shari'a* courts, and hence the livelihood of its advocates" (*Lawyers, the Rule of Law and Liberalism in Modern Egypt*, Stanford: Stanford University Press, 1968, pp. 58 and 59, respectively).

28. Nathan Brown, *The Rule of Law in the Arab World*, Cambridge, 1997, p. 18.

the history of reform (both, of course, in various ways participated in the changes). It is the determination of that new landscape, and the degree to which the languages, behaviors, and institutions it makes possible come to resemble those that obtain in the West European nation-states. This approach requires some reference to the necessities and potentialities of modernity (or "civilization") as these were presented by Europeans and interpreted by Egyptians.

Arguments about the defensive character of legal reforms are not new. The numerous reforms initiated by the Ottomans since the eighteenth century have long been described in precisely that way. My interest, however, is not in speculating about an old motive (resistance) but about new institutional and discursive spaces (themselves not immutably fixed) that make different kinds of knowledge, action, and desire possible. That the results of these changes were not exactly European has also long been recognized, but there are two ways of looking at this outcome: either (as the majority of historians have claimed) as evidence of "a failure to modernize properly," or (and this is just beginning to be proposed)[29] as expressions of different experiences rooted in part in traditions other than those to which the European-inspired reforms belonged, and in part in contradictory European representations of European modernity.

(By contradictory representations of modernity I refer, for example, to this: Whereas Max Weber wrote that the *sharī'a* was primitive because it lacked the criteria given to modern law by rational authority,[30] Anglo-American jurists had no hesitation in regarding English common law *modern* even though it did not embody the Weberian criteria of legal rationality. In other words, there is no consensus on what the decisive criteria are

29. My point here should not be confused with the rebuttal of the "Eastern-stagnation-versus-Western-development" thesis now being mounted by many historians of Asian countries. To argue that there were indigenous roots of modern development in the latter does not in itself interrogate the criteria by which "modern development" is described. That industrialization and modernization are to be seen as global processes that transform all component units differentially does not shift from the idea of teleological history. For a subtle study that does attempt to do just that, however, see Dipesh Chakrabarty's *Provincializing Europe; Postcolonial Thought and Historical Difference*, Princeton: Princeton University Press, 2000.

30. Weber derived his understanding of Islamic law largely from the Dutch orientalist Snouck Hurgronje, who was closely involved with projects of law reform in colonial Indonesia.

for regarding particular forms of law "modern" *in* the West. There "modernity"—like secularism, which is said to be part of the latter—is located in an argument about the importance of particularity. Even in the context of Western-dominated Egypt, European codes arrived as *exceptions* applicable only to particular categories of subject and not as *universal* law applicable to everyone.)

Brown connects the legal reforms with the needs of what he calls "centralization and state building."[31] Certainly the state's appropriation of the domain of criminal law, its monopolization of the definition of categories of crime—and of the treatment of criminals—was part of this process.[32] But there was more at work here than a single project of increasing state power. There was also the question of how liberal governance (political, moral, and theological) was to be secured during the different phases of state building and dismantling—of how, according to many reformers, liberty, modernity, and civilized life were to be achieved. It was in response to that question that the law had to acquire new substance and new functions and to employ new kinds of violence. For colonial punishment—the institution of a police force and a prison system—was central to the modernization and secularization of law in Egypt.[33] And it gradually replaced previous forms of violence.

Reforming Islam by reforming its law

The secularization of the law in Egypt has not only involved the circumscription and reform of the *sharīʿa*, it has been deeply entangled with the nineteenth-century reformulation of Islamic tradition generally. So before I proceed with the analysis of my texts I consider aspects of that reform.

Reinhard Schulze once asked a question most historians have taken for granted: Why did nineteenth-century Islamic reformers take so eagerly

31. Brown, pp. 56–60.

32. For example, in homicide cases, as Rudolph Peters points out, "according to the Sharia, the next of kin of the victim can play an active role in the proceedings, whereas, according to the secular, Western type laws, they are left out of the trial, unless summoned as witnesses" (R. Peters, "Murder on the Nile," *Die Welt des Islams*, vol. 30, 1990, p. 116.

33. See Harold Tollefson, *Policing Islam: The British Occupation of Egypt and the Anglo-Egyptian Struggle over Control of the Police, 1882–1914*, Westport, CT: Greenwood, 1999.

to the European interpretation of Islamic history as one of "civilizational decadence"?[34] The interesting answer he gives refers to political economic changes as well as to the cultural consequences of print. European capitalism, he points out, transformed the eighteenth-century mode of surplus extraction through rent into a system of unequal exchange between metropole and colony. Because the traditional forms of political legitimation were now no longer appropriate to the colonial situation, he argues, a new ideological need was created—and eventually met by the indigenous elite that emerged out of the social-economic disintegration of the old society and of the effects of print on its culture. European historical reason (including the notion of an Islamic Golden Age followed by a secular decline under the Ottomans) was adopted by the new elites, he suggests, via books from and about Europe, as well as the Islamic "classics" selected for printing by European orientalists and by Westernized Egyptians. That civilizational discourse could now be used, concludes Schulze, to legitimize the claim to equality and independence.

Ijtihād (a term used by earlier Muslim scholars to refer to independent legal reasoning on matters about which they were not in agreement) was made to mean the general exercise of free reason, or independent opinion, directed against *taqlīd* (the unreflective reproduction of tradition) and in the cause of progressive social reform. This extension of the sense of *ijtihād* has been commented on critically by generations of orientalists. Thus Charles Adams writes that "In orthodox Islam, the right of 'ijtihad' (independent opinion) in matters of law and religion, belonged only to the great masters of the early generations and has consequently not existed since the third century A.H. [ninth century C.E.]. Muhammad 'Abduh and his followers have, however, claimed this right for the present generation, as for every other, so that Islam, and particularly its legal system, may be adapted to present-day requirements."[35] And Aharon Layish pronounces on the intellectual inadequacy of Muhammad Abduh, Rashid Rida, and their followers: "the modernists did not succeed in shaping a new legal doctrine amalgamating Islam with liberal elements of Western civilization. Their attempt to improve the doctrine of selection and reopen the gates of

34. Reinhard Schulze, "Mass Culture and Islamic Cultural Production in 19th Century Middle East," in *Mass Culture, Popular Culture, and Social Life in the Middle East*, ed. G. Stauth and S. Zubaida, Boulder, CO: Westview, 1987.

35. Charles Adams, *Islam and Modernism in Egypt*, London: Oxford University Press, 1933, p. 70, n. 1.

ijtihād by refashioning traditional mechanisms was immature, unauthoritative and unenduring. Their efforts were not continued, at any rate not by the authorized exponents of the *sharī'a*."[36] Since it was precisely the "authorized exponents of the *sharī'a*" that Abduh and Rida sought to dislodge (and in some measure succeeded in dislodging) it is evident that Layish's critique—and others like it[37]—operates with an a priori concept of "orthodox Islam." Yet this concept seems to me misplaced in the discourse of scholars who aim to write a history of Islamic tradition. It belongs to religious dispute between reformers (who invoke the authority of the text over that of the interpretive community) and conservatives (for whom authority is vested in the community of interpreters, the keepers of texts), because both of them are committed to doing certain things *to* what they regard as the essential tradition.

In short, there is no such thing as "real" *ijtihād* waiting to be authenticated by orientalist method; there is only *ijtihād* practiced by particular persons who situate themselves in various ways within the tradition of *fiqh*. When Abduh and Rida draw explicitly on the precedence of the medieval theologian and jurist Ibn Taymiyya, who employed *ijtihād* to criticize the status quo of his time, they are invoking a tradition of several centuries— albeit in very changed circumstances—and not simply "refashioning [namely, departing from the legitimate uses of] traditional mechanisms." *That* tradition does not consist in employing the principle of universal reason. It provides specific material for reasoning—a theological vocabulary and a set of problems derived from the Qur'an (the divine revelation), the *sunna* (the Prophet's tradition), and the major jurists (that is, those cited as authoritative) who have commented on both—about how a contemporary state of affairs should be configured. Since *ijtihād* comes into operation precisely when *ijmā'* (the consensus of scholars) has failed, the disagreement of Abduh and Rida on this point with other Muslims, past and con-

36. Aharon Layish, "The Contribution of the Modernists to the Secularization of Islamic Law," *Middle Eastern Studies*, vol. 14, 1978, p. 267.

37. Layish's assessment of the work of the reformers as both inauthentic and a failure is of a piece with earlier verdicts by Elie Kedourie and Malcolm Kerr. See E. Kedourie, *Afghani and Abduh: An Essay on Religious Unbelief and Political Activism in Modern Islam*, London: Cass, 1966; M. H. Kerr, *Islamic Reform: The Political and Legal Theories of Muhammad Abduh and Rashid Rida*, Berkeley: University of California Press, 1966. I have written a review article dealing with the former: "Politics and Religion in Islamic Reform," *Review of Middle East Studies*, no. 2, 1976.

temporary, does not signify that their view is no longer "traditional." On the contrary, that disagreement or difference is what makes it part of the tradition of Islamic jurisprudence.

In fact, recent scholarship on the history of the *shariʿa* (by, for example, Wael Hallaq, Haim Gerber, and Baber Johansen[38]) has challenged the orientalist thesis, propounded in the West since at least the beginning of the twentieth century, that the Islamic legal tradition became static—that "the gates of *ijtihād* were closed," as the famous phrase has it—after the first formative centuries. That thesis reflects the more general notion that "the traditional" is opposed to "the modern" as the unthinking and unchanging is to the reasoned and new. But argued change was always important to the *shariʿa*, and its flexibility was retained through such technical devices as *ʿurf* (custom), *maslaha* (public interest), and *darūra* (necessity).

Schulze himself appears to be interested less in whether or not the reform movement led by Abduh and Rida was intellectually "immature." Instead, he tells us that advocating *ijtihād* in this new sense provoked the fear among more conventional *ʿulama* that they would lose their position of power as the new Islamic intelligentsia emerged, so they too began to take their distance from "tradition." Nevertheless, says Schulze, "traditional Islamic culture" did not disappear. The bastion of that tradition remained mysticism. The movements of rebellion against colonialism were based on this traditional culture, and the hostility between it and colonialism was extended to relations with the official Islam that colonialism had created. Thus Schulze too employs a notion of "traditional Islam" that he identifies with sufism and considers more authentic than the *salafiyya* attempts at reform. Schulze writes that the reform movement (*islāh*) openly turned against every manifestation of mysticism because mysticism represented what the European bourgeoisie disliked most about Islam—irrationalism, superstition, fanaticism. By taking their distance from what Schulze calls "tradition," the new Islamic elites signaled their abandonment of it and so asserted their claim to independence on the basis of civilized status.

This is a sophisticated account, and Schulze is right to draw our attention to the evolving class structure of nineteenth-century Egypt. But I am not persuaded by it as an explanation. To begin with a substantive point, it ignores the ways the Egyptian reformers were able to draw on

38. W. Hallaq, *Law and Legal Theory in Classical and Medieval Islam*, Aldershot: Variorum, 1995; H. Gerber, *Islamic Law and Culture, 1600–1840*, Leiden: Brill, 1999; B. Johansen, *Contingency in a Sacred Law*, Leiden: Brill, 1999.

some of the ideas and attitudes of the eighteenth-century Hanbalite Arabian reformer Muhammad bin Abdul-Wahhab, who was also very suspicious of "irrationalism" and "superstition," and who was prepared to use *ijtihād* to attack them in order to "purify" Islamic practice—but not because he wanted to get closer to the European bourgeoisie. Ibn Abdul-Wahhab, like ibn Taymiyya before him, was considered by the Egyptian reformers to be part of their tradition even where they disagreed with him.

Thus theoretically, Schulze's perspective on the reasons behind discursive and behavioral shifts in Islamic tradition is too instrumental. (Whereas Nathan Brown explains the reform of the Egyptian system of justice in terms of tools for resisting imperialism, Reinhard Schulze sees Islamic reform in general as a means of claiming political independence.) When major social changes occur people are often unclear about precisely what kind of event it is they are witnessing and uncertain about the practice that would be appropriate or possible in response to it. And it is not easy to shed attitudes, sensibilities, and memories as though they were so many garments inappropriate to a singular historical movement. New vocabularies ("civilization," "progress," "history," "agency," "liberty," and so on) are acquired and linked to older ones. Would-be reformers, as well as those who oppose them, imagine and inhabit multiple temporalities.

The concept of "tradition" requires more careful theoretical attention than the modernist perspective gives it. Talking of tradition ("Islamic tradition") as though it was the passing on of an unchanging substance in homogeneous time oversimplifies the problem of time's definition of practice, experience, and event. Questions about the internal temporal structure of tradition are obscured if we represent it as the inheritance of an unchanging cultural substance from the past—as though "past" and "present" were places in a linear path down which that object was conveyed to the "future." (The notion of invented tradition is the same representation used subversively.) We make a false assumption when we suppose that the present is merely a fleeting moment in a historical teleology connecting past to future. In tradition the "present" is always at the center. If we attend to the way time present is separated from but also included within events and epochs, the way time past authoritatively constitutes present practices, and the way authenticating practices invoke or distance themselves from the past (by reiterating, reinterpreting, and reconnecting textualized memory and memorialized history), we move toward a richer understanding of tradition's temporality. When settled cultural assumptions cease to be viable, agents consciously inhabit different kinds of time simultaneously and try to straddle the gap between what Reinhart Koselleck, speaking of "modernity," calls experience and expectation, an aspect of the contemporaneity of the noncontemporaneous.[39] But unilinear time together with its breaks— the homogeneous time of modern history—in spite of its being essential to thinking and acting critically, is only one kind of time people imagine, respond to, and use.

Modern history clearly links time past to time present, and orients its narratives to the future. But present experience is also, as Koselleck points out, a reencounter with what was once imagined as the future. The disappointment or delight this may occasion therefore prompts a reorientation to the past that is more complex than the notion of "invented tradition" allows. The simultaneity of time that this generates is not to be confused, incidentally, with what Benedict Anderson identifies as the premodern religious imagination in which cosmology and history are confused, or as the modern secular imagination that links together disparate events on the one hand and nationwide readers on the other hand—two kinds of linkage mediated through the daily newspaper.[40] Koselleck's notion of simultaneity relates neither to a confusion of religious imagination nor to coincidences apprehended within homogeneous time. It is intrinsic to the structure of time itself.

(The Arabic word *hadīth*, incidentally, captures nicely the double sense of temporality usually separated in English: on the one hand it denotes anything that is new or modern, and on the other hand a tradition that makes the past—and future—reencountered in the present.[41] For *ha-*

39. *Gleichzeitigkeit der Ungleichzeitigen.* Koselleck sees "modernity" (*Neuzeit*) as being located precisely in the rupture between the two: "the divide between previous experience and coming expectation opened up, and the difference between past and present increased, so that lived time was experienced as a rupture, as a period of transition in which the new and the unexpected continually happened" (*Futures Past: On the Semantics of Historical Time*, Cambridge, Mass.: MIT Press, 1985, p. 257). Koselleck does not add that in this rupture the old might be remembered in unexpected ways because the future looked forward to is not experienced as such when it arrives. One should not take it as given, as progressivists tend to do, that all positive invocations of the past are inevitably "nostalgic."

40. Benedict Anderson, *Imagined Communities*, London: Verso, 1983, chapter 2.

41. In an excellent (unpublished) paper entitled "The Birth of Tradition and Modernity in 18th and 19th Century Islamic Culture—The Case of Printing,"

dīth means "discourse" in the general, secular sense as well as the remembered discourse of the Prophet and his Companions that is actualized in the disciplined body/mind of the faithful Muslim—and thus becomes the tradition, the *sunna.*)

But I have empirical concerns about Schulze's account too. Muhammad Abduh's relation to sufism was more complicated than it suggests. For although Abduh was critical of Sufis who promoted doctrines and practices he considered contrary to the *shari'a* (*ghulāt al-sūfiyya*), and who served the political ambitions of rulers by providing them with what he called "corrupt fatwas," he strongly endorsed the sufi understanding of ethics and spiritual education (*'ilm al-akhlāq wa tarbiyyat al-nufūs*).[42] The complexity in Abduh's views brings out the inadequacy of the kind of binary thinking (familiar to Western students of Islam since Goldziher) that opposes as mutually exclusive "orthodox Islam" to "*sufi* Islam," "doctors of law" to "saints," "rule-following" to "mystical experience," "rationality" to "tradition," and so forth.[43] This is not to say that Muslims never themselves employ such binaries—especially for polemical purposes—but this situated deployment should not be mistaken by the nonparticipatory scholar as objective evidence of a continuous split in the Islamic tradition. The difference that does exist is between would-be authorizer and practioner. The participant's engagement with his tradition is in part an involvement with

---

Reinhard Schulze traces the shifting semantic field of such Arabic words as "new" (*hadīth*), "free from precedent" (*ijtihād*), "original" (*asli*), and so forth, which reenforces the point I am making.

42. See, for example, the summary of a conversation in 1898 between Abduh and Rida (published under the heading "*al-tasawwuf wa al-sūfiyya*" in volume three of *al-A'māl al kāmila,* edited by Muhammad Imara) in which he also declares to the latter that "All the blessings of my religion that I have received—for which I thank God Almighty—are due to sufism" (p. 552).

43. The idea that these contrasts are at once mutually exclusive and fundamental to Islamic thought and practice was taken up and repeated by an older generation of social anthropologists (for example, E. E. Evans-Pritchard, E. Gellner, and C. Geertz). Unfortunately even recent anthropological monographs on mystical Islam (for example, by K. Ewing, who employs psychoanalytic theory in her work) have, by their exclusion of any discussion of the connections between sufism and *shari'a,* tended to reinforce that binary. But this has now begun to be disputed by scholars. See G. Makdisi, "Hanbalite Islam and Sufism," in *Studies on Islam,* ed. and trans. M. Swartz, London: Oxford University Press, 1981. See also the comments in Julian Baldick's *Mystical Islam,* London: I. B. Tauris, 1989, pp. 7–8.

its multiple temporalities, his selection, affirmation, and reproduction of its authoritative practices. I will return to this point later.

In his informative study of the connection between late-nineteenth-century Islamic reform and the modernizing state, Jakob Skovgaard-Petersen has taken the argument about the ideological role of the new Islamic elites further, with specific reference to a sociology of secularization within Egypt.[44] He underlines the well-known social developments from the late nineteenth-century onward—the centralization of state authority, the creation of new state institutions, the standardization of administrative rules—and like Schulze he considers the spread of printing and the emergence of a reading public as critical developments. These new developments, he tells us, enabled Islamic reformers to advocate a more "rational and ethical" Islam, especially through the institution of the *fatwa* (jurisprudential opinion on matters of religious conduct), in which the idea of self-regulation is crucial. Borrowing from Peter Berger's ideas on secularization, he proposes that freeing the individual from religious authority has a double consequence: on the one hand it greatly expands the choices available, and on the other hand religious commitments come to depend on subjective judgment. Because the choices are now situated in a "disenchanted" world,[45] the judgment tends to employ secular reason.

There is some truth in this, but as I proposed earlier, terms such as "rational and ethical" as well as "disenchantment" are problematic (see Chapter 1). Perhaps more important is the mistaken assumption (gaining some popularity in Islamic studies) that modernity introduced subjective interiority into Islam, something that was previously absent. But subjective interiority has always been recognized in Islamic tradition—in ritual worship (*'ibadāt*) as well as in mysticism (*tasawwuf*). What modernity does bring in is a new *kind* of subjectivity, one that is appropriate to ethical autonomy and aesthetic self-invention—a concept of "the subject" that has a new grammar.

In this connection Skovgaard-Petersen makes the familiar progressivist claim that "the room for choice is constantly expanding in the case of sexual relations, as it is in most other walks of life"[46]—presumably because sex is no longer hedged around by religio-legal taboos. However, this state-

44. Jakob Skovgaard-Petersen, *Defining Islam for the Egyptian State: Muftis and Fatwas of the Dar al-Ifta*, Leiden: Brill, 1997.

45. Ibid. pp. 23–24.

46. Ibid., p. 384.

ment of increasing freedom obscures a complicated picture. Consider the many legal restrictions in modern life (minimum age of marriage, restrictions on polygyny, the requirement of state registration of marriage and divorce, and so on) that were previously absent. So what one gets is a different pattern of constraint and possibility reflected in a reformulated criminal law. Consider, further, the fact that many social relations—such as those between adults and children—become sexualized in modern life, and thus become the object of public anxiety (an uncontrollable emotion) and administrative regulation (involving judgment and intervention). This very modern instance of the interweaving of fantasy and exploitation, forbidden pleasure and governmental power is not well represented in the old formula of a "disenchanted world" in which triumphant rationality affords increasing choice.[47] "The room for choice" is not a homogeneous space of which secular liberal society happens to have the most.

Nevertheless, one can draw out a conclusion from Skovgaard-Petersen that he leaves implicit but which I consider especially important for my story. The individual is now encouraged—in morality as well as in law—to govern himself or herself, as befits the citizen of a secular, liberal society. But two points should be borne in mind in relation to this conclusion. First, this autonomy depends on conditions that are themselves subject to regulation by the law of the state and to the demands of a market economy. Second, the encouragement to become autonomous is primarily directed at the upper classes. The lower classes, constituted as the objects of social welfare and political control, are placed in a more ambiguous situation.

This conclusion seems to me to have particular implications for an analysis of the modernist movement in Islam. It prompts one to ask of the *salafiyya* reformers not why they failed to produce a sufficiently impressive Islamic theology or legal theory, nor why they became willing ideologists for the state (both being tendentious and question-begging formulations), but how the reordering of social life (a new moral landscape) presented certain priorities to Islamic discursive tradition—a reordering that included a new significance being given to the family, a new distinction being drawn between law and morality, and new subjects being formed. How the Is-

47. See Ian Hacking, *Rewriting the Soul: Multiple Personality and the Sciences of Memory*, Princeton: Princeton University Press, 1995, a fascinating discussion of child abuse as subjective experience, emancipatory politics, and psychological knowledge.

lamic discursive tradition responded to and intervened in the newly emerging moral landscape is a complex matter. In this chapter I consider only one small aspect of it, having to do with the reform of the law.

Moral autonomy and family law

"The *shari'a* was not abandoned," writes Nathan Brown, "but it was restricted to matters of personal status and to areas where it could be clearly and easily codified."[48] But when the *shari'a* is structured essentially as a set of legal rules defining personal status, it is radically transformed. This is not because the *shari'a*, by being confined to the private domain, is thereby deprived of political authority, something that advocates of an Islamic state argue should be restored. On the contrary, what happens to the *shari'a* is best described not as curtailment but as transmutation. It is rendered into a subdivision of legal norms (*fiqh*) that are authorized and maintained by the centralizing state.

In the perspective on law reform in Egypt that I adopt, a citizen's rights are neither an ideological legitimation of class rule ("Marxism") nor a means for limiting arbitrary government ("liberalism"). I see them as integral to the process of governance, to the normalization of social conduct in a modern, secular state. In this scheme of things the individual acquires his or her rights mediated by various domains of social life—including the public domain of politics and the private domain of the family—as articulated by the law. The state embodies, sanctions, and administers the law in the interests of its self-governing citizens. The state's concern for the harms and benefits accruing to its subjects is not in itself new. But—as Foucault argued—the modern state expresses this concern typically in the form of a new knowledge (political economy) and directs it at a new object (population). It is in this context that "the family" emerges as a category in law, in welfare administration, and in public moralizing discourse. The family is the unit of "society" in which the individual is physically and morally reproduced and has his or her primary formation as a "private" being. It is often assumed that colonial governments were reluctant to interfere with family law because it was the heart of religious doctrine and practice. I argue, on the contrary, that the *shari'a* thus defined is precisely a secular for-

48. Hacking, p. 58.

mula for privatizing "religion" and preparing the ground for the self-governing subject.

This brings me to Muhammad Abduh's report on the *shari'a* courts written in 1899, the year he was appointed Grand Mufti of Egypt.[49] Abduh's recommendations in this remarkable mandate for reform cover a range of technical topics—improving court buildings, increasing the salaries of judges and clerks and raising their standard of education, expediting the hearing of cases and the execution of judgments, instituting regular inspections and a better system of record-keeping, simplifying interaction with litigants and clarifying the official language used, and so on. The reforms Abduh proposes here are therefore largely to do with procedure and setting. The *shari'a*, he insists, is not itself in need of improvement but the books in which it is written are unnecessarily difficult for litigants to understand, and it could therefore do with the kind of rationalizing work that the Ottoman state undertook for the *majalla*.[50] But what is striking is the way Abduh approaches the basic social function of the *shari'a* courts in terms of something that has come to be called "the family."

These courts, he writes, intervene between husband and wife, father and son, a guardian and his ward, and between brothers. There is no right relating to kin over which these courts do not have jurisdiction. This means, says Abduh, that *shari'a* judges look into matters that are very private and listen to what others are not allowed to hear. For even as they provide the framework of justice, so they are a depository for every kind of family secret. In other words, the courts are expected both to guard the privacy of the words and acts of domestic life and to work through the sentiments on which social life ultimately depends. Since the *shari'a* code of 1897 explicitly required a public hearing of cases (something Abduh must have been aware of in writing his report) his emphasis on secrecy expresses the old liberal dilemma of addressing both *privacy* and *publicity* in the legal culture.

Abduh observes that in these modern times, "Most of the lower class and a fair number of the middle and upper classes have abandoned kinship

49. Muhammad Abduh, "*Taqrīr islāh al-mahākim al-shar'iyya*," in *Al-A'māl al-kāmila lil-imām Muhammad 'Abduh*, ed. Muhammad Imara, vol. 2, Beirut, 1980, pp. 217–97. Surprisingly, it is not mentioned in modern histories of law in Egypt.

50. Ibid., p. 295.

and affinal sentiments, and so they resort to the *shari'a* courts in the matter of domestic relations. With regard to such matters as daily expenses, the accommodation and comfort of the wife in disputes with the husband's family, with regard to provisioning and other affairs of the children, to their education until a pre-determined age, and to everything needed for such matters, the resort among those we have mentioned is now to the *shari'a* courts. It is obvious," Abduh goes on, "that a people (*sha'b*) is composed of households that are called families (*al-buyūt allati tusamma 'ā'ilāt*) and that the basis of every nation (*umma*) is its families, because a totality is logically made up of its parts. Since the welfare of families is connected in its most detailed links with the *shari'a* courts—as is the case today—the degree to which the nation needs the reform of these courts becomes clear. It is apparent that their place in the structure of Egyptian government is foundational, so that if they were to weaken, the effects of this weakness would be evident in the entire structure."[51]

Among the many recommendations in his report, Abduh stresses the need for a more careful separation of functions between administration and jurisprudence (*al-idāra wa al-fiqh*), and he urges greater independence of the *shari'a* courts from state control. Thus even though he considers the *shari'a* system to be integral to governance, he does not consider the state to be the source of its authority. Nevertheless, he regards the *shari'a* to be essential to the restoration of "the family," especially among the lower classes. Without the work of the *shari'a* courts—which are in effect "family courts"—he sees social life itself in danger of moral collapse. By being identified with the family the *shari'a* thus becomes functionally central at once to political order and to the total body that will eventually be represented as "society." The modern Arabic word for society (*mujtama'*) is not yet linguistically available, nor is the modern concept to which it now refers. For insofar as that concept is political, it signifies a population held together by social relations where "the social" is constituted by the theoretical equivalence of autonomous individuals.[52] The theological concept *umma* that Abduh employs has the sense of a collective body of Muslims bound together by their faith in God and the Prophet—a faith that is em-

51. Ibid., pp. 219–20.
52. The entry for "society" in Badger's *English-Arabic Lexicon*, London (1881), gives neither the word *mujtama'*, nor any reference to the modern concept. Lane's *Arabic-English Lexicon*, London (1872), also has no reference to the modern concept of "society"; the sense of *mujtama'* is still only "a meeting place."

bodied in prescribed forms of behavior. It is therefore quite different from the idea of a society made up of equal citizens governing themselves individually (through conscience) and collectively (through the electorate). That idea was just beginning to be deployed in Western Europe in the nineteenth century as the object of knowledge-based interventions[53]—by movements for universal franchise,[54] as well as movements for the moral improvement of the poor, for the practical reform of education and the law, and for the organization of sanitation and hygiene in urban space.

It is in this context that I think one may place the reform that eventually translates the *shari'a* as "family law." For the family is not merely a conservative political symbol or a site of gender control. By virtue of being a legal category it is an object of administrative intervention, a part of the management of the modern nation-state—not least in the twentieth-century projects of birth control. (Paradoxically, the "family" becomes salient precisely when modern political economy, the principal source of government knowledge and the principal object of its management, begins to represent and manipulate the national population in terms not of "natural units" but of statistical abstractions—economic sectors, consumers, active labor force, property owners, recipients of state benefits, demographic trends, and so forth. At the level of public knowledge and activity "the individual" becomes marginalized.)

It is because the legal formation of the family gives the concept of individual morality its own "private" locus that the *shari'a* can now be spoken of as "the law of personal status"—*qānūn al-ahwāl al-shakhsiyya*. In

53. The National Association for the Promotion of Social Science was home to everyone "engaged in all the various efforts now happily begun for the improvement of the people," as the official account of its foundation in England in 1857 put it. "It divided itself into five 'departments': legal reform, penal policy, education, public health, and 'social economy'. . . . [T]he bulk of its members were drawn from . . . professions most actively engaged with practical social problems—doctors, coroners, charity organizers, and the like" (Stefan Collini, *Public Moralists: Political Thought and Intellectual Life in Britain, 1850–1930*, Oxford: Clarendon, 1991, p. 210).

54. For an excellent history of the suffrage in France, see Pierre Rosanvallon, *Le Sacre du Citoyen*, Paris: Gallimard, 1992.

this way it becomes the expression of a secular formula, defining a place in which "religion" is allowed to make its public appearance through state law.[55] And the family as concept, word, and organizational unit acquires a new salience.

The modern "family"

The sense of the word *'ā'ila* (translated into English as "family") as used by Abduh and other reformers is modern—a fact reflected not only in its relatively recent coupling with *sharī'a* law, but also in changing literary Arabic. Eighteenth-century dictionaries do not give the modern sense of *'ā'ila* and *usra*, meaning a unit consisting of parents and children. One can see how the modern usage was probably derived: the form *'iyāla* is given as meaning "to give help and support to dependents," but also as "the process of having more children"; *usra* meant "tribe," or "agnates" (relatives on the father's side).[56] By the late nineteenth century, *'ā'ila* becomes a part of common usage and generally signifies "a man and his wife and his children and those who are dependent on him from his paternal relatives"[57]— such as younger siblings or aged parents. A modern dictionary has a definition in terms of unit of habitation: *'ā'ila* means "those who are gathered

55. Hamid Zaki states that the term *al-aḥwāl al-shakhsiyya* (personal status) is new to Egypt, having been introduced from Europe with the laws now administered by the National Courts, and he notes its absence in the codes administered by the *sharī'a* courts. Accordingly, he traces the definition of the term through French legal authorities, from the division between "personal status" and "real status" in the Napoleonic Code, to the contemporary recognition of multiple status categories. The term "personal status" (*al-aḥwāl al-shakhsiyya*) now refers, Zaki notes, to the ensemble of juridical institutions that define the human person independent of his wealth, obligations, and transactions ("*Al-Mahākim al-ahliyya wa al-aḥwāl al-shakhsiyya*," in *Majallat al-qānūn wa al-iqtiṣād*, December 1934, pp. 793–95). This abstraction subverts the old *sharī'a* categorization of the human person. In the writings of medieval Islamic jurists the particular categories of male and female, free and slave, are essential to the legal interpretation of the human body, intention, and agency (see Baber Johansen, "The Valorization of the Human Body in Muslim Sunni Law," in D. J. Stewart, B. Johansen, and A. Singer, *Law and Society in Islam*, Princeton: Markus Wiener, 1996).

56. See *Tāj al-'Urūs*.

57. See *Muḥīt al-Muḥīt*.

together in one house, including parents, children and near relatives."[58] So much for shifting referents.[59]

The things signified are also being transformed. Social historians have traced the rearticulation of kinship units and networks among the rural population in mid-century and ascribed it both to state and market: forced labor and military conscription, a general decline in the economic condition of handicraft workers and petty traders due to the penetration of European capitalism, as well as the reform of landholding and taxation systems. Thus Judith Tucker notes that although it was common for several brothers to live and work together with their wives and children, sharing goods, livestock, and land in a unit recognized in law as a partnership (*shirka*), the state's draconian measures seriously affected the structure of such units and networks. For example, "Despite the migration of women and children in the wake of drafted husbands in a conscious attempt to maintain the family unit, conscription made inroads on traditional [that is, existing] structures. The military family was a nuclear family; the man, wife and children were removed from their village community, and more importantly, from the extended family which had formed their social and economic environment. A network of economic relations and social responsibilities bound them to their parents, brothers and sisters, and relatives by marriage. The formation of a nuclear family unit at some distance away weakened these ties. If the woman remained without her husband in the village, the man's absence affected patterns of material support and the division of tasks."[60] (It is of some interest that the "family" makes its appearance as a category in the census registers of Egypt only in 1917.[61])

So if Muhammad Abduh regards the family as the basic unit of society, it is not because he invokes a nostalgic past but because something new is now emerging in the changing social structure.

Among the urban upper classes, Western-type schooling (in European languages) and the adoption of Western domestic styles and manners

58. See *al-Mu'jam al-Wasīt*.

59. The *Qur'an*, which is the basic source for the *sharī'a*, contains neither *'ā'ila* nor *usra*. The words that are used there, *bayt* and *ahl*, and that are translated into English as "family," have much wider or looser connotations.

60. Judith Tucker, "Decline of the Family Economy in Mid-Nineteenth-Century Egypt," in *Arab Studies Quarterly*, vol. 1, no. 3, 1979, p. 262.

61. See François Ireton, "Element pour une sociologie historique de la production statistique en Egypte," *Peuples méditerranéen*, no. 54–55, 1991, p. 80.

also produced a discourse of the ideal family—typically expressed in terms of "the problem of the status of Muslim women"—among Western-educated reformers in the late nineteenth century. Perhaps the most famous text that exemplifies this is Qasim Amin's controversial book on *The Emancipation of Woman*,[62] long regarded as a major step in the history of Egyptian feminism. In a powerful critique of that work, Leila Ahmed has argued that "In calling for women's liberation the thoroughly patriarchal Amin was in fact calling for the transformation of Muslim society along the lines of the Western model and for the substitution of the garb of Islamic-style male dominance by that of Western-style male dominance. Under the guise of a plea for a 'liberation' of woman, then, he conducted an attack that in its fundamentals reproduced the colonizer's attack on native culture and society."[63] It was designed, in other words, to help eradicate bad habits among the natives.

Amin's book is devoted to a sustained condemnation of the seclusion of women (symbolized by the veil) and a reiteration of the condition that makes for happiness in the family. As he puts it, when a "woman learns of her rights and acquires a sense of her self-worth, marriage will become the natural means for realizing the happiness of both the husband and wife. Then marriage will be based on the inclination of two persons to love each other completely—with their bodies, their hearts, and their minds."[64] Thus the nuclear family is the essential site for the happiness of the married couple through the fulfillment of their dreams. The material conditions of their existence are irrelevant. "Look at spouses who love one another, and you will see that they enjoy the blessings of paradise. What do they care if they are penniless, or if they have only lentils and onions to eat? Their cheerfulness throughout the day is enough for them—a cheerfulness that energizes the body, reassures the self, awakens feelings of joy in life, and renders it beautiful."[65] The core of the happy modern family is a monogamous relationship; a polygynous household can only be a space of conflict, hatred, and misery. But if even monogamous families are not to-

62. Qasim Amin, *Tahrir al-mar'a*, Cairo: Dar al-Ma'arif, 1970 [1899]. Amin was a lawyer by profession, initially trained in Egypt but with several years' further education in France.

63. Leila Ahmed, *Women and Gender in Islam*, New Haven: Yale University Press, 1992, p. 161.

64. Ibid., p. 145.

65. Ibid., pp. 145–46.

day full of happiness and true love, if on the contrary they are usually the site of continuous quarrels, it is because the uncivilized practice of veiling prevents the wife from acquiring the minimal education and from interacting with men in order to make the (middle-class) family successful.[66]

Ahmed is right to describe Amin's text, with its contempt for Egyptian domesticity and its insistence on the supreme importance of abolishing the veil, as the reproduction of a "Western colonial discourse." But here I want to focus on something else: the appearance of the conception that love between a man and a woman is the necessary basis of the only kind of family life that can have any value, and the assumption that legal conditions are necessary for ensuring domestic bliss. Of course monogamy in itself is not a Western phenomenon, nor was affection between husband and wife unknown in Egypt until Westernized reformers proposed it—although Amin, like many other Egyptian reformers of his time, believed that that was so. My concern is simply to draw attention to the condition of equality in the mutual sentiments of love between a man and a woman that Amin regards as essential to the private institution called "family"[67]— and to the fact that this equality is entangled with legal definitions.

It is for this reason—to secure mutual love within a monogamous family—that the reform of marriage and divorce provisions in the *sharīʿa*

66. The Islamic journal *al-Manār*, edited by Muhammad Abduh's disciple Rashid Rida, was very favorable to Qasim Amin's book—as well as to its sequel *The New Woman*. See Sami Abdulaziz al-Kumi, *as-Sahāfa al-islāmiyya fi misr fi-l-qarn at-tāsiʿ ʿashara*, Mansura: Dar al-Wafaʾ, 1992, pp. 96–97.

67. In his magisterial study of European bourgeois sexuality in the long nineteenth century, Peter Gay observes: "Intimate love, intimate hatred, are timeless; Freud did not name the Oedipus complex after an ancient mythical hero for nothing. But the nineteenth-century middle-class family, more intimate, more informal, more *concentrated* than ever, gave these universal human entanglements exceptional scope and complex configurations. Potent ambivalent feelings between married couples, and between parents and children, the tug between love and hate deeply felt but rarely acknowledged, became subject to more severe censorship than before, to the kind of repression that makes for neurosis. The ideology of unreserved love within the family was attractive but exhausting. Father's claims on daughters and mother's claims on sons, assertions of authority or demands for devotion often masquerading as excessive affection, acquired new potency precisely as the legal foundations for authority began to crumble. Increasingly, family battles took place, as it were, not in the courtroom, but in individual minds" (*The Education of the Senses*, New York: Norton, 1984, pp. 444–45).

plays such an important role throughout Amin's text. Thus polygyny, which unfortunately for Amin seems to be condoned by the Qur'an, should be legally circumscribed as much as possible. Indeed he argues, like other reformers before and since, that the intention of the relevant Qur'anic verses is that polygyny be allowed only if it is secured against injustice. "If there is injustice among the wives as is evident in our times," Amin writes, "or if moral corruption comes to families from the plurality of wives, and if the limits of the law that should be respected are transgressed, and if there is enmity among members of a single family and it spreads to the point that it becomes general—then it is allowed to the ruler who cares for public welfare [*al-maslaha al-ʿāmma*] to prohibit polygyny, conditionally or unconditionally, according to what he sees as suitable to public welfare."[68] Thus although state legislation is necessary for creating the conditions for moral behavior, the argument for overriding the Qur'anic permission of polygyny is simply a generalized sense of public welfare that is still justified in Islamic terms.[69] Although, paradoxically, the ideal that exemplifies the solution is the monogamous nuclear family among the Westernized classes (whose men now engage in the publicly regulated professions of law, medicine, the higher civil service), increasingly separated from "public life," and becoming the principal domain in which moral behavior is to be learned and always to be practiced.

Defining secular law for modern morality

I am suggesting, in effect, that the social and cultural changes taking place in the late nineteenth and early twentieth centuries—whether deliberately initiated or not—created some of the basic preconditions for secular modernity. These involved the legal constitution of fundamental social spaces in which governance could be secured through (1) the political authority of the nation-state, (2) the freedom of market exchange, and (3) the moral authority of the family. Central to this schema is the distinction between law (which the state embodied, produced, and administered) and

68. Amin, pp. 154–55.

69. This position is quite different from that of Ahmad Safwat, which I discuss below, but it is not unrelated to arguments produced by recent Muslim modernists, such as Fazlur Rahman—see, for example, his "Law and Ethics in Islam," in *Ethics in Islam*, ed. R. G. Hovannisian, Malibu, CA: Undena Publications, 1985.

morality (which is the concern ideally of the responsible person generated and sustained by the family), the two being mediated by the freedom of public exchange—a space that was restructured in Egypt by the penetration of European capital and the adoption of the European law of contract,[70] a space in which debates about Islamic reasoning and national progress, as well as about individual autonomy, could now take place publicly. The reform of the *shari'a* in Egypt should be seen in relation to this re-ordering, although it was not the only way the reform could conceivably have been carried out.

Ahmad Safwat's attempt at the beginning of the twentieth century to formulate for Egypt a secular distinction between law and morality claims our detailed attention, because it applies *ijtihād* (in the wider sense popularized by the *salafiyya* reformers) in the cause of a modernized and modernizing state. It is also, to my knowledge, the first work to argue this case rigorously and without having to depend logically on Islamic ideas of *maslaha*. Safwat was a British-trained lawyer and an advocate of *shari'a* reform, who first presented his ideas in a book entitled "An Inquiry into the Basis of Reform of the Law of Personal Status." Three years later he published a short statement of his position in English.[71]

The former, being addressed to an Egyptian audience, is largely preoccupied with the problem of changing the existing laws relating to marriage and divorce, the social problem with which it begins. There is a popular feeling, Safwat claims, that the *shari'a* is sacred (*shu'ūr 'āmat al-nās bi qadāsatihi*),[72] and yet it is precisely its details, such as inequality in the marriage contract, that make for difficulties now that social life has changed. This constitutes a danger to the whole of society. "If we wish to discover a cure for the present situation then let us think of how we want our family life to be organized, and see how we can put that into effect in agreement with religious rules. Previously marriage was (and continues to be in the customary practice of the lower classes) an institution designed for sexual pleasure and procreation, but now it has become a partnership

70. See Hossam M. Issa, *Capitalisme et sociétés anonymes en Égypte: Essai sur le rapport entre structure sociale et droit*, Paris: R. Pichon et R. Durand-Auzias, 1970, especially part one.

71. *Bahth fi qā'idat islāh qanūn al-ahwāl al-shakhsiyya*, Alexandria: Jurji Gharzuri Press, 1917; "The Theory of Mohammedan Law," in *The Journal of Comparative Legislation and International Law*, vol. 2, 1920.

72. Safwat, *Bahth*, p. 2.

in a joint mode of life." This means that the marriage contract can be binding only with the complete agreement of both sides with no inter-ference from anyone.[73] The freedom of contract between equal parties—a freedom already central to the sphere of commercial exchange—is thus a basic principle of Safwat's proposals for reform, one on which he lays great stress.

The improved conditions of domestic life among the upper classes, Safwat believes, point to the way that marriage for all of society must be civilized with the aid of a civilized law. Safwat's attribution of people's feel-ings of "sacredness" toward the *shariʿa* is a formulation symptomatic of the newly emerging secular discourse. It is clearly intended to signal the pres-ence of "irrational" sentiments toward the law assumed to be based on the belief that it cannot be touched by "profane" hands ("taboo"). But the Ara-bic word *qadāsa* ("sacred") is not used classically to qualify the *shariʿa*. (See Chapter 1.) The most common adjective used, at least in the nineteenth century and later, is "Islamic." It is when something is described as be-longing to "religion" and it can be claimed that it does not that the secular emerges most clearly.

Safwat insists that such reforms are not contrary to the fundamental principles of the *shariʿa*, and proposes a reexamination of the basic sources of that law: Qurʾan (the divinely revealed text), *sunna* (the tradition of the Prophet), *ijmāʿ* (consensus of scholars), and *qiyās* (analogical reasoning). Since analogy is not a source but a method of reasoning, it can be set aside, he says. Furthermore, since the consensus established in the past by jurists, and even the tradition of the Prophet himself, depend for their au-thority on the Qurʾan, Safwat suggests that it is the latter one must attend to above all.

Safwat notes that the commandments in the Qurʾan may be classified as follows: (1) acts that are forbidden (*harām*), (2) acts that are mandatory (*wājib*), and (3) acts that are permitted (*jāʾiz*).[74] This latter residual cate-gory consists of everything that (from the point of view of religion) the in-dividual has the right to do, and as the members of an infinite residual cat-egory they cannot be exhaustively enumerated. The legal status of such acts mentioned in the Qurʾan is no different from those that are not men-tioned. They are all equally optional. The few that are specified have the

73. Ibid., pp. 3–5.
74. Ibid., p. 24.

function of defining forbidden acts—as when the Qur'anic statement that Muslims may have up to four wives defines a limit (that is, that having *more* than four at the same time is forbidden). But as optional acts are not mandatory, they cannot be granted absolutely by the state since they may conflict with the freedom of others in particular social circumstances. And this is where the positive law of the state comes in, because its function is to limit—in the interest of all—the options of the individual that the *shari'a* permits. That is why a large number of activities are possible only by prior permission of the government in which particular conditions are stipulated—for example, the professional practice of medicine or law, or (this is Safwat's example) of plural marriage.

The almost indefinite extension of "natural" rights may thus be curtailed by the state through legislation without infringing the rules of (religiously derived) morality, because the state's jurisdiction lies beyond the two Qur'anic classes of forbidden and obligatory acts. The argument by which Safwat delimits the sphere of religious rules and opens up the space for secular state law is, I think, one of the earliest and most rigorous of its kind in modern Islamic reform. Thus although he repeatedly adverts to the importance of recent historical changes and to the need for responding to them, he does not make that the basic *method* of reform. He does not, for example, take the easy way out (as others have done since) by resorting directly to the slippery notion of "public interest" (*istislāh*) in order to adjust *shari'a* rules to "modern standards." He first clears a theoretical space in which the state *can* judge and act freely in limiting the liberties of its individual citizens in the public interest—an interest that presupposes the conditions in which civilized life can be lived by all.

It is in the English article (addressed to European readers) that Safwat more boldly represents the Qur'an as a religious text that mixes together moral and legal rules: "the liberty of a Mohammedan is only restricted by the positive commandments of the Koran. I say 'positive' to distinguish the positive rules of law from those of morality, which in the Koran are mixed together, and to distinguish them, we have to look for the nature of the sanction."[75]

The distinction between law and ethics is itself made in jurisprudential terms that are traceable in European thought at least as far back as Grotius,[76]

75. Safwat, "Theory," p. 314.

76. See J. B. Schneewind, *The Invention of Autonomy: A History of Modern Moral Philosophy*, Cambridge: Cambridge University Press, 1998, chapter 4, espe-

a distinction expressing the idea that law is the domain of obedience to a civil sovereign and morality the domain of individual sovereignty in accordance with inner freedoms (conscience). The idea of an inner, conscience-driven moral law is taken for granted by Safwat. Where the disregard or breaking of a rule leads to punishment imposed by the state, says Safwat, there is (secular) law; where transgression is sanctioned only by punishment in the next world, there is (religious) morality. The interesting point here is not simply that law and morality are distinguished (medieval Islamic jurists made that distinction too, as we shall see in the next section), but that the distinction between "morality" and "law" can be defined in parallel ways as rules, and that their obligatory character is constituted by the punishment attached to them.

There are at least two ways in which Safwat's clear separation between the scope of morality and of law may be described, the first of which one might call ethnographic. Thus even in the Western liberal scheme morality is connected to law in complicated ways. The authority of legal judgments is dependent on the ways justice, decency, reasonableness, and the like are culturally interpreted; the credibility of witnesses is linked to ways "good" or "bad" character are culturally recognized, assessed, and responded to. Furthermore, there is the general sense that the laws in force should be consistent with the prevailing morality.[77] In Egypt the codes introduced at the turn of the century were largely European and secular while morality was largely rooted in Islamic tradition.[78] This fact

cially pp. 75–78; and Richard Tuck, *The Rights of War and Peace*, Cambridge: Cambridge University Press, 1999, chapter 3.

77. James Fitzjames Stephen expresses this negatively in relation to criminal law thus: "If a man is punished by law for an act for which he is not blamed by morals, law is to that extent put out of harmony with morals, and legal punishment would not in such a case, as it always should, connote, as far as may be possible, moral infamy" (*A History of The Criminal Law of England*, London: Macmillan, 1883, vol. 2, p. 172). Paul Vinogradoff makes the more general point that "law cannot be divorced from morality in so far as it clearly contains, as one of its elements, the notion of right to which the moral quality of justice corresponds." But then he proceeds to address the precise distinction (so crucial to the modern conception and practice of law) "between moral and legal rules, between ethical and juridical standards" (*Common-Sense in Law*, London: Thornton Butterworth, 1913, pp. 24, 25).

78. See Tariq al-Bishri, *al-Sharī'a al-islāmiyya wa al-qanūn al-wad'i*, Cairo: Dar al-Sharuq, 1996, pp. 30–32. But while al-Bishri is thinking of the content of moral rules my concern is with the grammar of "the moral" itself.

leads to the question of how interpretive tendencies and assumptions of "secular" law engage with sensibilities and predispositions articulating "religious" morality. If traditionally embodied conceptions of justice and unconsciously assimilated experience are no longer relevant to the maintenance of law's authority, then that authority will depend entirely on the force of the state expressed through its codes.

It might appear at first sight that I am making a familiar argument about the introduction of "foreign codes." But my concern here is neither with the geographical origin of the law nor with codification as such. I argue that it is the power to make a strategic separation between law and morality that defines the colonial situation, because it is this separation that enables the legal work of educating subjects into a new public morality.[79] The European task of establishing order in Egypt was based on a new notion of "order," as Timothy Mitchell has rightly argued.[80] But it also required a new conception of what law can do and how it should do it.

Of course I am not proposing that Safwat's theoretical text is a complete copy of Western secularism—he is concerned, after all, to adapt *Islamic* ethics and law to Western jurisprudential thinking, and the *Qur'an* is his theoretical starting point. Nor do I assume that the clarity of his the-

79. James Fitzjames Stephen (one-time legal member of the viceroy's council) describes the principles that animate the task of the colonial government in India as follows: "The government which now exists [in India] has not been chosen by the people. It is not, and if it is to exist at all, it cannot look upon itself as being, the representative of the general wishes and average way of thinking of the bulk of the population which it governs. It is the representative of a totally different order of ideas from those prevalent amongst the natives of India. To these ideas, which are those of educated Europeans, and particularly of educated Englishmen, it attaches supreme importance; they are the ideas on which European civilization is founded. They include all the commonly accepted principles of European morality and politics—those for instance which condemn cruel acts like the burning of widows, or the offering of human sacrifices in the name of religion, or the infliction of disabilities, as for instance disability to marry, on account of widowhood or a change of religion, and others of the same sort" (J. F. Stephen, "Foundations of the Government of India," *The Nineteenth Century*, no. 80, October 1883, p. 548). The law, while not itself a moral system, is indispensable to the replacement of an inferior morality by a superior one.

80. Timothy Mitchell, *Colonizing Egypt*, Cambridge: Cambridge University Press, 1988.

ory is a reflection of institutional practice (the insertion of discourses such as Safwat's into processes of institutional legal reform in modern Egypt still needs to be researched). I am looking for systematic shifts in reasoning about legal reform that indicate ways in which "the secular" are understood and applied in colonial Egypt.

The second way of describing Safwat's division between (secular) law and (religious) morality is analytic. It follows the conceptual implications of the fact that his reading cuts right across the famous *shariʿa* classification—*ʿibādāt* (rules governing relations between God and the faithful), *muʿāmalāt* (rules governing proper behavior between the faithful), and *hudūd* (rules defining limits to the behavior of the faithful through penalties). Modern secular law not only excludes the first as being beyond its purview. It also redraws the distinctions applicable to proper behavior and punishments in terms of "civil law" and "criminal law." It does all this in accordance with different principles. Furthermore, Safwat's division deliberately ignores the fivefold *shariʿa* ranking of acts—required (*wājib*), recommended (*mustahabb*), indifferent (*mubāh*), discouraged (*makrūh*), and forbidden (*harām*).

The grid separating "law" from "morality" that Safwat imposes on the *shariʿa* differs sharply from its traditional language. The concept of virtue (*fadīla*) in the latter cannot be defined simply in terms of the type of sanction (this-worldly versus otherworldly) or of the type of governance (subjective freedom versus obedience to external authority). It constitutes a dimension of all accountable behavior (including justiciable acts), in the sense that while all such behavior is the responsibility of a free agent, it is also subject to assessments that have practical consequences for the way one lives in this world *and* the next. And all practical programs for the cultivation of moral virtues presuppose authoritative models. In the case of the *shariʿa* the ultimate model is that of the Prophet Muhammad as embodied in the discursive tradition known as *hadīth*. In other words, the *shariʿa* in this conception is the process whereby individuals are educated and educate themselves as moral subjects in a scheme that connects the obligation to act morally with the obligation to act legally in complicated ways.

A digression on medieval 'fiqh'

This point is important for my argument. The conception of the law assumed in Safwat's texts clears the space not only for the modern, reforming state, but also for a secular morality. In this section I shall try to develop this theme through a dialog with one of the most impressive contributions to appear in recent years to the study of premodern *fiqh* (Islamic jurisprudence), Baber Johansen's *Contingency in a Sacred Law.*[81] It will, I hope, help us to clarify some crucial ways in which modern concepts replaced earlier ideas in the tradition of Islamic jurisprudence and ethics in Egypt.

Johansen reminds us of the colonial context of orientalist studies of the *shari'a,* and observes that Snouck Hurgronje, the first Western authority on the subject, regarded *fiqh* as an incoherent mixture of religion, ethics, and politics—not as a functioning law but as a theory of the ideal Muslim society that had practical significance only in matters relating to ritual devotions, family relations, and endowments. This view, says Johansen, has had a profound effect on Western students of Islam who have tended to see *fiqh* as a deontology—a system of religious and moral duties—rather than as a law in the rational sense.

Joseph Schacht, perhaps the most important orientalist of the twentieth century to specialize in Islamic law, drew on Max Weber's distinction between procedural and substantive rationality, but retained his notion of the *shari'a* as "sacred law."[82] However Schacht did see that *fiqh* was not simply a compendium of religious duties but a system of subjective rights, and so inaugurated a new, and more fruitful, approach because *fiqh* could

81. Baber Johansen, *Contingency in a Sacred Law: Legal and Ethical Norms in the Muslim Fiqh,* Leiden: Brill, 1999.

82. See Joseph Schacht, *Introduction to Islamic Law,* Oxford: Oxford University Press, 1964. But his most influential, and most controversial, work is *The Origins of Muhammadan Jurisprudence,* Oxford: Clarendon, 1950. Its thesis—that the prophetic traditions (*hadīth*) are historical inventions—is an early example of what anthropologists now call "the invention of tradition." Schacht wrote that just conceivably some traditions might be authentic but orientalists had found it impossible to determine with certainty which these were. A scholarly defense of the authenticity of those traditions is Muhammad M. Al-Azami, *On Schacht's Origin of Muhammadan Jurisprudence,* New York: John Wiley & Sons, 1985. On this matter orientalists tend to see the latter as biased by their religious belief; Muslim scholars see the former as biased by their anti-Islamic prejudice. However, both critics and defenders share the assumption that the time of tradition must always be vindicated by the time of history, that the question of "historical fact" is always integral to the constitutive work of tradition.

now be seen as a legal system that private individuals could use "for their individual strategies of claims and counter-claims. It is a law in which individuals can create individual norms through their actions and can pursue individual claims against others. It enters into the world of social relations and ceases to be an abstract religious duty."[83]

The aim of treating *fiqh* as real law, with changing implications for everyday life, is extremely important, and Johansen's formulation of this point opens the way for a comparative study of Islamic law that is not mired in dubious evolutionary assumptions—and therefore also for serious consideration of the relations between law and ethics in the Islamic tradition. But the following question suggests itself: Is the manipulative model the only way of representing law as "real"? And is this why we are urged to see *fiqh* as essentially individualistic? There seems to be a connection between the two in Johansen's argument, and in particular in his opposing "the world of social relations" to "abstract religious duties." And yet, are religious duties not themselves partly constitutive of the world of social relations? For although not all social relations entail religious duties (buying and selling legitimate goods, for example), some do (an offspring's obligations to his or her parents, for instance). Another way of putting this is to say that no religious duty can be entirely abstracted from social relations. Thus although one may perform the *salāt* by oneself, one has to learn their *correct* performance from others. Besides, Friday prayers, 'Id prayers, and so on cannot be performed alone. And of course the concept and practice of *nasīha*—of the duty of "promoting what is right and discouraging what is wrong"—presupposes social relations in the making. Thus it is precisely *how* "religious" duties are embedded in social relations (learning and teaching correct religious practices, giving moral advice to fellow Muslims, and so on) and *what* specific duties are entailed by social relations that need to be analyzed in *fiqh*.

Johansen extracts two major questions that he finds implicit in Schacht: (1) how the legal dimension relates to the ethical and religious dimension, and (2) how subjective rights relate to religious duties. The difficulty with Schacht, as well as with contemporary Arab jurists such as Sanhuri and Shahata who have taken a similar line, is that while they recognize the distinctive character of the legal dimension of *fiqh*, they ignore its ethical dimension. Johansen makes this point as follows: "in all these attempts

83. Johansen, pp. 54–55.

to bring the *fiqh* back into law those who want to do so act as jurists who refer to legal texts. The liturgical acts, the ethical content of those norms which cannot be applied by courts but which address the conscience of the individual believers, their *forum internum*, in short, the religious dimension of the *fiqh*, has hardly been considered as an object of legal reconstruction and would need a completely different approach."[84] Johansen quite rightly insists that attention must be paid to *both* the religious *and* the ethical dimensions if the connections between Islamic law and ethics are to be explained. Thus Schacht failed to consider that "ownership" is given a different moral and religious value in different domains,[85] a difference reflected in the fact that, as Johansen observes, in some cases "intention"—regarded as an inner, psychological state—is considered legally critical for the transfer of ownership, and in others it is only the form of words used in the transaction that is relevant.

Finally, Johansen argues that Schacht and Hurgronje (and Weber) seriously underestimated the scope and significance of doctrinal disagreements between the schools. Dissent on details was not regarded as heresy. Johansen elaborates this point with skill and erudition and sums it up as follows: "The respect for normative pluralism (*ikhtilāf*) is possible only because the *fiqh* scholars conceive an ontological difference between the knowledge as revealed by God in Koranic texts, the prophet's praxis or the community's consensus on the one hand, and the knowledge which human beings acquire through their own reasoning. The first one contains absolute truth, the second one is fallible human reasoning. The second one has to interpret the first but cannot aspire to reach its rank. Therefore Muslim jurists recognize the contingency of all results of scholarly reasoning. The acknowledgment of the contingency of all human action and reasoning is at the basis of the *fiqh* as a discipline which comprises different methods and schools of thought (*madhāhib*) and different organizations of scholars and upholds the cohesion of the scholars and doctrines."[86]

Johansen's overall argument is complicated. There is, on the one hand, the thesis that Islamic jurists have traditionally held all human (and therefore legal) reasoning to be based on probability not certainty, and, on the other hand, the proposition that Islamic law has always distinguished

84. Ibid., p. 59.
85. Ibid., p. 64.
86. Ibid., pp. 65–66.

moral judgments from legal ones. Both theses are brilliantly expounded. The two then seem to be linked together through the idea that "certainty" (*'ilm yaqīn*) depends on observability—on the *forum externum*—with which the law deals, as opposed to the *forum internum*, the domain of "conscience" and so of ethics. It is not always clear whether the absolute certainty referred to in this argument relates to the authority of the divine text or to that of conscience.[87] In any case, it seems to me that when it is conceived as the hidden seat of self-government, "conscience" refers to something at once modern and Christian.

What defines "conscience," in modern Christianity, is not simply that it is "interior" and "hidden" (the mind of someone who calculates his or her own interests is also hidden to others) but that it is the seat of a moral function responding sovereignly to the question: "What should I do if I am to do that which is good?" This conception of ethics has a history,[88] of course, and its great theorist was Kant. "The question here is not," wrote Kant, "how conscience ought to be guided (for conscience needs no guide; to have a conscience suffices), but how it itself can serve as a guide in the most perplexing moral decisions."[89] This proposition, with its emphasis on the absolute moral autonomy of the subject, would surely be rejected by medieval Islamic theologians and jurists. Wouldn't Kant's equation of morality with the certainty of sovereign, internal judgment also come into question? "It is a basic moral principle, which requires no proof," Kant insisted, "that *one ought to hazard nothing that may be* wrong . . . Hence the *consciousness* that an action *which I intend to perform* is right, is unconditioned duty. . . . [C]oncerning the act which *I* propose to perform I must not only judge and form an opinion, but I must be *sure* that it is not wrong; and this requirement is a postulate of conscience, to which is opposed *probabilism*, i.e., the principle that the mere opinion that an action may well be right warrants its being performed."[90]

87. "The *forum internum* is the instance of the religious conscience," writes Johansen, "the seat of the relation between God and the individual, of veracity and of absolute identity between the truth on the one hand, rights or obligations on the other. The *forum externum* is an instance of contingent decisions which are legally valid and whose assertions about the facts of the cases are probable" (ibid., p. 36).

88. See Alasdair MacIntyre, *A Short History of Ethics*, London: Macmillan, 1966.

89. Immanuel Kant, *Religion Within the Limits of Reason Alone*, New York: Harper and Row, 1960, p. 173.

90. Ibid., pp. 173–74; emphases in original.

Kant detested the old Catholic discipline of moral casuistry because it sought to guide the conscience, especially in situations of uncertainty, and would also surely have detested the practice of seeking *fatwas*. His standpoint suggests that a category like *makrūh* (reprehensible) has no place in a truly moral vocabulary because it dilutes the absolute wrongness of an act to which it is applied.[91] But seen simply as the products of ethical judgment one misses the practical use of the words *makrūh* (reprehensible) and *mustahabb* (desirable) in cultivating virtuous thought and behavior—forms of behavior that, incidentally, carry no punitive sanctions.

This modern view not only takes the moral question to be quite different from the "social" question "How should I behave if I want to do well?" but assumes that doing well and having it socially recognized that one is doing well have nothing to do with acting morally. And yet it is precisely the way in which the answers to these two questions have been connected (and disconnected) in Muslim societies that needs systematic investigation—that is, how learning forms of thought and behavior properly (that would be socially recognized and admired as demonstrations and exemplars of religious virtues) comes to be a precondition for acting ethically. Johansen's general approach makes it possible to investigate this connection fruitfully.

Johansen is absolutely right to maintain that Islamic law has always distinguished between justiciable norms and those that are not subject to the court's ruling. Indeed this point is often missed by contemporary scholars dealing with "intentionality" in Islamic law. But is this point best made by equating legal norms with observable acts and ethical norms with nonobservable ones? I think not. Acting in a way that people generally recognize as *makrūh* (reprehensible) is observable, since an act is what it is because of the description under which it falls, and yet as Johansen himself is at pains to point out, this behavior does not entail a judgment by the court in spite of its being "observable." On the other hand, acts that are justiciable (for example, contracts) may require an inquiry into aspects of behavior that are "nonobservable" (such as intention)—as Johansen himself clearly notes.

91. Kant's requirement that in order to act morally the conscience must be certain of its rightness would also, incidentally, rule out the discourse of modern bioethics that deals in probabilities rather than certainties—but that's another matter.

Johansen's attempt to identify the ethical dimension of *fiqh* in its relation to the law is of the greatest importance, but his characterization of it in terms of disembodied "conscience" does not seem to me quite appropriate. Besides it is, so I would argue, not essential to his basic view of *fiqh*. My position, at any rate, is that one should not try to map the interior/exterior binary directly onto ethics/law. The latter has to do with authoritative judgments in cases of dispute over transactions and dispositions and in cases where transgressions against particular norms are alleged to have occurred. Both kinds of judgment carry important social consequences, and both often depend on reconstructing what was not "visible." The crucial point is that they are, as justiciable cases, sanctioned by the use of violence that the court can authorize. One might therefore reformulate the matter by saying that it is not strictly the literal visibility of a justiciable event that is at issue here but its objectification. Punishment inflicted on the body-and-mind is possible only when a justiciable event can be constituted as a discursive object.

While the formation and exercise of virtues (a disciplinary process in which rites of worship are involved) do overlap with what in modern parlance is called "ethics," one must be careful not to assume that ethics as such is essentially a matter of internal conditions, with conscience as a sovereign matter. That conscience is a purely private matter at once enabling and justifying the self-government of human beings is a necessary (though not sufficient) precondition of modern secular ethics. The *sharī'a*, in contrast, rejects the idea that the moral subject is completely sovereign (Kant's "conscience needs no guide; to have a conscience suffices"). Islamic jurists certainly recognized that a Muslim's relation to God (*fīmā baynahu wa bayn allāh*) cannot be the object of a judge's (*qādi*'s) verdict. But this is not because they thought this matter was practically inaccessible; it is simply that being set doctrinally outside the jurisdiction of an earthly court of law, they regarded it as legally inviolable.[92] Nevertheless, they regard the individual's ability to judge what conduct is right and good (for oneself as well as for others) to be dependent not on an inaccessible conscience but on embodied relationships—heavily so in the learning process of childhood, but also

92. Hence, as Johansen has himself pointed out, classical Hanafi doctrine forbade torture to extract evidence, but later *fiqh* accepted it for reasons of expediency (op. cit., pp. 407–8). See also his excellent essay, "La découverte des choses qui parlent: La légalisation de la torture judiciaire en droit musulman (XIIIe–XIVe siècles)," *Enquête*, no. 7, 1998.

in adulthood where the intervention of authorities, relatives, and friends in particular situations may be critical for the exercise of that ability or for dealing with the consequences of its failure. Here body-and-mind is the object of moral discipline.

In brief, I submit that although the *shari'a* does distinguish between "law" and "ethics," neither term should be understood in its modern, secular sense.

'Shari'a' as a traditional discipline

In Safwat's proposal for reform, the basic moral appeal is to conscience in the Kantian sense. The *shari'a* comes to be equated with jurisprudential rules concerning marriage, divorce, and inheritance, with the resolution of disputes arising from such relationships, and also with the rules for proper worship. The consequence of that equation is not simply abridgement but a rearticulation of the concepts of law and morality. The latter comes increasingly to be seen as rules of conduct whose sanctions are essentially different from those of legal rules—that is, not subject to institutionalized, worldly punishments. This is precisely what one finds in the liberal reform lawyers who describe the *shari'a* as "the law of personal status" (*qānūn al-ahwāl al-shakhsiyya*), that is, as rules for regulating "the family," a modern institution built around the married couple. And one finds it also generally among recent Islamists.

But in Abduh, the modernizing Azharite steeped in *tasawwuf* (mysticism), there is a tension that is absent in the proposed reforms of European-trained lawyers such as Safwat. For Abduh also invokes an older conception of the *shari'a*. Thus on the one hand Abduh complains that teaching and examining the *shari'a* in al-Azhar pays far too much attention to *'ibādāt* (rituals of worship) and far too little to *mu'āmalāt* (rules for social relations).[93] But he also says that the judge's authority requires more than intellectual competence, that it depends on his developing certain moral aptitudes and predispositions.

In Abduh's words, "the Islamic *shari'a* has intricate details which cannot be taken into account except by someone who has informed himself thoroughly of all its legal provisions, enquired properly into its objectives and arrived at its precise meanings—that is, someone who knows its lan-

93. Muhammad Abduh, *Taqrīr*, p. 295.

guage as well as its masters do. No man can attain to that state unless he has acquired the *shariʿa* from its practitioners, and has been brought up according to the true religious tradition (*al-sunna al-dīniyya al-sahīha*). Furthermore, the judge cannot be a preserver of family and domestic organization merely by learning *shariʿa* injunctions. The injunctions must become an authoritative part of himself [*thumma la yakūnu al-qādi hāfizan nizām al-usr wa al-buyūt baʿd al-ihāta bi ahkāmi al-sharʿi hatta yakūnu li al-sharʿi wa ahkāmihi sultān—ayy sultān ʿala nafsihi*]."[94] That is to say, the *shariʿa* must become part of the judge's moral and physical formation, ceasing in that context to be mere "rules"—although rules are what he deploys in his judgments. (Incidentally, I make no claims about Abduh's "real motives"—a topic on which historians and biographers have been happy to speculate—but about what the text says.)

What such a passage reveals is not the banal recognition that rituals of worship are a vital part of every pious Muslim's upbringing. Nor does it simply indicate that they are an integral part of the Islamic tradition. Its interest, I suggest, lies in the claim that increasingly correct social practice is a moral prerequisite for the acquisition of certain intellectual virtues by the judge. A knowledge of legal rules will not suffice—so Abduh insists—because the judge's task is not simply the application of those rules. It is necessary for him to know *how* to apply the rules in such a way that he helps "to preserve the family." The thought presented here is not that by being seen to be religious the judge acquires the charisma to reinforce his authority. Nor is it that faith and probity are essential *criteria* for eligibility to the status of judge.[95] On the contrary, Abduh is saying that the authoritative character of the law can be recognized, and its rules properly applied, only after a process of personal discipline that depends on *al-sunna al-dīniyya al-sahīha*—"the true religious tradition." The tradition is not based on rationally founded belief but on commitment to a shared way of life divinely mandated. The techniques of the body (kinesthetic as well as sensory) employed in rituals of worship are taught and learnt within the tradition, helping to form the abilities to discriminate and judge correctly, for these abilities are the precondition not only of Islamic ethics in general but also—and this is the point I want to stress—of the law's moral authority

94. Ibid., p. 219.

95. On some medieval discussions about the preconditions for authoritative legal reasoners, see Wael Hallaq, *A History of Islamic Legal Theories* (Cambridge: Cambridge University Press, 1997), pp. 117–21.

for the model judge. Whether, and if so how and to what extent, such cultivation actually works, how it combines or conflicts with extra-*shariʿa* conditions, are of course different questions—and questions for historical and ethnographical research. But the conception here is that being a defective judge is not unlike being a defective teacher in as much as both intervene wrongly or inadequately in the developing lives of others. In other words, it is when the *shariʿa* fails to be embodied in the judge that it becomes a set of sacred rules—"sacred" because of the source of their sanction, "rules" because of their impersonal and transcendent application.

The view that Abduh takes here of the moral subject is not concerned with state law as an external authority. It presupposes that the capability for virtuous conduct, and the sensibilities on which that capability draws, are acquired by the individual through tradition-guided practices (the *sunna*). *Fiqh* is critical to this process not as a set of rules to be obeyed but as the condition that enables the development of virtues. Abduh therefore repudiates the liberal conception of the right to self-invention. Implied in this conception of *fiqh* is not simply a comprehensive structure of norms (*ahkām*), but a range of traditional disciplines, combining both sufism and the *shariʿa*, on which the latter's authority depends. In other words, Abduh sees the "Islamic tradition" (the *sunna*) not merely as a law whose authority resides in a supernatural realm, but as the way for individuals to discipline their life together as Muslims. The role of pain—penalty—is not to constitute moral obligation, but (as indicated in Chapter 2) to help develop virtue as a habitus.

The fourteenth-century jurist Ibn Taymiyya, whose authority Abduh often invoked, expounded a doctrine of sufism that I think underlies Abduh's views. According to Ibn Taymiyya the only point of spiritual discipline (the point that makes sufism essential) is to promote a convergence between human willing and the commands of God as expressed in the *shariʿa*. Thus for Ibn Taymiyya (and for Abduh) "at every stage the servant must desire to do that which has been commanded him in the *shariʿa* and avoid what has been forbidden him in the *shariʿa*. When [the mystic Abd al-Qadir] commands the servant to leave off his desiring, that pertains to those things which have been neither commanded nor forbidden."[96] In this

96. Cited in Thomas Michel, "Ibn Taymiyya's *Sharh* on the *Futuh al-Ghayb* of Abd al-Qadir Jilani," *Hamdard Islamicus*, 4/2, 1981, p. 5. Michel, in his very interesting analysis of Ibn Taymiyya's theological tract on sufism, goes on to comment: "Ibn Taymiyya stresses that this primacy of the *shariʿa* forms the soundest tradition in Sufism, and to argue his point he lists over a dozen early masters, as

view, the performance of the *shari'a*—spiritual cultivation of the self through *'ibādāt*, the entire range of embodiments that define worship, together with supererogatory exercises as well as the norms of social behavior (called *mu'amalāt*)—are all interdependent. *Together they occupy the space that Ahmad Safwat would pre-empt for the legislative authority of the sovereign state and the moral authority of the sovereign subject.*

There is, of course, a partial resemblance between this idea and the one familiar to the social sciences as "habitus," made famous by Pierre Bourdieu but first introduced into comparative sociology by Marcel Mauss in his famous essay "Techniques of the Body." Mauss himself acquired the concept from medieval Christian discourse, which continued and built on the Aristotelian tradition of moral thinking[97]—a tradition that is also shared with Islam.

The concept of *habitus* invites us to analyze any assemblage of embodied aptitudes not as systems of meanings to be deciphered. In Mauss's view, the human body was not to be regarded simply as the passive recipient of "cultural imprints" that can be imposed on the body by repetitive discipline—still less as the active source of "natural expressions" clothed in local history and culture—but as the self-developable means by which the subject achieves a range of human objects—from styles of physical movement (for example, walking), through modes of emotional being (for ex-

---

well as more contemporaneous *shaykhs* like his fellow Hanbalis, al-Ansari al-Harawi and Abd al-Qadir, and the latter's own *shaykh*, Hammad al-Dabbas. Conversely no *maqam* or *hal*, no spiritual exercises, no status as spiritual guide—even when these are accompanied by miracles and wonders—can be considered valid unless they promote obedience to the *shari'a* command. However, within this carefully delimited interpretation, the Sufi path is considered a salutary effort and even essential within the life of the Islamic community. Its goal is to imitate those who have approached near to God through supererogatory works in imitation of the Prophet and the '*shaykhs* among the *salaf*.' The goal is not the unity of *being* between God and the believer, as is spoken of by many mystical writers, but a unity of *will*, where the believer actively wants and desires nothing but what God desires and performs in his life. . . . Ibn Taymiyya is an activist, convinced that God calls upon Muslims to undertake the responsibility of combatting external enemies as well as internal evils, and that *sabr* [fortitude, patience] is the proper Islamic response only to those things that cannot be prevented or controlled after all man's efforts" (pp. 5–6, 7).

97. See Mary Carruthers, *The Book of Memory*, Cambridge: Cambridge University Press, 1990.

ample, composure), to kinds of spiritual experience (for example, mystical states).

It is the final paragraph of Mauss's essay that carries what are perhaps the most far-reaching implications for an anthropological understanding of secularism. Beginning with a reference to Granet's remarkable studies of Taoist body techniques, he goes on: "I believe precisely that at the bottom of all our mystical states there are body techniques which we have not studied, but which were studied fully in China and India, even in very remote periods. This socio-psycho-biological study should be made. I think that there are necessarily biological means of entering into 'communion with God'."[98] Thus the possibility is opened up of inquiring into the ways in which embodied practices (including language-in-use) form a precondition for varieties of religious (and secular) experience.[99] The inability to "enter into communion with God" not only becomes a function of untaught bodies but it shifts the direction in which the authority for conduct can be sought. And authority itself comes to be understood not as an ideologically justified coercion but as a predisposition of the embodied self.

Conclusions

The importation of European legal procedures and codes in nineteenth-century Egypt were seen at the time, by Westerners and Egyptians alike, as aspects of becoming Europeanized (*mutafarnij*) or civilized (*mutamaddin*). Today most people prefer to speak of that process as sec-

98. Ibid., 122.

99. In *Genealogies of Religion* I attempted to explore this question with reference to medieval Christian monastic discipline. I deal there with how bodily attitudes were cultivated, but also with how sexuality (libido) was differently managed among Benedictines (who recruited children) and Cistercians (who recruited adults only) in the education of Christian virtues. In the one case this involved trying to direct the body's experience; in the other, to reconvert the experienced body. My suggestion was that not only the force and direction of universal desire but desires in the form of specific Christian virtues may be historically constituted. Incidentally, this line of thought should not be confused with the conditioning thesis—the notion that "beliefs" are "inculcated" by bodily repetition, as though the self were an empty container to be filled with "belief" through ritual performance. I argue specifically against that in my book—see chapter 4 of *Genealogies of Religion*, and especially pp. 143–44.

ularization and modernization. The need to unpack these terms is rarely recognized.

The increasing restriction of *shariʿa* jurisdiction has been seen as a welcome measure of progress by secular nationalists, and as a setback by political Islamists. But both secularists and Islamists have taken a strongly statist perspective in that both see the *shariʿa* as "sacred law" that is presently circumscribed but should in any case be properly administered or further reformed by state institutions. This is not surprising since the unprecedented powers and ambitions of the modern state and the forces of the capitalist economy have been central to the great transformation of our time.

Nevertheless, a modern autonomous life (which is, paradoxically, regulated by a modern bureaucratic state and enmeshed in a modern market economy) requires particular kinds of law as well as particular kinds of subjects of law. It is because the ideology of self-government seems also to call for the "civilizing" of entire subject populations through the law that the authority of the law and its reconstructive power come to be taken as supremely important. Ideally that project requires the installation of a particular conception of ethics and its formal separation from the authority of law, both also delinked from "religion." Thus a useful study of Egyptian *shariʿa* courts during the first half of the twentieth century concludes that "The state's leaders and legislators were reluctant . . . to create a split with tradition in this sensitive field of family law; they felt the society was not yet ready for more drastic change and that it was therefore preferable to introduce a modest reform in the framework of the existing legal system."[100] My argument, on the contrary, is that whatever the intentions of legislators, the legal reforms marked a revolutionary change.

Interestingly, the project of "civilizing" a population is one that secularists and Islamists share, albeit differently. Both of them agree that the rural and urban lower classes are immersed in "non-Islamic beliefs and practices," in a deep-rooted culture that owes more to Pharaonic and Coptic Egypt than it does to Islam brought by the sixth-century Arab con-

100. Ron Shaham, *Family and the Courts in Modern Egypt: A Study Based on Decisions by the Shariʿa Courts, 1900–1955*, Leiden: Brill, 1997, p. 228. However, the study also shows that judges (*qādis*) were often quite innovative in adjusting their decisions to changing socioeconomic circumstances.

querors.[101] Both agree also that these classes need to be educated out of their superstition, an obstacle to their becoming "truly modern." And both agree, finally, that the social power that can carry out this mission is the one that already represents them as a nation and directly intervenes in their lives: the modernizing state. Of course the two tendencies are by no means the same; they do not draw on the same sensibilities. Each attaches to itself elements of what is generally represented in political discourse as "the secular," but not entirely the same elements.

Thus for secularists each citizen is equal to every other, an equal legal and political member of a state that itself claims a single personality. In their scheme the categories "majority" and "minority" technically relate to electoral politics only, but in practice they reflect entrenched social inequalities. For Islamists they are basic cultural categories that define citizens as necessarily unequal. In the modern state, both make it difficult, if not impossible, for people who belong to different religions (Muslims, Christians, and Jews) to live in accordance with their traditions without—on the one hand—having also to be grouped invidiously as *dhimmis* (non-Muslim protected subjects of a Muslim state) or—on the other hand—as "ethnicities" (that is, as "minorities" unwilling or unable to assimilate to "the national culture").

In so far as "religion" is recognized in the texts of modern legal re-

101. This view has been greatly strengthened by the efforts of folklorists who have constructed a secular, mass "culture" for Egypt (embracing tribes and urbanites, upper Egyptians and inhabitants of the Delta) within an evolutionary framework that secures its continuous national personality. See, for instance, the standard survey of Egyptian folklore by Ahmad Rushdi Salih, *Al-adab al-shaʿbi* (Cairo, first edition, 1954); the famous study of "immortality" in Egyptian cultural heritage—"an extremely ancient and continuous heritage"—by Sayyid ʿUways in his *Al-khulūd* (Cairo, 1966); and the interesting dictionary of customs, manners, and sayings compiled by Ahmad Amin: *Qamūs al-ʿādāt wa al-taqālīd wa al-taʿābīr al-misriyya*, Cairo, 1953. Such writers, most of whom date from the Nasir period (1952–70), are clearly inspired by a secular vision that denies the existence of any significant "cultural" distinction between Christians and Muslims within a unified Egyptian nation. They draw freely from the writings of European folklorists and travelers from previous centuries. Ahmad Amin's unacknowledged reproduction of numerous etchings from Edward Lane's early nineteenth-century classic, *An Account of the Manners and Customs of the Modern Egyptians*, reinforces the reader's impression of a timeless and general Egyptian people. (For national history, homogeneous time belongs to the larger frame within which "epochs" and "events" can be plotted.)

formers—Amin, Safwat, and so forth—it comes to be thought of in moral terms. The essence of religion—as Kant put it, and other moderns agreed—was its ethics. (In contrast, the Kierkegaardian view makes a sharp distinction between "religion" and "ethics.")[102] This meant that the attempt to allocate "religion" or its surrogate to its own private sphere, defined and policed by the law, was also an attempt to clear a space within the state for modern ethics.

Put another way: whereas ethics could at one time stand independently of a political organization (although not of collective obligations), in a secular state it presupposes *a specific political realm*—representative democracy, citizenship, law and order, civil liberties, and so on. For only where there is this public realm can *personal ethics* become constituted as sovereign and be closely linked to a personally chosen style of life—that is, to an aesthetic.

A secular state is not one characterized by religious indifference, or rational ethics—or political toleration. It is a complex arrangement of legal reasoning, moral practice, and political authority. This arrangement is not the simple outcome of the struggle of secular reason against the despotism of religious authority. We do not understand the arrangements I have tried to describe if we begin with the common assumption that the essence of secularism is the protection of civil freedoms from the tyranny of religious discourse, that religious discourse seeks always to end discussion and secularism to create the conditions for its flourishing.

One of the many merits of Johansen's account of classical Islamic law is his demonstration that the *shariʿa* is a field of debate and dissent in which the distinction between certainty and probability is pivotal, and that this law has evolved in the context of changing social circumstances and arguments. But just as important is his implicit suggestion that the authoritative closure of a debate is not necessarily a sign of discursive failure, that it indicates a different kind of discursive performance altogether—the carrying out of *legal judgment*. For legal judgment is not confined to the cog-

102. "The ethical expression for what Abraham did is, that he would murder Isaac; the religious expression is, that he would sacrifice Isaac; but precisely in this contradiction consists the dread which can well make a man sleepless, and yet Abraham is not what he is without this dread" (Søren Kierkegaard, *Fear and Trembling (&) The Sickness Unto Death*, Princeton: Princeton University Press, 1954, p. 41). Thus even in his conception of "religion" as deeply personal and experiential, Kierkegaard stands in sharp opposition to the liberal, secularized view.

nitive domain of truth, to a recognition of transcendent rules; it is also central to the practical domain of punishment and pain.

The judicial process is an institution integral to every kind of state, and it is always based on coercion. In order to understand "secularism" I therefore did not begin with an a priori definition of that concept ("the universal principles of freedom and toleration" or "a particular cultural import from the West"). I tried to look at aspects of *shari'a* reform as both the precondition and the consequence of secular processes of power. For the law always facilitates or obstructs different forms of life *by force*, responds to different kinds of sensibility, and authorizes different patterns of pain and suffering. It defines, or (as in the present moment of genetic and cognitive revolutions) tries to redefine the concept of the human—and so to protect the rights that belong essentially to the human and the damage that can be done to his or her essence. And it punishes transgressions (of commission and omission) by the exercise of violence.

Index

Cultural Memory | *in the Present*

Timothy J. Reiss, *Against Autonomy: Global Dialectics of Cultural Exchange*

Hent de Vries and Samuel Weber, eds., *Religion and Media*

Niklas Luhmann, *Theories of Distinction: Redescribing the Descriptions of Modernity*, ed. and introd. William Rasch

Johannes Fabian, *Anthropology with an Attitude: Critical Essays*

Michel Henry, *I Am the Truth: Toward a Philosophy of Christianity*

Gil Anidjar, *"Our Place in Al-Andalus": Kabbalah, Philosophy, Literature in Arab-Jewish Letters*

Hélène Cixous and Jacques Derrida, *Veils*

F. R. Ankersmit, *Historical Representation*

F. R. Ankersmit, *Political Representation*

Elissa Marder, *Dead Time: Temporal Disorders in the Wake of Modernity (Baudelaire and Flaubert)*

Reinhart Koselleck, *The Practice of Conceptual History: Timing History, Spacing Concepts*

Niklas Luhmann, *The Reality of the Mass Media*

Hubert Damisch, *A Childhood Memory by Piero della Francesca*

Hubert Damisch, *A Theory of /Cloud/: Toward a History of Painting*

Jean-Luc Nancy, *The Speculative Remark (One of Hegel's Bons Mots)*

Jean-François Lyotard, *Soundproof Room: Malraux's Anti-Aesthetics*

Jan Patočka, *Plato and Europe*

Hubert Damisch, *Skyline: The Narcissistic City*

Isabel Hoving, *In Praise of New Travelers: Reading Caribbean Migrant Women Writers*

Richard Rand, ed., *Futures: Of Derrida*

William Rasch, *Niklas Luhmann's Modernity: The Paradox of System Differentiation*

Jacques Derrida and Anne Dufourmantelle, *Of Hospitality*

Jean-François Lyotard, *The Confession of Augustine*